SOUTH-WESTERN

BASIC ENGLISH REVIEW

fourth edition

NORMAN SCHACHTER • ALFRED T. CLARK, JR.

Los Angeles City Unified School District
Los Angeles, California

SOUTH-WESTERN PUBLISHING CO.

Managing Editor: Karen Schneiter
Developmental Editor: Marilyn Hornsby
Production Editor: Shannon O'Connor

ISBN: 0-538-70621-X

Library of Congress Catalog Card Number: 91-66734

  2 3 4 5 6 7 8 H 99 98 97 96 95 94 93

Printed in the United States of America

Preface

Basic English Review, Fourth Edition, is an easy-to-learn presentation of English grammar. This short yet intensive text-workbook provides practical, varied, and meaningful new content and varied exercises geared to your interests.

Basic English Review, Fourth Edition, meets a wide range of your needs and expectations. *Basic English Review* can be used as a text for basic English, basic English review, or remedial courses, or as a supplemental text for other courses in which only a limited time can be given to English fundamentals. This text-workbook employs a self-teaching, highly motivational, classroom-tested plan of instruction and instructional material.

In this fourth edition there are completely *new* sentences and examples for all application practice exercises. Included are sentences that are related to topics of current interest as suggested by students and teachers.

The content is organized in an orderly, sequential manner. Each of the eleven units and Appendixes A and B consists of the following:

1. *Student objectives* to direct you to the purposes of each unit.

2. *Sections* with short reading explanations which include new and instructive examples with analytical explanations in a clear and informative manner.

3. *Illustrative drawings* that provide additional clarification and reinforcement of the material.

4. *Tryout exercises* designed to help you better understand the reading assignment and to determine the extent to which you have mastered the material.

5. *Application practices* in which to apply the fundamentals you have just studied. The exercise content and difficulty are sufficiently varied to challenge a wide range of ability and interest. Application practices relate to specific content areas. Drills for vocabulary building and spelling are included in separate appendixes.

6. *New Appendix A* with spelling rules and spelling application practices and new *Appendix B* with guidelines and applications for vocabulary, homonyms and homophones, synonyms, and antonyms.

7. *Scoring guides and review notes* that instruct you to review particular sections when weaknesses exist.

8. *Periodic review exercises* that cover the subject matter presented in each unit and material studied at an earlier time.

A test package is available to accompany this text. Included are one four-page pretest, achievement tests for each of the eleven units, one two-page review test, and one four-page posttest.

Basic English Review, Fourth Edition, has utilized many improvements suggested by students and teachers who have tested the material in actual classrooms in a number of schools. In response to their recommendations and ideas, additional pages of vocabulary drills dealing with synonyms, antonyms, spelling, and definitions are included. Further emphasis has been given to Unit 11 which deals with writing sentences and paragraphs. This allows you an opportunity to demonstrate your writing ability in short, meaningful ways. All examples and application practices have been revised to make each exercise more stimulating regardless of your age or academic ability.

The authors hope that *Basic English Review*, Fourth Edition, will contribute substantially to the improvement of your communication skills.

Norman Schachter

Alfred T. Clark, Jr.

Contents

Unit 5 *The Time of Verbs*

Unit 6 *Adjectives and Adverbs*

Unit 7 *Prepositions and Conjunctions*

OBJECTIVES
1. To understand that a sentence expresses a complete thought.
2. To recognize the different kinds of sentences.
3. To identify the eight parts of speech.

A *sentence* expresses a complete thought through a series or group of words. A simple sentence consists of two important parts, the *subject* (*a noun or pronoun*) and the *verb*. The subject noun is a person, place, or thing spoken of, and the verb is the word that tells what the subject does or is. A group of words is not a sentence unless it contains both a subject and a verb.

Below are examples of complete and incomplete sentences with subjects underlined once and verbs underlined twice. Remember that a complete sentence must have a subject and a verb.

COMPLETE SENTENCE

INCOMPLETE SENTENCE

Example 1

Susan walked through the shopping mall.

Analysis:

Susan—person spoken of—subject
walked—tells what Susan did—verb

Example 2

Her aunt paid for the lunch.

Analysis:

aunt—person spoken of—subject
paid—tells what her aunt did—verb

Example 3

Carl in the swift-flowing Colorado River.

Analysis:

Carl—person spoken of—subject
There is no verb to tell what Carl did—the sentence is incomplete. (A verb such as *swam*, *played*, or *fished* is needed to complete the sentence.)

TRYOUT EXERCISE   **Directions:** Identify the subjects of the following sentences by underlining them once. Identify the verbs by underlining them twice. Check your answers on page 245 or with your teacher before continuing with your assignment.

1. The guide explained the different trails.

2. We watched the movie in the Grand Canyon Lodge.

3. Our friend lives in Hawaii.

4. Mrs. Mauro mailed a new record to my cousin.

5. Grant bought several souvenirs.

6. Christy sent many scenic postcards.

Complete Application Practices 1-3, pages 3-5, at this time.

Kinds of Sentences

The *declarative* sentence makes a statement. It ends with a period.

Our boss toured in New Zealand.

He enjoyed the different native animals.

The *interrogative* sentence asks a question. It ends with a question mark.

Have you visited a zoo lately?

Why didn't you bring me back a stuffed bear?

The *exclamatory* sentence expresses surprise, disbelief, or deep feeling. It ends with an exclamation point.

What a cute monkey that is!

Watch out for that snake!

The *imperative* sentence gives a command, requests someone to do something, or begs. It usually ends with a period, but a strong command may be ended with an exclamation point (see the last sentence above). The subject *you* is often omitted, but understood.

Read your signs carefully. (*You* understood)

Keep your hands away from the deer. (*You* understood)

You must listen to the zoo director.

Don't bother the baby cubs! (imperative and exclamatory)

TRYOUT EXERCISE **Directions:** Classify the following sentences by placing a check mark in the proper blank at the right. *D* stands for declarative, *Int* for interrogative, *Excla* for exclamatory, and *Imp* for imperative. Check your answers on page 245 or with your teacher before continuing with your assignment.

	D	Int	Excla	Imp
1. Was Alaska or Hawaii the last state admitted to the United States?	___	___	___	___
2. I drove the car on the Alcan Highway in Alaska.	___	___	___	___
3. Wear your heavy sweater.	___	___	___	___
4. Look out for that falling rock!	___	___	___	___

Complete Application Practices 4-6, pages 6-8, at this time.

Subject and Verb Recognition

application practice **1**

1-A Practice Procedure Identify the subjects of the following sentences by underlining them once. Identify the verbs by underlining them twice. Score one point for each correctly identified subject and one point for each correctly identified verb.

Your Score

1. Betty visited a television studio.   1. _____
2. She laughed at the comedian.   2. _____
3. Tom looked at the stage sets.   3. _____
4. Alicia applied for a job at the studio.   4. _____
5. The teacher explained the duties of the camera technicians.   5. _____
6. Pam got several autographs from the actors.   6. _____
7. The audience applauded the young singer.   7. _____
8. Miss Jenkins worked with the writers.   8. _____
9. Her uncle produced the comedy series.   9. _____
10. The guide introduced us to the studio manager.   10. _____

1-B Practice Procedure Follow the procedure given for 1-A.

1. My friend drives at a high speed.   1. _____
2. Pete forgot his parking spot.   2. _____
3. Mr. and Mrs. Weber traveled through Canada.   3. _____
4. Rita Thompson flew to Milwaukee.   4. _____
5. The plane left an hour late.   5. _____
6. The pilot walked through the cabin.   6. _____
7. Elroy received a free trip.   7. _____
8. Our neighbor bought a painting at the art show.   8. _____
9. The exhibit featured many famous artists.   9. _____
10. We spent an hour at the coin collection.   10. _____
11. The orchestra plays soft music.   11. _____
12. My hobby relaxes me.   12. _____
13. The store sold coins from foreign countries.   13. _____
14. Mr. Navarro collects silver dollars.   14. _____
15. Ellen Corbett studies Mexican customs.   15. _____

Your Total Score _____ /50

If your score was 39 or less for 1-A and 1-B, review page 1 before continuing.

/50

Subject and Verb Recognition

2 Practice Procedure Identify the subjects of the following sentences by underlining them once. Identify the verbs by underlining them twice. Score one point for each correctly identified subject and verb.

Your Score

1. The company looks for energetic workers.
2. Sharon earned an excellent salary.
3. She trained for the computer job.
4. The company listed the requirements for the position.
5. Carla worked at the hospital.
6. Our doctor opened a new office.
7. She named it "Brookline Emergency Clinic."
8. Dr. Hobbs graduated from medical school five years ago.
9. She specializes in internal medicine.
10. Dr. Powers started his practice in Canada.
11. He reads many medical journals.
12. Mabel received her first paycheck today.
13. Aunt Liz took Mabel to dinner as a reward.
14. The weather kept me at home today.
15. The rain created a major traffic problem.
16. The store opened at the usual time.
17. Pete helped Mabel in the interview.
18. The design for the new product pleased the boss.
19. Mr. Kaii added the bonus to her paycheck.
20. The employees liked their company.
21. Many qualified people took the exam.
22. Their business improved with better service.
23. Certain firms offer outstanding benefits.
24. A temporary job often becomes a steady job.
25. Bill wanted to become an auto mechanic.

1. _____
2. _____
3. _____
4. _____
5. _____
6. _____
7. _____
8. _____
9. _____
10. _____
11. _____
12. _____
13. _____
14. _____
15. _____
16. _____
17. _____
18. _____
19. _____
20. _____
21. _____
22. _____
23. _____
24. _____
25. _____

Your Total Score _____ /50

If your score was 39 or less, review page 1 before continuing.

Complete or Incomplete Sentences

3-A Practice Procedure Identify the incomplete sentences by placing a check mark in the blank at the right. In the space provided below the sentences, rewrite each of the incomplete sentences adding whatever words are necessary to make them complete. Remember that a sentence expresses a complete thought and has a subject and verb. Score one point for each incomplete sentence identified.

Answers

1. Gary moved the calculator.   1. _____
2. The principal in her office with a parent.   2. _____
3. The faculty came early to school.   3. _____
4. Donna and the Pledge of Allegiance.   4. _____
5. Mr. Duncan sang the national anthem before the start of the program. 5. _____
6. A computer salesclerk sold me a word processor.   6. _____
7. The manager with the many different machines in the shop.   7. _____

_____

_____

_____

_____

3-B Practice Procedure Follow the procedure given for 3-A.

1. Juan made the plans for the Alaskan trip.   1. _____
2. Mrs. Rivas paid for the airplane tickets.   2. _____
3. The trip in British Columbia on June 19.   3. _____
4. The best hotel rooms in scenic Vancouver.   4. _____
5. We joined the group for dinner aboard the ship.   5. _____
6. The tour manager on the exciting days ahead.   6. _____
7. We went ashore at Anchorage.   7. _____
8. Many houses on the mountainside and boardwalk.   8. _____
9. Morning sightseeing abundant wildlife and Mount McKinley National Park. 9. _____
10. The United States purchased Alaska for 7.2 million dollars.   10. _____

_____

_____

_____

_____

_____

Your Total Score _____ /8

If your score was 5 or less for 3-A and 3-B, review page 1 before continuing.

Name

Date

Score

/8

Types of Sentences

4-A Practice Procedure Indicate whether the following sentences are declarative, interrogative, exclamatory, or imperative by placing a check mark at the right. *D* stands for declarative, *Int* for interrogative, *Excla* for exclamatory, and *Imp* for imperative. Score one point for each correct answer.

	D	Int	Excla	Imp

1. The Declaration of Independence is a historic document.   1. ____ ____ ____ ____
2. The thirteen original states ratified it on July 4, 1776.   2. ____ ____ ____ ____
3. Who wrote that famous document?   3. ____ ____ ____ ____
4. What a magnificent heritage that is!   4. ____ ____ ____ ____
5. Read the article about Thomas Jefferson.   5. ____ ____ ____ ____
6. John Hancock signed his name first.   6. ____ ____ ____ ____
7. Don't touch that paper!   7. ____ ____ ____ ____
8. How many signed the Declaration of Independence?   8. ____ ____ ____ ____
9. Please pass the book to Hillary.   9. ____ ____ ____ ____
10. Is the United States Constitution different from the Declaration of Independence?   10. ____ ____ ____ ____

4-B Practice Procedure Follow the procedure given for 4-A.

1. We enjoyed our visit to the Colonial Historic Park.   1. ____ ____ ____ ____
2. Have you ever heard of it?   2. ____ ____ ____ ____
3. What a beautiful setting that is!   3. ____ ____ ____ ____
4. Tell me about Yellowstone National Park.   4. ____ ____ ____ ____
5. It is the world's greatest geyser area.   5. ____ ____ ____ ____
6. Where is the Booker T. Washington National Monument located?   6. ____ ____ ____ ____
7. The Bronx Zoo has many interesting animals.   7. ____ ____ ____ ____
8. Who is buried in Grant's Tomb?   8. ____ ____ ____ ____
9. Listen to the teacher read.   9. ____ ____ ____ ____
10. Stand up for the national anthem!   10. ____ ____ ____ ____
11. Is a group of elephants called a herd?   11. ____ ____ ____ ____
12. Which is the fastest animal?   12. ____ ____ ____ ____
13. Look at that cheetah run!   13. ____ ____ ____ ____
14. A baby whale is called a calf.   14. ____ ____ ____ ____
15. Remember not to litter in the national parks.   15. ____ ____ ____ ____

Your Total Score _____ /25

If your score was 19 or less for 4-A and 4-B, review page 2 before continuing.

Kinds of Sentences

5 Practice Procedure In the spaces provided below, compose five examples of each kind of sentence (declarative, interrogative, exclamatory, and imperative). Score one point for each correct sentence.

Declarative Sentences

1. _____
2. _____
3. _____
4. _____
5. _____

Interrogative Sentences

1. _____
2. _____
3. _____
4. _____
5. _____

Exclamatory Sentences

1. _____
2. _____
3. _____
4. _____
5. _____

Imperative Sentences

1. _____
2. _____
3. _____
4. _____
5. _____

Your Total Score _____ /20

If your score was 15 or less, review page 2 before continuing.

6-A Practice Procedure Indicate whether the following sentences are complete or incomplete. Write a *C* for complete or an *I* for incomplete in the space provided to the right of the sentence. Remember that a complete sentence must have a subject and a verb. Score one point for each correct answer.

Answers

1. Mr. Quon taught typing in his school.　　　　1. ___C___
2. Students with their machines on their desks.　　2. ___I___
3. Business courses offer a wide range of opportunities.　3. ___C___
4. The computer manager brought many samples of the newest machines.　4. _____
5. Her assistant with many slides of the latest calculators.　5. _____
6. Our school prepares many pupils for employment in industry.　6. _____
7. The counselor introduced the owner of the engineering firm.　7. _____
8. Kevin filled out the application form.　　　8. _____
9. Different types of jobs for different people.　　9. _____
10. Teresa Martinez got a job with a medical company.　10. _____

6-B Practice Procedure Indicate whether the following sentences are declarative, interrogative, exclamatory, or imperative by writing *D* for declarative, *Int* for interrogative, *Excla* for exclamatory, and *Imp* for imperative in the spaces proviced at the right of the sentences. Score one point for each correct answer.

1. The library received three new books about famous explorers.　1. ___D___
2. Please handle these books with care.　　　2. ___Imp___
3. Who was Christopher Columbus?　　　　3. ___In___
4. What beautiful books these are!　　　　4. ___Ex___
5. In 1492 Columbus sailed with three tiny ships.　5. _____
6. Did the same explorer discover the Pacific Ocean?　6. _____
7. Don't throw that book!　　　　　　7. _____
8. Why do we remember Hernando de Soto?　　8. _____
9. James Cook was one of the greatest Pacific explorers.　9. _____
10. What a thrilling story that is!　　　　10. _____
11. Give a report tomorrow on Jacques Cartier and the St. Lawrence River.　11. _____
12. Ponce de Leon named Florida.　　　　12. _____
13. He heard fabulous stories about the water there.　13. _____
14. No one believed that story!　　　　　14. _____
15. Has anyone visited Alaska?　　　　　15. _____

Your Total Score _____ /25

If your score was 19 or less for 6-A and 6-B, review pages 1 and 2 before continuing.

Parts of Speech

Most of the words that are used to make sentences can be sorted into eight classifications called *parts of speech*. The eight parts of speech are discussed briefly here. They will be treated in greater detail in later units.

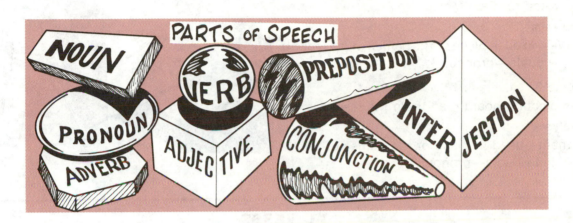

3-A NOUNS

A *noun* names a person, a place, or a thing. (See page 25 for a detailed treatment of nouns.)

Example 1

Linda rode in the boat on the Potomac River.

Analysis:

Linda—names a person—noun
boat—names a thing—noun
Potomac River—names a place—noun

Example 2

Jose Canseco hit the ball in Yankee Stadium.

Analysis:

Jose Canseco—names a person—noun
ball—names a thing—noun
Yankee Stadium—names a place—noun

Example 3

Ann Lee owned a video store in Cincinnati.

Analysis:

Ann Lee—names a person—noun
store—names a thing—noun
Cincinnati—names a place—noun

Example 4

Cindy Howell played the piano in the Bijou Theater.

Analysis:

Cindy Howell—names a person—noun
piano—names a thing—noun
Bijou Theater—names a place—noun

3-B PRONOUNS

A *pronoun* is a word used as a substitute for a noun. (Pronouns are discussed in greater detail on page 43.)

Example 1

She won the election for mayor.

Analysis:

She—used in place of the name of the individual—pronoun

Example 2

We voted for Paul Moss.

Analysis:

We—used in place of the names of the individuals—pronoun

Example 3

The election board read them the results.

Analysis:

them—used in place of the names of the individuals—pronoun

Example 4

I felt sorry for the losers.

Analysis:

I—used in place of the name of the individual—pronoun

PRONOUNS TAKE THE PLACE OF NOUNS

3-C VERBS

A *verb* tells what the subject does or is, or what happens to it. It can make a statement, ask a question, or give a command. (See page 71 for a detailed treatment of verbs.)

Example 1

Mark Twain wrote popular books.

Analysis:

wrote—tells what the subject *Mark Twain* did—verb

Example 2

Was the thief ever caught?

Analysis:

Was caught—asks a question about the subject *thief*—verb

Example 3

Watch your step on that ledge!

Analysis:

Watch—gives a command to the understood subject *you*—(You watch your step on that ledge!)—verb

TRYOUT EXERCISE

Directions: Identify the nouns, the verbs, and the pronouns in the following sentences. Underline the nouns once, the verbs twice, and the pronouns three times. Check your answers on page 245 or with your teacher before continuing with your assignment.

1. They gave excellent campaign speeches.

2. He lost by a few votes.

3. The people gave them three cheers.

4. She read the victory speech to the students.

Complete Application Practices 7-8, pages 11-12, at this time.

Nouns, Verbs, and Pronouns

application practice **7**

7 Practice Procedure Identify the nouns, the verbs, and the pronouns in the following sentences. Underline the nouns once, the verbs twice, and the pronouns three times. Score one point for each correct identification.

Your Score

1. He told Mrs. Wales about the bears in Sequoia National Park.   1. _____

2. The deer approached them very carefully.   2. _____

3. We watched a movie about the Great Smokey Mountains.   3. _____

4. The ranger showed her the pretty slides of the forest.   4. _____

5. I went to the ranger station for more information.   5. _____

6. They handed me an application for a job.   6. _____

7. She enjoyed the colors of the trees.   7. _____

8. Ms. Marion raised horses for us in Maine.   8. _____

9. Beverly and he rode the horses every day.   9. _____

10. Yosemite Valley gave her many pleasant experiences over the years.   10. _____

11. They took pictures of the peaks of the Alaskan range for the class.   11. _____

12. We watched the climbers on the mountaintop.   12. _____

13. Flo warned them about the dangerous areas.   13. _____

14. I thanked Sue for the extra sweaters.   14. _____

15. She almost fell off the high ledge.   15. _____

16. Tina and I prepared a hot breakfast for the climbers.   16. _____

17. The storekeeper sold us clothes for the trip.   17. _____

18. We paid him for the maps and food.   18. _____

19. They pointed us in the right direction.   19. _____

20. Jan and I enjoy stories about the trails on Mount Rainier.   20. _____

21. We drove them to Dawson Creek and through Alaska.   21. _____

22. Burt and I flew to the mountains in Canada.   22. _____

23. They named a mountain for him and her.   23. _____

24. He camps every summer with the family.   24. _____

25. The guide told them about the highest mountain in the United States.   25. _____

Your Total Score _____ /115

If your score was 91 or less, review pages 1 and 9-10 before continuing.

8 Practice Procedure Identify the nouns, the verbs, and the pronouns in the following sentences. Underline the nouns once, the verbs twice, and the pronouns three times. Score one point for each correct identification.

Your Score

1. Miss Carlson told us about the different jobs in industry.

1. _____

2. He spoke about jobs for beginners in the company.

2. _____

3. Many agencies provided help for us.

3. _____

4. They listed the library as an important source for information.

4. _____

5. She explained to me about other opportunities in medicine.

5. _____

6. We listened to the speech by Ms. Dunkin, the president of the bank.

6. _____

7. The representative from the Ace Company handed us pamphlets for the field of communication.

7. _____

8. I check the newspapers for work in the neighborhood.

8. _____

9. He looked for a position in a legal office.

9. _____

10. The teacher gave him and her many helpful hints for an interview.

10. _____

11. Ted Hernandez mentioned to them the importance of references.

11. _____

12. Many businesses posted the salary for a new employee.

12. _____

13. I went to the companies in the field of computers.

13. _____

14. Ann Kelly and he asked questions about law.

14. _____

15. They attended the lecture on television and radio.

15. _____

16. Some students joined him in the auditorium.

16. _____

17. Miss Shimahara spoke to them about engineering.

17. _____

18. Ida Diaz and she received the most applause.

18. _____

19. We seek trainees in sales and bookkeeping.

19. _____

20. Sandy Woo asked him for a reference from the teacher.

20. _____

21. The company offered him and me good salaries.

21. _____

22. I drew a poster for the manager of the firm.

22. _____

23. He noticed the date for the interview.

23. _____

24. They advertised for chemists on the radio.

24. _____

25. Ruben graduated from school with honors.

25. _____

Your Total Score _____ /120

If your score was 95 or less, review pages 9-10 before continuing.

3-D ADJECTIVES

An *adjective* modifies (describes) a noun or a pronoun. It answers such questions as these: How many? How big? What kind? Which? (See page 127 for a detailed treatment of adjectives.) *A, an,* and *the* are adjectives. *Definite* (the) and *indefinite* (a, an) *adjectives* are referred to as articles.

Example 1

The two puppies chewed on an old shoe.

Analysis:

The—definite adjective
two—tells how many *puppies*—adjective
an—indefinite adjective
old—tells what kind of *shoe*—adjective

Example 2

A funny clown entertained thirty children.

Analysis:

A—indefinite adjective
funny—tells what kind of *clown*—adjective
thirty—tells how many *children*—adjective

Example 3

The author wrote an exciting story.

Analysis:

The—definite adjective
an—indefinite adjective
exciting—tells what kind of *story*—adjective

Example 4

A barking dog chased the cute kitten.

Analysis:

A—indefinite adjective
barking—tells what kind of *dog*—adjective
the—definite adjective
cute—tells what kind of *kitten*—adjective

3-E ADVERBS

An *adverb* modifies (describes) a verb, an adjective, or another adverb. It answers these questions: When? Where? How? Most words ending in *ly* are adverbs. Five common exceptions are *friendly, lively, lonely, lovely,* and *ugly,* which are adjectives. (See page 135 for a detailed treatment of adverbs.)

Example 1

Beth quietly opened the door.

Analysis:

quietly—modifies *opened* by telling *how*—adverb

Example 2

The Pony Express finally went out of business.

Analysis:

finally—modifies *went* by telling *when*—adverb

Example 3

The coach yelled <u>loudly</u> and <u>excitedly</u> at the team.

Analysis:

<u>loudly</u>, <u>excitedly</u>—modify *yelled* by telling *how*—adverbs

Example 4

The herd of elephants moved <u>west</u> to the water hole.

Analysis:

<u>west</u>—modifies *moved* by telling *where* or in what direction—adverb

---

TRYOUT EXERCISE   **Directions:** Identify the verbs, the adjectives, and the adverbs in the following sentences. Underline the verbs once, the adjectives twice, and the adverbs three times. Check your answers on page 245 or with your teacher before continuing with your assignment.

1. The experienced pilot flew the plane skillfully.

2. Heavy storms frequently cancel some flights.

3. The eager flight attendant worked quickly and quietly.

4. The airplane flies north on a regular schedule.

Complete Application Practices 9-10, pages 15-16, at this time.

9-A Practice Procedure Identify the verbs, the adjectives, and the adverbs in the following sentences. Underline the verbs once, the adjectives twice, and the adverbs three times. Score one point for each correct verb, adjective, and adverb identified.

Your Score

1. The happy child ran quickly toward a giraffe.   1. _____

2. The animal stood there quietly in the open area.   2. _____

3. Many people always waited in a long line.   3. _____

4. A full-grown giraffe often reaches to a height of twenty feet.   4. _____

5. The graceful stride of the animal frequently surprises many people.   5. _____

6. The strange beast mostly eats tender shoots and leaves from the tallest trees.   6. _____

7. Youngsters generally enjoy movies about the huge animals in the wild.   7. _____

8. Chet and Carmen willingly visited four famous zoos last year.   8. _____

9. Melissa remained here during the hot summer.   9. _____

10. Mr. Hopkins goes regularly to the prehistoric shows.   10. _____

11. Many countries unfortunately pushed the large animals into crowded areas.   11. _____

12. Lions and leopards recently attacked two young hippos.   12. _____

13. A hippopotamus invariably returns to a favorite watering hole.   13. _____

14. She heard the rhino roar in the mud south of the camp.   14. _____

15. The crocodile barely noticed her there from forty feet.   15. _____

9-B Practice Procedure Indicate whether the following words are verbs, adjectives, or adverbs. Score one point for each correct answer.

1. arrives   _____

2. beautiful   _____

3. here   _____

4. disturb   _____

5. several   _____

6. gracious   _____

7. certainly   _____

8. always   _____

9. nervous   _____

10. buys   _____

11. seven   _____

12. carefully   _____

Your Total Score _____ /92

If your score was 73 or less for 9-A and 9-B, review pages 10 and 13-14 before continuing.

Name

Date

Score

/92

10-A Practice Procedure Identify the pronouns in the following sentences by underlining them once. Score one point for each correct identification.

Your Score

1. We visited the Baseball Hall of Fame.

2. Uncle Jack gave us plane tickets to Cooperstown, New York.

3. He told them to check the names of the players there.

4. She wrote an entertaining report for him.

5. The teacher gave her an *A* on the paper.

6. We had heard stories about the players.

7. He and I showed slides of the old-timers.

8. They especially liked the stories about Babe Ruth and Henry Aaron, home run hitters.

9. Coleen handed them a rare baseball card.

10. Samira liked baseball more than Cory and she.

11. They brought us a World Series pennant from the game.

12. I told him and them how Jack Fette knew the coach of the Los Angeles Dodgers.

13. Years ago he showed her a picture of the coach's college team.

14. He and they attended school together in Riverside.

15. The team's owner gave us an autographed ball signed by all the players.

1. _____
2. _____
3. _____
4. _____
5. _____
6. _____
7. _____
8. _____
9. _____
10. _____
11. _____
12. _____
13. _____
14. _____
15. _____

10-B Practice Procedure Indicate whether the following words are nouns, pronouns, or verbs. Score one point for each correct answer.

1. teach _____

2. we _____

3. them _____

4. field _____

5. worked _____

6. stadium _____

7. she _____

8. salary _____

9. paid _____

10. I _____

11. learned _____

12. people _____

13. wait _____

14. he _____

Your Total Score _____ /37

If your score was 29 or less for 10-A and 10-B, review pages 9-10 before continuing.

/37

Score

Date

Name

3-F PREPOSITIONS

A *preposition* shows the relationship between a noun or pronoun to some other word in the sentence. (See page 141 for a detailed treatment of prepositions.)

Example 1

My family went <u>from</u> Missouri <u>to</u> New Mexico <u>by</u> auto.

Analysis:

<u>from</u>—shows relationship between *Missouri* and *New Mexico*—preposition
<u>to</u>—shows relationship between *Missouri* and *New Mexico*—preposition
<u>by</u>—shows relationship between *went* and *auto*—preposition

Example 2

The dog chased the cat <u>across</u> the yard <u>toward</u> the tree <u>near</u> the alley.

Analysis:

<u>across</u>—shows relationship between *chased* and *yard*—preposition
<u>toward</u>—shows relationship between *chased* and *tree*—preposition
<u>near</u>—shows relationship between *tree* and *alley*—preposition

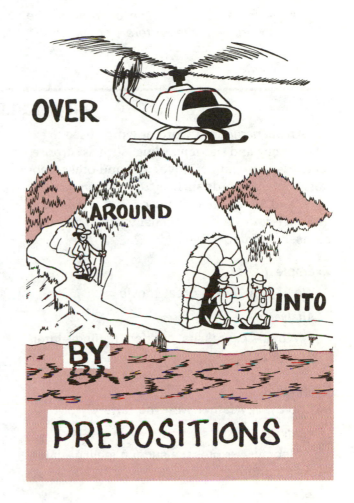

3-G CONJUNCTIONS

A *conjunction* joins words, phrases, and clauses. (See page 145 for a detailed treatment of conjunctions and page 152 for clauses.)

Example 1

Thomas Jefferson <u>and</u> James Madison were born in Virginia.

Analysis:

<u>and</u>—joins *Jefferson* and *Madison*—conjunction

Example 2

Was John Adams <u>or</u> James Monroe the second President of the United States?

Analysis:

<u>or</u>—joins *Adams* and *Monroe*—conjunction

Example 3

The children of the players <u>and</u> the writers sat in the press box.

Analysis:

<u>and</u>—joins phrases—*The children of the players* with *the writers*—conjunction

Example 4

<u>Before</u> my sister left for work, she cooked breakfast for me.

Analysis:

<u>Before</u>—connects the dependent clause with the main clause—conjunction

---

3-H INTERJECTIONS

An *interjection* is a word or words used to express strong and sudden feeling, such as surprise, fear, suspense, anger, love, joy, and other emotions. Special words such as *wow, horrors, hurrah, ouch,* and *hooray* are often used, but words such as *help, beware,* and *stop* (usually verbs) may also be used as interjections.

Example 1

<u>Wow!</u> That was a great movie.

Analysis:

<u>Wow!</u>—expresses sudden feeling—interjection

Example 2

<u>Hooray!</u> My father won the lottery.

Analysis:

<u>Hooray!</u>—expresses sudden feeling—interjection

TRYOUT EXERCISE

Directions: Identify the prepositions, the conjunctions, and the interjections in the following sentences. Underline the prepositions once, the conjunctions twice, and the interjections three times. Check your answers on page 245 or with your teacher before continuing with your assignment.

1. Hurrah! Mr. Owen and the neighbors planned a picnic with a dessert from the pastry shop.

2. Wow! School ended in June, and Holly and I flew to Hollywood.

3. Gosh! The famous television and movie actor visited with the students.

4. The hotel or motel near the airport was nice.

5. Jennifer and Chris brought their pictures and autographs to school.

Complete Application Practices 11-16, pages 19-24, at this time.

Parts of Speech Drill

application practice **11**

11-A Practice Procedure Identify the prepositions in the following sentences by underlining them once. Identify the conjunctions by underlining them twice. Score one point for each correct identification.

Your Score

1. Is soccer or swimming more popular during the summer with young people?   1. _____

2. My brother and sister played basketball on the team at college.   2. _____

3. The referee with his whistle and fine attitude worked a good game.   3. _____

4. Mr. and Mrs. Wetzel enjoy fishing for trout or salmon in Washington.   4. _____

5. Surfing and skiing are two popular activities for youngsters in California and Hawaii.   5. _____

6. Surfers with their surfboards and wet suits come to our beach during the month of June.   6. _____

7. When the surf is high, dozens of surfers with their boards under their arms arrive early.   7. _____

Your Total Score _____ /25

If your score was 19 or less for 11-A, review pages 17-18 before continuing.

11-B Practice Procedure Identify the interjections in the following sentences by underlining them once. Identify the verbs by underlining them twice. Score one point for each correct identification.

1. Wow! That elephant weighs six tons.   1. _____

2. Hooray! I finally saw a koala.   2. _____

3. The whale show pleased the entire audience. Terrific!   3. _____

4. Oops! My sister slipped on the wet aisle at the show.   4. _____

5. Phooey! The pandas were in a separate building.   5. _____

Your Total Score _____ /10

If your score was 7 or less for 11-B, review pages 10 and 18 before continuing.

11-C Practice Procedure Identify the following words by writing the part of speech for each. Score one point for each correct answer.

1. she _____   7. usually _____

2. ouch! _____   8. and _____

3. understand _____   9. between _____

4. with _____   10. handsome _____

5. explorer _____   11. them _____

6. smart _____   12. song _____

Your Total Score _____ /12

If your score was 9 or less for 11-C, review Section 3, pages 9-18 before continuing.

12-A Practice Procedure Identify the nouns, verbs, adjectives, and prepositions in the following sentences. Place *N* for noun, *V* for verb, *Adj* for adjective, or *Prep* for preposition above the word. Score one point for each correct response.

Your Score

1. Active people of all ages enjoy swimming, hiking, tennis, or golf.   1. _____

2. Individual sports are the oldest and most popular in the nation.   2. _____

3. Pleasant activities include bowling, archery, and fishing.   3. _____

4. With the enormous interest in health at this time, jogging and walking appeal to concerned people.   4. _____

5. Uncle Dave gave me a weight machine and a book about conditioning.   5. _____

6. Many spectators appreciate the amazing ability of the professional athletes.   6. _____

7. Other activities besides walking, jogging, or weights combine fun with healthy exercise.   7. _____

8. The parents in the neighborhood, with help from the coach, organized a conditioning program.   8. _____

9. Popular sporting events in the community provide competition for all people.   9. _____

10. The marathon started with loud shouts and yells from the cheerful crowd.   10. _____

Your Total Score _____ /107

If your score was 85 or less for 12-A, review pages 9-10, 13, and 17 before continuing.

12-B Practice Procedure Identify the pronouns, conjunctions, interjections, and adverbs in the following sentences. Place *Pro* for pronoun, *C* for conjunction, *I* for interjection, or *Adv* for adverb above the word. Score one point for each correct response.

1. Hooray! They happily celebrated Washington's birthday today.   1. _____

2. When we went to the nation's capital, he and I visited the Smithsonian Museum.   2. _____

3. Gosh! I finally saw the exhibit there.   3. _____

4. He obviously enjoyed the guided tour.   4. _____

5. Yippee! We gratefully and respectfully observed Independence Day.   5. _____

6. Oops! They unintentionally and unknowingly forgot Cinco de Mayo Day.   6. _____

7. Elena reminded him and her about the dinner at Arturo's or Juan's house.   7. _____

8. Gee! They solemnly promised to attend.   8. _____

9. Chun and Kwan generously prepared a tasty Chinese dinner for us.   9. _____

10. Terrific! The meal was carefully and slowly cooked by them.   10. _____

Your Total Score _____ /40

If your score was 31 or less for 12-B, review pages 10, 14, 17, and 18 before continuing.

Parts of Speech Review

application practice **13**

13-A Practice Procedure Identify the nouns, verbs, adjectives, and prepositions in the following sentences. Place *N* for noun, *V* for verb, *Adj* for adjective, or *Prep* for preposition above the word. Score one point for each correct response.

Your Score

1. The generous Mr. Biller gave me a new word processor for graduation.   1. _____

2. Greta enjoyed the three courses in computers at school during the year.   2. _____

3. The teacher presented the lessons in a pleasant and relaxed manner.   3. _____

4. The new local store demonstrated the machines for the class.   4. _____

5. The two owners invited five pupils to the comfortable and calm presentation. 5. _____

6. The salesperson explained about the numerous computers and new calculators.   6. _____

7. Ms. Gabriel and Mr. Dugan worked with the different types of machines.   7. _____

8. Nicola, Carla, and Yoko learned about the various machines in three weeks.   8. _____

13-B Practice Procedure Identify the pronouns, adverbs, conjunctions, and interjections in the following sentences. Place *Pro* for pronoun, *Adv* for adverb, *C* for conjunction, or *I* for interjection above the word. Score one point for each correct response.

1. Whew! We enthusiastically visited Washington, D.C., and Williamsburg.   1. _____

2. The guide carefully arranged transportation for me.   2. _____

3. Gosh! I proudly and humbly looked at the White House with them.   3. _____

4. Tomorrow they eagerly plan a tour of the National Gallery or the Supreme
   Court Building.   4. _____

5. She gladly viewed the National Archives and White House yesterday.   5. _____

6. He planned a drive for us later to Mount Vernon or Williamsburg. Wow!   6. _____

7. Fantastic! They finally toured us through Richmond and Williamsburg.   7. _____

8. Oh! Alma secretly planned a luncheon for him or me.   8. _____

Your Total Score _____ /117

If your score was 93 or less for 13-A and 13-B, review Section 3, pages 9-18, before continuing.

Reinforcement Review of Parts of Speech

application practice **14**

14-A Practice Procedure Identify the underlined nouns, verbs, adjectives, and prepositions in the following sentences. Place *N* for noun, *V* for verb, *Adj* for adjective, or *Prep* for preposition above each underlined word. Score one point for each correct response.

Your Score

1. Young and <u>older</u> people <u>exercise</u> on <u>a</u> regular <u>schedule</u>.   1. _____

2. <u>Miss Naulls</u> <u>arranged</u> <u>a</u> program <u>for</u> the health <u>club</u>.   2. _____

3. My <u>mother</u> <u>enjoys</u> walking <u>in</u> the <u>park</u> <u>with</u> me.   3. _____

4. <u>Karen</u>, the <u>tall</u> <u>lifeguard</u>, <u>swims</u> every <u>day</u>.   4. _____

5. Olivia <u>improved</u> her <u>posture</u> walking <u>two</u> miles <u>a</u> <u>day</u>.   5. _____

6. Dr. Kerlan, <u>the</u> <u>famous</u> orthopedist, <u>considers</u> walking a <u>basic</u> sport <u>for</u> most people.   6. _____

7. <u>By</u> swimming and eating properly Phil <u>maintained</u> a <u>slim</u> <u>figure</u>.   7. _____

8. <u>Jogging</u> <u>is</u> fashionable <u>with</u> many <u>celebrities</u>.   8. _____

9. <u>Three</u> qualified <u>nutritionists</u> <u>wrote</u> <u>an</u> article <u>for</u> the <u>magazine</u>.   9. _____

10. The <u>physical</u> <u>therapist</u> <u>treated</u> my <u>young</u> brother <u>with</u> a <u>massage</u>.   10. _____

Your Total Score _____ /48

If your score was 37 or less for 14-A, review pages 9-10, 13, and 17 before continuing.

14-B Practice Procedure Identify the underlined pronouns, adverbs, conjunctions, and interjections in the following sentences. Place *Pro* for pronoun, *Adv* for adverb, *C* for conjunction, or *I* for interjection above each underlined word. Score one point for each correct response.

1. He and <u>she</u> <u>often</u> gave <u>me</u> certain jobs to do.   1. _____

2. <u>Golly!</u> <u>I</u> <u>quickly</u> learned to finish the work on time.   2. _____

3. <u>We</u> <u>seldom</u> received any instructions <u>late</u> in the day.   3. _____

4. <u>Wow!</u> The manager was <u>always</u> ready <u>or</u> eager to help <u>us</u>.   4. _____

5. Simple instructions are more <u>readily</u> understood by <u>him</u> <u>and</u> <u>me</u>.   5. _____

6. Susan <u>surely</u> was happy to receive her paycheck from <u>them</u> <u>or</u> <u>him</u>.   6. _____

7. <u>You</u> should <u>certainly</u> ask questions if you need help.   7. _____

8. <u>Whew!</u> My salary was <u>usually</u> more than <u>I</u> expected.   8. _____

9. Her husband and <u>she</u> <u>generally</u> were kind <u>and</u> helpful.   9. _____

10. <u>I</u> <u>gratefully</u> accepted the help that <u>he</u> and she offered <u>me</u> and her.   10. _____

Your Total Score _____ /33

If your score was 25 or less for 14-B, review pages 10, 14, and 17-18 before continuing.

22

15-A Practice Procedure Identify the nouns, verbs, adjectives, and prepositions in the following sentences. Place *N* for noun, *V* for verb, *Adj* for adjective, or *Prep* for preposition above the word. Score one point for each correct response.

Your Score

1. The librarian recommended a good book to Jim and Peg.   1. _____
2. She took the popular magazine from the top shelf.   2. _____
3. Miss Anton spoke about the various jobs with noisy Hank and attentive Fran.   3. _____
4. Peg accepted a fair offer for the new job from the committee.   4. _____
5. Lois and a late applicant had the highest marks in the interview.   5. _____
6. Ms. Mills hoped for an excellent position with Ms. Ortiz.   6. _____
7. Will drove through the heavy rainstorm in a battered, old car.   7. _____
8. Talkative Magda sat behind Will and the frisky dog in the front seat.   8. _____
9. Nellie and the timid girl listened to the informative lecture by the assistant

   manager.   9. _____
10. The operator of the camera placed the expensive equipment behind the

   last row of seats.   10. _____

15-B Practice Procedure Identify the pronouns, adverbs, conjunctions, and interjections in the following sentences. Place *Pro* for pronoun, *Adv* for adverb, *C* for conjunction, or *I* for interjection above the word. Score one point for each correct response.

1. Golly! I really enjoyed the program given by Miss Olsen.   1. _____
2. Lindsey and Marta carefully listened to the speaker.   2. _____
3. Wow! She often spoke to groups or classes.   3. _____
4. He and Mr. Riggs left soon after the movie.   4. _____
5. They seldom displayed the shells or jewelry to us.   5. _____
6. We traveled to Fiji and Samoa with the manager and him.   6. _____
7. Fantastic! Tim and I once visited them there with the folks and him.   7. _____
8. Fiji or Samoa is sometimes too warm for me.   8. _____
9. Gosh! He later went there with us for a vacation.   9. _____
10. Originally, Fiji was annexed quickly by the British Crown Colony.   10. _____
11. Golly! They still inhabit about 100 or 110 islands in the South Pacific now.   11. _____
12. The Fiji Islands are an independent country now, and the inhabitants still

    speak English.   12. _____

Your Total Score _____ /157

If your score was 125 or less for 15-A and 15-B, review Section 3, pages 9-18, before continuing.

16-A Practice Procedure Identify the nouns, verbs, adjectives, and prepositions in the following sentences. Place *N* for noun, *V* for verb, *Adj* for adjective, or *Prep* for preposition above the word. Score one point for each correct response.

Your Score

1. The capable Miss Kelly received a good salary from the supervisor.   1. _____

2. Mr. Dunn dictated long memorandums to the large staff.   2. _____

3. Sally Munoz, with excellent references, got a good position.   3. _____

4. The cordial receptionist greeted salespeople in a pleasant manner.   4. _____

5. Joe Torres recognized the regular customers without any trouble.   5. _____

6. A professional secretary performs many complex duties during an entire day.   6. _____

7. Jane places the daily schedule for the staff on the bulletin board.   7. _____

8. The supervisor evaluated the employees in a clear and logical way.   8. _____

9. An alert executive realizes the importance of a steady worker.   9. _____

10. The experienced Mrs. Johnson walked around the office.   10. _____

16-B Practice Procedure Identify the pronouns, adverbs, conjunctions, and interjections in the following sentences. Place *Pro* for pronoun, *Adv* for adverb, *C* for conjunction, or *I* for interjection above the word. Score one point for each correct response.

1. He works carefully and slowly on the computer.   1. _____

2. I am now responsible for the letters and accounts.   2. _____

3. Whew! We prepare forms often for tax reporting or payrolls.   3. _____

4. She finally learned the job from Stella and him.   4. _____

5. Golly! They seldom forget the daily routine or a customer.   5. _____

6. Gosh! He probably misplaced the files or letters there.   6. _____

7. He soon found the records by the window and desks.   7. _____

8. They usually get a raise or extra benefits from her.   8. _____

9. Oh! I never knew what he or she did in the office.   9. _____

10. Wow! They always remember the good work he does and never notice the mistakes he makes.   10. _____

11. She was soon responsible for the hiring and firing of employees.   11. _____

12. Stop! You are foolishly typing the wrong address.   12. _____

Your Total Score _____ /143

If your score was 113 or less for 16-A and 16-B, review Section 3, pages 9-18, before continuing.

Score _____ /143

Date

Name

Major Classes of Nouns

1. To recognize the three types of nouns.
2. To learn how to form noun plurals and noun possessives.

4-A COMMON NOUNS

Common nouns are names given to words identifying persons, places, or things in a special class. A common noun does not refer to a *particular* person, place, or thing.

Example 1

Dozens of hikers walked with their equipment on their backs.

Analysis:

Dozens, hikers, equipment, backs—general terms not naming anyone or anything in particular—common nouns

Example 2

The donkeys were led along the path by the guide.

Analysis:

donkeys, path, guide—general terms not

naming anyone or anything in particular—common nouns

Example 3

The cook prepared the meals for the boys and girls.

Analysis:

cook, meals, boys, girls—general terms not naming anyone or anything in particular—common nouns

Example 4

The parents watched a movie in the theater.

Analysis:

parents, movie, theater—general terms not naming anyone or anything in particular—common nouns

---

4-B PROPER NOUNS

Proper nouns are names of particular persons, places, or things. Proper nouns should always be capitalized. (See page 183 for the section on capitalization.)

Example 1

Beth Mauro visited a friend in London, England.

Analysis:

Beth Mauro—name of a particular person—proper noun
London, England—names of particular places—proper nouns

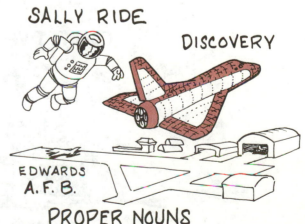

SALLY RIDE

DISCOVERY

EDWARDS A.F.B.

PROPER NOUNS

Example 2

George Washington was born in Virginia on February 22, 1732.

Analysis:

George Washington—name of a particular person—proper noun

Virginia—name of a particular place—proper noun

February 22—name of a particular thing—proper noun (1732 is a common noun)

Example 3

Thanksgiving Day is observed nationally on the fourth Thursday in November.

Analysis:

Thanksgiving Day—name of a particular thing—proper noun

Thursday, November—names of particular things—proper nouns

Example 4

Scott Brown walked across the Golden Gate Bridge from San Francisco.

Analysis:

Scott Brown—name of a particular person —proper noun

Golden Gate Bridge—name of a particular thing—proper noun

San Francisco—name of a particular place —proper noun

4-C COLLECTIVE NOUNS

Collective nouns are names of groups or collections, such as *mob, crowd, committee*. Parts of numbers or sums of money are collective nouns (*three-fifths, one-third, $100*).

Example 1

The audience applauded the speeches of the candidates.

Analysis:

audience—name of a group of persons—collective noun

Example 2

A crowd quickly gathers for the actress' entrance.

Analysis:

crowd—name of a group of persons—collective noun

Example 3

One-third of the band played in the brass section.

Analysis:

One-third—part of a number—collective noun

band—name of a group of persons—collective noun

Example 4

The committee selected the orchestra.

Analysis:

committee, orchestra—names of groups of persons—collective nouns

COLLECTIVE NOUN

FLOCK

CROWD

Collective nouns may take either the singular or the plural form of the verb, depending on the use in the sentence. If a collective noun refers to a group acting as a whole, a singular verb is used. If a collective noun refers to a group in which the members act individually, a plural verb is used. However, collective nouns usually take a singular verb.

Example 1

The committee is against the tax increase.

Analysis:

> committee—collective noun. The singular form of the verb is used because the committee is thought of as a group. Every member of the committee is against the tax increase.

Example 2

The crowd is cheering the players to victory.

Analysis:

> crowd—collective noun. The singular form of the verb is used because the crowd is thought of as a group. Every member of the crowd is cheering the players to victory.

Example 3

The office force were hurrying to finish their jobs.

Analysis:

> office force—collective noun. The plural form of the verb is used because the members of the office force are thought of as individuals.

Example 4

The group were talking among themselves about the new television show.

Analysis:

> group—collective noun. The plural form of the verb is used because the members of the group are thought of as individuals.

Example 5

The faculty have not yet agreed upon their regular rooms.

Analysis:

> faculty—collective noun. The plural form of the verb is used because the members of the faculty are thought of as individuals.

Sometimes it may be difficult to determine whether the singular or plural form of the verb should be used with a collective noun. When in doubt, decide whether you want to refer to the group as a whole or to the individuals in the group, and then use a singular or a plural verb.

Frequently Used Collective Nouns

army	company	herd	office force
assembly	congregation	jury	panel
audience	corps	legislature	platoon
band	crew	majority	police
cast	crowd	mass	public
choir	faculty	mob	school
chorus	family	nation	staff
class	flock	navy	swarm
club	gang	number	team
committee	group	orchestra	trio

Directions: Identify the nouns in the following sentences by underlining them once. Above each noun place the abbreviation *P* if it is a proper noun, *C* if it is a common noun, or *Col* if it is a collective noun. Check your answers on page 245 or with your teacher before continuing with your assignment.

1. Shirley Modesti was the leader of the class on the trip to Australia last August.

2. A committee of parents watched the students leave from the Los Angeles International Airport.

3. A band from the local high school met the group at the airport in Cairns, Australia.

4. The next morning the faculty cruised to the Outer Barrier Reef for a view of the fish and coral.

5. Miss Oswald of the Palace Hotel and her staff arranged tours for the students.

Complete Application Practices 17-18, pages 29-30, at this time.

Noun Identification

17 Practice Procedure Identify each noun and tell whether it is a proper, a common, or a collective noun. Place the abbreviation *P* for proper, *C* for common, or *Col* for collective above the noun. Score one point for each correct response.

Your Score

1. The band from the navy played patriotic songs.

1. _____

2. The crowd of parents loudly sang the popular tunes.

2. _____

3. Gina Orsatti led the choir in a rendition of *The Grand Old Flag*.

3. _____

4. One-fifth of the group did not know the words.

4. _____

5. Mr. Eaton was pleased at the behavior of the audience.

5. _____

6. Jesse Jackson spoke to the faculty about the value of education.

6. _____

7. The speech was favorably received by the majority of the people.

7. _____

8. A number of youngsters met Mr. Jackson and his staff.

8. _____

9. Madge Drake led the orchestra in the musical program.

9. _____

10. A crowd met with the president of the *Aero Club*.

10. _____

11. One-fourth of the group had never heard of Neil Armstrong.

11. _____

12. Dr. Smith showed a tape of the first walk on the moon by Armstrong.

12. _____

13. The second astronaut on the moon was ''Buzz'' Aldrin.

13. _____

14. John Glenn, an astronaut, piloted the first orbital spacecraft.

14. _____

15. He was later elected to the U.S. Senate from Ohio.

15. _____

16. Dr. Sally Ride was the first woman to ride in space.

16. _____

17. She received her doctorate in physics from Stanford University.

17. _____

18. Men and women from the army and navy marched proudly on Veterans Day in Washington, D.C.

18. _____

19. Three-fourths of our class knew Martin Luther King had won a Nobel Peace Prize.

19. _____

20. A committee of citizens has called Dr. King a crusader.

20. _____

21. Dennis Chavez was once a leader in the U.S. Senate.

21. _____

22. He had been a chairman of the committee for Public Works.

22. _____

23. Mrs. Maxson gave a stirring talk to the faculty about the Nobel Peace Prize.

23. _____

24. Alfred Nobel was the inventor of dynamite.

24. _____

25. Bill Beverly, the pilot of the crew, flew through fog and snow.

25. _____

Your Total Score _____ /88

If your score was 69 or less, review pages 25-28 before continuing.

Name

Date

Score

/88

Noun Identification

application practice **18**

18 Practice Procedure Identify each noun and tell whether it is a proper, a common, or a collective noun. Place the abbreviation *P* for proper, *C* for common, or *Col* for collective above the noun. Score one point for each correct response.

Your Score

1. A panel of geographers spoke about the seven continents. 1. _____
2. Continents are the great dry-land divisions in the world. 2. _____
3. Dr. Tunney talked about Asia, Africa, and Europe. 3. _____
4. Her staff discussed South America and North America. 4. _____
5. Miss Adams showed film of her trip to Australia and Antarctica. 5. _____
6. More than one-half of the people in the world live in Asia. 6. _____
7. A number of large countries in Asia were listed. 7. _____
8. China, India, Burma, Japan, and Korea were listed on the chart. 8. _____
9. Mt. Everest in Nepal-Tibet is the highest mountain in the world. 9. _____
10. A hiker from the army brought a film about the Himalayan Mountains. 10. _____
11. The audience was fascinated by the movie. 11. _____
12. The continent of Australia is about equal in area to the U.S. if Alaska and Hawaii are excluded. 12. _____
13. Captain Cook in 1770 claimed possession of Australia for Great Britain. 13. _____
14. A group from the local bank told us about the monetary unit of Britain. 14. _____
15. A majority of the faculty was interested in North America. 15. _____
16. Our country has unusual scenic sights. 16. _____
17. The original Americans were the Indians and Eskimos. 17. _____
18. Liz Cooper listed the U.S. as having the greatest number of people in North America. 18. _____
19. The class, under the guidance of Ms. Rich, toured Africa. 19. _____
20. Cory Sloan had pictures of cheetahs and leopards. 20. _____
21. A herd of elephants was featured in the photos. 21. _____
22. A group of natives helped the crowd of workers. 22. _____
23. The Amazon River is the second longest river in the world. 23. _____
24. The orchestra played many stirring songs of Brazil. 24. _____
25. A mob gathered at the airport to welcome the singer from Argentina. 25. _____

Your Total Score _____ /94

If your score was 74 or less, review pages 25-28 before continuing.

30

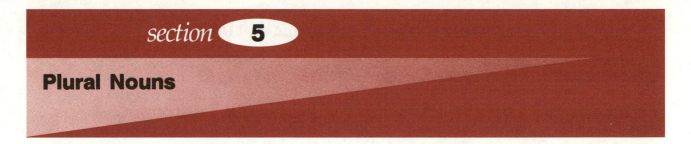

Plural Nouns

Remember that a noun names a person, a place, or a thing. It is a *singular noun* when it names one person, one place, or one thing. It is a *plural noun* when it names more than one. You must know whether a noun is singular or plural. To form the plural of nouns, remember a few rules.

5-A FORMING THE PLURAL OF NOUNS

Simple Plurals

Rule 1: Most nouns become plural by adding the letter *s* to the singular noun. Study the following examples.

Singular	Plural
book	books
cat	cats
desk	desks
girl	girls
river	rivers
tiger	tigers

Rule 2: For words ending in *s, x, z, sh,* or *ch,* you must add *es* to form the plural. Study the examples below.

Singular	Plural
beach	beaches
bunch	bunches
bus	buses
glass	glasses
dish	dishes
fox	foxes
waltz	waltzes

Plurals of Words with Special Endings

Rule 3: *Y*-Ending Plurals. If a noun ends in *y* and is preceded by a consonant, change the *y* to *i* and add *es*. Study the examples below.

Singular	Plural
baby	babies
city	cities
melody	melodies
spy	spies

Rule 4: *O*-Ending Plurals. If a noun ends in *o* and is preceded by a consonant, add *es* to form the plural. Study the examples below.

Singular	Plural
echo	echoes
hero	heroes
tomato	tomatoes
potato	potatoes

There are several exceptions to this rule: solo, solos; piano, pianos; auto, autos; silo, silos; soprano, sopranos.

If a noun ends in *o* and is preceded by a vowel (a, e, i, o, u), add *s* to form the plural. Study the examples below.

Singular	Plural
studio	studios
patio	patios
radio	radios
stereo	stereos
shampoo	shampoos

Rule 5: *F*- or *Fe*-Ending Plurals. To form the plural of a noun ending in *f* or *fe*, change the *f* or *fe* to *v* and add *es*. Study the examples below.

Singular	Plural
calf	calves
knife	knives
wife	wives
wolf	wolves

Note these common exceptions to the above rule: roof, roofs; safe, safes; belief, beliefs; sheriff, sheriffs; chief, chiefs.

5-B WORDS WITH IRREGULAR PLURALS

The following twelve words have no set rules for forming the plurals. Some of these words do not change at all from the singular to the plural. Study these words carefully for they are often used incorrectly.

Singular	Plural
moose	moose
deer	deer
child	children
trout	trout

Singular	Plural
man	men
woman	women
sheep	sheep
foot	feet
goose	geese
ox	oxen
tooth	teeth

Note: Some nouns have unusual plural forms. Here are a few of them.

Singular	Plural
cupful	cupfuls
birdhouse	birdhouses
bookcase	bookcases
man-of-war	men-of-war
daughter-in-law	daughters-in-law

5-C NOUNS ALWAYS IN PLURAL FORM

Some nouns are always written in the plural form. The more commonly used ones are shown at the right.

athletics	pants	scissors
earnings	proceeds	shears
economics	riches	thanks

5-D PLURAL FORMS WITH SINGULAR MEANING

Several nouns have a plural form but a singular meaning. Watch verb agreement with these nouns. These nouns require a singular verb.

civic	news
measles	physics
mumps	politics

TRYOUT EXERCISE   **Directions:** Write the plural form of each of the following singular nouns. Check your answers on page 245 or with your teacher before continuing with your assignment.

1. road _____

2. army _____

3. bench _____

4. potato _____

5. shelf _____

6. tooth _____

Complete Application Practices 19-20, pages 33-34, at this time.

19 Practice Procedure Write the plural form of each of the following singular nouns. Score one point for each correct response.

Singular	Plural	Singular	Plural
1. nurse	_____	26. history	_____
2. noun	_____	27. singer	_____
3. baby	_____	28. patio	_____
4. rabbit	_____	29. class	_____
5. spy	_____	30. spoonful	_____
6. tooth	_____	31. woman	_____
7. storm	_____	32. couch	_____
8. duplex	_____	33. tomato	_____
9. business	_____	34. echo	_____
10. coat	_____	35. authority	_____
11. dress	_____	36. committee	_____
12. piano	_____	37. computer	_____
13. man	_____	38. silo	_____
14. ship	_____	39. half	_____
15. community	_____	40. infant	_____
16. wolf	_____	41. security	_____
17. basket	_____	42. church	_____
18. foot	_____	43. quality	_____
19. delivery	_____	44. lunch	_____
20. football	_____	45. zoo	_____
21. sheep	_____	46. bush	_____
22. toy	_____	47. mother	_____
23. activity	_____	48. life	_____
24. address	_____	49. duty	_____
25. school	_____	50. key	_____

Your Total Score _____ /50

If your score was 39 or less, review pages 31-32 before continuing.

/50

Score

Date

Name

20 Practice Procedure Write the plural form of each of the following singular nouns. (Refer to the plural lists on pages 31-32 if necessary.) Score one point for each correct response.

Singular	Plural	Singular	Plural
1. bunny	_____	26. trout	_____
2. loaf	_____	27. child	_____
3. index	_____	28. athletics	_____
4. alley	_____	29. stereo	_____
5. handful	_____	30. sketch	_____
6. cattle	_____	31. mouse	_____
7. lullaby	_____	32. roof	_____
8. tariff	_____	33. chief	_____
9. fish	_____	34. measles	_____
10. thief	_____	35. sofa	_____
11. sister-in-law	_____	36. deer	_____
12. zero	_____	37. ox	_____
13. soprano	_____	38. patio	_____
14. corps	_____	39. politics	_____
15. torpedo	_____	40. birdhouse	_____
16. handkerchief	_____	41. scissors	_____
17. radio	_____	42. leaf	_____
18. sheriff	_____	43. glassful	_____
19. knife	_____	44. kangaroo	_____
20. potato	_____	45. series	_____
21. coach	_____	46. goose	_____
22. trio	_____	47. cameo	_____
23. moose	_____	48. navy	_____
24. topaz	_____	49. trousers	_____
25. bunch	_____	50. news	_____

Your Total Score _____ /50

If your score was 39 or less, review pages 31-32 before continuing.

Nouns and the Possessive Form

Nouns used in the *possessive form* show ownership or possession. The *apostrophe* (') is used to show the possessive form. Guides for forming possessives are given below. (For use of the apostrophe in a contraction, see page 178.)

6-A SINGULAR POSSESSIVE

To show the possessive form of a singular noun, merely place the apostrophe (') after the last letter of the word and add *s*.

Example 1

The sergeant's pen is on the table.

Analysis:

sergeant's—singular noun—apostrophe after *sergeant* and before *s* tells whose pen it is (the pen of the sergeant)

Example 2

The boy's tie is a new one.

Analysis:

boy's—singular noun—apostrophe after *boy* and before *s* tells whose tie it is (the tie of the boy)

To show the singular possessive form of a noun of *one syllable* ending in an *s, x, ch,* or *sh* sound, place the apostrophe after the last letter and add *s*. However, to show the singular possessive form of a noun of *more than one syllable* ending in an *s, x, ch,* or *sh* sound, add only the apostrophe.

Example

Mr. Ross's car needs new tires, but Miss Perkins' auto is in perfect condition.

Analysis:

Ross's—singular proper noun of one syllable—apostrophe and *s* added to show possession

Perkins'—singular proper noun of two syllables—apostrophe alone added to show possession

---

6-B PLURAL POSSESSIVE

To show the possessive form of a plural noun not ending in *s*, add the apostrophe (') and the *s*.

Example 1

The women's luggage went to the wrong airport.

Analysis:

women's—plural form of *woman*—apostrophe is placed before the *s* because the noun does not end in *s* (the luggage of the women)

Example 2

The children's toys were stored in a large box.

Analysis:

children's—plural form of *child*—apostrophe is placed before the *s* because the noun does not end in *s* (the toys of the children)

To show the possessive form of a plural noun ending in s, merely place the apostrophe after the s.

Example 1

The clowns' costumes were funny.

Analysis:

clowns'—plural form of *clown*—apostrophe is placed after the s to indicate plural possession (the costumes of the clowns)

Example 2

The Jeffersons' car was shipped to London.

Analysis:

Jeffersons'—plural of *Jefferson*—apostrophe is placed after the s to indicate plural possession (the car of the Jeffersons)

Example 3

The neighbors' trees provided shade in the summer.

Analysis:

neighbors'—plural form of *neighbor*—apostrophe is placed after the s to indicate plural possession (the trees of the neighbors)

Example 4

The Changs' airplane flew to Toledo.

Analysis:

Changs'—plural form of *Chang*—apostrophe is placed after the s to indicate plural possession (the airplane of the Changs)

TRYOUT EXERCISE

Directions: Write the singular possessive and the plural possessive of each of the following expressions. Make both nouns plural in the plural possessive. Check your answers on page 245 or with your teacher before continuing with your assignment.

Example: the bill of the doctor

the doctor's bill

the doctors' bills

1. the tail of the cat

2. the book of the author

3. the chair of the mother

Directions: Find the possessive nouns in the following sentences and place the apostrophe in the right spot. Check your answers on page 245 or with your teacher before continuing with your assignment.

1. My two uncles experiences were very funny.
2. The man s cars were repaired by his cousins.
3. The owner s life was insured by several companies.

Complete Application Practices 21-26, pages 37-42, at this time.

21 Practice Procedure Use the apostrophe (') to form the possessives of the following nouns. Form the singular possessive and the plural possessive of each singular expression. Make both nouns plural in the plural possessive. Score one point for each correct response.

Examples	Singular Possessive	Plural Possessive
a. purse of the girl	a. *girl's purse*	a. *girls' purses*
b. file of the clerk	b. *clerk's file*	b. *clerks' files*
c. dress of the woman	c. *woman's dress*	c. *women's dresses*
d. tooth of the dog	d. *dog's tooth*	d. *dogs' teeth*
1. sign of the store	1.	1.
2. tail of the tiger	2.	2.
3. phone of the girl	3.	3.
4. car of the family	4.	4.
5. howl of the wolf	5.	5.
6. bus of the school	6.	6.
7. echo of the valley	7.	7.
8. duty of the man	8.	8.
9. silo of the farmer	9.	9.
10. trick of the fox	10.	10.
11. class of the lady	11.	11.
12. studio of the actor	12.	12.
13. story of the writer	13.	13.
14. life of the sheriff	14.	14.
15. bench of the worker	15.	15.
16. jewel of the queen	16.	16.
17. desk of the coach	17.	17.
18. wish of the hero	18.	18.
19. puppy of the dog	19.	19.
20. shelf of the child	20.	20.
21. mask of the thief	21.	21.
22. tire of the bus	22.	22.
23. deer of the forest	23.	23.
24. foot of the ox	24.	24.
25. mouse of the cat	25.	25.

Your Total Score _____ /50

If your score was 39 or less, review pages 31-32 and 35-36 before continuing.

Name

Date

Score

/50

22 Practice Procedure Write the plural form of each of the following singular nouns in the blanks provided. (Refer to the plural lists on pages 31-32, if necessary.) Score one point for each correct response.

Singular	Plural	Singular	Plural
1. galaxy		26. Japanese	
2. gulf		27. hysterics	
3. quail		28. tray	
4. clothes		29. X ray	
5. trolley		30. toothbrush	
6. species		31. zebra	
7. handful		32. economics	
8. scarf		33. tattoo	
9. louse		34. sheep	
10. motto		35. axis	
11. Chinese		36. trout	
12. strawberry		37. half	
13. child		38. civics	
14. analysis		39. fish	
15. navy		40. piccolo	
16. notary public		41. Eskimo	
17. teaspoonful		42. elf	
18. salmon		43. ethics	
19. lottery		44. cattle	
20. giraffe		45. bus	
21. turkey		46. series	
22. foot		47. cello	
23. photo		48. ally	
24. stereo		49. editor-in-chief	
25. alumnus		50. fowl	

Your Total Score _____ /50

If your score was 39 or less, review pages 31-32 before continuing.

23 Practice Procedure Find the noun in each sentence that requires an apostrophe ('). In the answer column, write the correct possessive form of the noun with the apostrophe in the correct place. Score one point for each correct answer.

Examples:

Answers

a. The girls in Jennifers class enjoyed hiking. a. **Jennifer's**

b. Mr. Smiths house was at Elm and Maple Streets. b. **Smith's**

c. The mices problems were the cats in the house. c. **mice's**

1. An Indian chiefs daughter led the Pledge of Allegiance to our flag. 1. _____

2. Many Indians have become famous in our countrys history. 2. _____

3. Ted Foss store sold many artifacts from the different Indian tribes. 3. _____

4. All of the Indians saddle blankets were handwoven. 4. _____

5. Many families hunted for a certain birds feathers. 5. _____

6. All of the pupils applause at the end of the speech pleased the visitors. 6. _____

7. Art Cross unusual blankets of moccasins and wampum belts were displayed. 7. _____

8. Some of the womens dresses were worn by students. 8. _____

9. One of Mrs. Burns sons did the Buffalo Dance. 9. _____

10. Several of their warriors clothes were made from the skins and furs of animals. 10. _____

11. Frances uncles used their trucks for hauling the various displays. 11. _____

12. The ladies headdresses were made from horns of buffalo. 12. _____

13. Crazy Horse and the Sioux Indians defeated General Custers army at Little Bighorn. 13. _____

14. The childrens visits to the Indian Museum were fun and educational. 14. _____

15. Mr. Charles Russells paintings of cowboy life are expensive. 15. _____

16. A cowboys equipment included boots, spurs, and chaps. 16. _____

17. Large profits were made by the sale of the cattlemens steers. 17. _____

18. Daniel Boones companions helped explore the West. 18. _____

19. Scouting and trailing were two of many pioneers abilities. 19. _____

20. Kit Carson looked after some of the traders oxen, horses, and mules. 20. _____

21. Carson served with General Kearnys army during the Mexican War. 21. _____

22. That writers books were sold at many stores. 22. _____

23. Charles job was walking horses after a race. 23. _____

24. The programs for the rodeo were printed by Ms. James company. 24. _____

25. The companies feed bills were higher this month. 25. _____

Your Total Score _____ /25

Name

Date

Score

/25

If your score was 19 or less, review pages 35-36 before continuing.

/30

Score

Date

Name

24-A Practice Procedure Use the apostrophe (') to form the possessives of the following nouns. Form the singular possessive and the plural possessive of each singular expression. Make both nouns plural in the plural possessive. Score one point for each correct response.

Examples	Singular Possessive	Plural Possessive
a. brush of the lady	a. *lady's brush*	a. *ladies' brushes*
b. fax of the office	b. *office's fax*	b. *offices' faxes*
1. cello of the child	1. _____	1. _____
2. foot of the ox	2. _____	2. _____
3. life of the woman	3. _____	3. _____
4. galaxy of the sky	4. _____	4. _____
5. class of civics	5. _____	5. _____
6. salmon of the river	6. _____	6. _____
7. gas of the refinery	7. _____	7. _____
8. cattle of the range	8. _____	8. _____
9. story of the Chinese	9. _____	9. _____
10. hysterics of the calf	10. _____	10. _____

24-B Practice Procedure Find the noun in each sentence that requires an apostrophe ('). In the answer column, write the correct possessive form of the noun with the apostrophe in the correct place. Score one point for each correct answer.

Examples:

Answers

a. The mens businesses were successful.　　　　a. *men's*

b. Mr. Jones garages were located in two cities.　　b. *Jones's*

c. Carlos wishes involved certain businesses.　　　c. *Carlos'*

1. Miss Ross relatives were in politics.　　　　　　1. _____

2. Two of the Riggs children visited the grandparents.　2. _____

3. Stacey Moss three insurance companies were busy.　3. _____

4. The womens careers progressed very rapidly.　　　4. _____

5. Various farmers crops brought high prices.　　　　5. _____

6. Her mothers knives were cleaned and polished.　　6. _____

7. Five of the Sanders relatives were teachers.　　　7. _____

8. Californias earthquakes scared many tourists.　　8. _____

9. Brenden Flores neighbors spoke many languages.　9. _____

10. That golf courses owners were Brooks and Timms.　10. _____

Your Total Score _____ /30

If your score was 23 or less, review pages 31-32 and 35-36 before continuing.

Matching Definitions and Plural Possession

25-A Practice Procedure Match each item in Column A with the item it describes in Column B. Write the identifying letter from Column A in the blank provided at the right. Score one point for each correct answer.

Column A	Column B	Answers
a. do not refer to a particular person, place, or thing	**1.** the pupil's pen	**1.** _____
b. common noun	**2.** possessive noun	**2.** _____
c. names more than one person, place, or thing	**3.** singular noun	**3.** _____
d. shows ownership	**4.** common nouns	**4.** _____
e. names of groups or parts of numbers	**5.** proper nouns	**5.** _____
f. possessive noun	**6.** horse	**6.** _____
g. proper noun	**7.** plural noun	**7.** _____
h. collective noun	**8.** three-fifths	**8.** _____
i. nouns which should always be capitalized	**9.** Susan B. Anthony	**9.** _____
j. names one person, one place, or one thing	**10.** collective noun	**10.** _____

Your Total Score _____ /10

If your score was 7 or less, review pages 25-28, 31-32, and 35-36 before continuing.

25-B Practice Procedure Find the noun in each sentence that requires an apostrophe ('). In the answer column, write the correct possessive form of the noun with the apostrophe in the correct place. Score one point for each correct answer.

Answers

1. My three cousins partners hired my sister and me. 1. _____

2. The policewomens uniforms were comfortable. 2. _____

3. The storms blew and a trees leaves dropped off. 3. _____

4. Dot Moss children visit their aunts every week. 4. _____

5. Freds employers gave him health benefits. 5. _____

6. The mens horse blankets were stolen. 6. _____

7. Connie Jones clothes are expensive and attractive. 7. _____

8. Swimming and walking were my mothers exercises. 8. _____

9. Jim Burgess cars raced at many different speedways. 9. _____

10. Many of our friends jobs were different from mine. 10. _____

11. My junk may be other childrens treasures. 11. _____

12. The mices favorite foods are cheese and crackers. 12. _____

Your Total Score _____ /12

If your score was 9 or less, review pages 35-36 before continuing.

Plural Nouns and Noun Possession

26-A Practice Procedure Write the plural form of each singular noun. (Refer to the plural lists on pages 31-32, if necessary.) Score one point for each correct response.

	Singular	Plural		Singular	Plural
1.	athletics	_____	11.	alley	_____
2.	torpedo	_____	12.	cupful	_____
3.	holiday	_____	13.	study	_____
4.	teaspoonful	_____	14.	mother-in-law	_____
5.	politics	_____	15.	zero	_____
6.	corps	_____	16.	stand-by	_____
7.	knife	_____	17.	handkerchief	_____
8.	roof	_____	18.	skateboard	_____
9.	scissors	_____	19.	beauty	_____
10.	radio	_____	20.	box	_____

Your Total Score _____ /20

If your score was 15 or less, review pages 25-28, 31-32, and 35-36 before continuing.

26-B Practice Procedure Find the noun in each sentence that requires an apostrophe ('). In the answer column, write the correct possessive form of the noun with the apostrophe in the correct place. Score one point for each correct answer.

Examples:

Answers

a. The mices hiding places were in the garage.

a. ___*mice's*___

b. That companys lists of addresses needs updating.

b. ___*company's*___

c. Franks sisters helped him with his payments.

c. ___*Frank's*___

1. My mothers office doesn't need any typists.

1. _____

2. Two of the womens sweaters were misplaced.

2. _____

3. The boys moustaches changed their appearances.

3. _____

4. Her childs toys were left in the back alleys.

4. _____

5. The secretaries register kept ringing up the sales.

5. _____

6. Two donkeys areas were stocked with food and water.

6. _____

7. The athletics programs at both schools were good.

7. _____

8. Our customers accounts were handled by two firms.

8. _____

9. The hurricane blew off several neighbors roofs.

9. _____

10. The ladys gardens won all of the prizes.

10. _____

Your Total Score _____ /10

If your score was 7 or less, review pages 35-36 before continuing.

OBJECTIVES
1. To know that pronouns are words used as substitutes for nouns.
2. To recognize and use different types of pronouns.

Personal pronouns are used in place of the person *speaking* (*I, me, we, us*), in place of the person *spoken to* (*you*), and in place of the person *spoken of* (*he, him, she, her, they, them*). Personal pronouns replace nouns. The old, second-person singular pronoun (*thou, thy, thee*) is still used in poetry.

Personal Pronouns

	Singular	Plural
1st person	I, me, my, mine	we, us, our, ours
2nd person	you, your, yours	you, your, yours
3rd person	he, him, his, she, her, hers, it, its	they, them, their, theirs

Person speaking: *I* went to the hobby show.

Person spoken to: *You* drove the family to the show.

Person spoken of: *He* spoke with the manager's daughter.

7-A PRONOUN AGREEMENT IN PERSON AND NUMBER

A pronoun must agree with its antecedent in person, number (singular or plural), and gender (masculine, feminine, or neuter sex). The *antecedent* is the word for which the pronoun stands. If the antecedent is singular, a singular form of the pronoun is used. If the antecedent is plural, a plural form of the pronoun is used.

Example 1

Peter met his friend at the beach.

Analysis:

his—singular pronoun—agrees in person, number, and gender with antecedent *Peter*

Example 2

Helen wore her new swimsuit.

Analysis:

her—singular pronoun—agrees in person, number, and gender with antecedent *Helen*

Example 3

One of the teachers left a package at school, but she wasn't worried about it.

Analysis:

she—agrees in person and in number with antecedent *One* (*He* could be used in place of *she* as antecedent *One* does not indicate gender.)

Example 4

Guzman and Torres sold their business to a national firm.

Analysis:

their—plural pronoun—agrees in person and number with antecedents *Guzman* and *Torres*

Example 5

The officers meet every Thursday for their luncheon.

Analysis:

their—plural pronoun—agrees in person and in number with antecedent *officers*

7-B CASE FORMS OF PERSONAL PRONOUNS

The three case forms of personal pronouns are nominative, objective, and possessive.

The *nominative case* pronouns (*I, you, he, she, it, we, they*) are used as subjects or as predicate pronouns (in place of predicate nouns) of sentences.

The *objective case* pronouns (*me, you, him, her, it, us, them*) are used as objects of verbs, indirect objects, or objects of prepositions.

The *possessive case* pronouns (*my, mine, your, yours, his, hers, its, our, ours, their, theirs*) are used to denote ownership.

Nominative Case

Pronouns (and nouns) used as subjects are in the *nominative* case. Remember that the *subject noun* is the person, place, or thing spoken of. The *subject pronoun*, however, may be the person, place, or thing spoken of, spoken to, or speaking.

Example 1

I went to the hobby show.

Analysis:

I—person speaking—subject—nominative case

Example 2

You bought some unusual foreign stamps.

Analysis:

You—person spoken to—subject—nominative case

Example 3

She read the baseball card catalog.

Analysis:

She—person spoken of—subject—nominative case

Personal pronouns may be used as *compound* subjects. *Compound* means more than one. Use a plural verb form with a compound subject. (See page 81 for plural forms with compound subjects.)

Example

He and his parents sell coins from the different countries.

Analysis:

He—singular pronoun. Since it is used with the word *parents* as part of the compound subject, a plural verb is required.

When a pronoun (or noun) is used after a verb and refers to the same person or thing as the subject of the verb, it is called a *predicate pronoun* (or noun). A predicate pronoun means the same thing as the subject to which it refers and is in the nominative case.

Example 1

The best teacher in school is he.

Analysis:

he—predicate pronoun—nominative case—follows the verb *is* and refers to the subject *teacher*

Example 2

It is I.

Analysis:

I—predicate pronoun—nominative case—follows the verb *is* and refers to the subject *It*

Example 3

Albert Einstein was a famous scientist.

Analysis:

scientist—predicate noun—nominative case—follows verb *was* and refers to the subject *Albert Einstein*

Most predicate pronouns (or nouns) follow a form of the verb *be* (*is, am, are, be, was, were, has been, have been, had been*). Forms of *be* are called *linking verbs*. Other linking verbs that take a predicate pronoun or noun are forms of the verbs *seem, feel,* and *become*. (See page 74 for use of verbs with predicate nouns, pronouns, and adjectives.)

Example

George Burns became a comedian as a young man.

Analysis:

comedian—predicate noun—nominative case—follows the verb *became* and refers to the subject *George Burns*

Objective Case

Pronouns (and nouns) are in the *objective* case if they are used as objects of verbs, indirect objects, or objects of prepositions. If a pronoun (or noun) answers the question "what" or "whom" after the verb and receives the action, it is the object of the verb.

Example 1

His family visited <u>her</u> in the hospital.

Analysis:

<u>her</u>—personal pronoun—objective case—answers the question "whom" after the verb *visited*—visited whom?

Example 2

The doctor told <u>them</u> about the operation.

Analysis:

<u>them</u>—personal pronoun—objective case—answers the question "whom" after the verb *told*—told whom?

Example 3

Dr. Nina Murphy explained <u>it</u>.

Analysis:

<u>it</u>—personal pronoun—objective case—answers the question "what" after the verb *explained*—explained what?

A pronoun (or noun) that follows a preposition (see page 142 for a list of prepositions) is the *object of the preposition*. These pronouns or nouns must be in the objective case. (See page 44 for a list of objective pronouns.)

Example 1

The nurse drew a picture for <u>them</u>.

Analysis:

<u>them</u>—personal pronoun—objective case—object of the preposition *for*

Example 2

Her parents stayed all day with <u>her</u>.

Analysis:

<u>her</u>—personal pronoun—objective case—object of the preposition *with*

Pronouns used as *compound* (more than one) *objects* of verbs or prepositions cause some confusion. Omit one of the compond objects, and it becomes very easy.

NOMINATIVE/OBJECTIVE

Example 1

The employer gave <u>them</u> and <u>me</u> application forms.

Analysis:

<u>them</u>—objective case—object of the verb *gave*—gave them
<u>me</u>—objective case—object of the verb *gave*—gave me

Example 2

The manager left with <u>her</u> and <u>me</u>.

Analysis:

<u>her</u>—objective case—object of the preposition *with*—with her
<u>me</u>—objective case—object of the preposition *with*—with me

An *indirect object* tells *to* or *for whom* something is done, or *to* or *for what* something is done. The pronoun used as an indirect object is always in the objective case.

Example 1

Norma Mendoza sent <u>me</u> a map of Mexico.

Analysis:

<u>me</u>—indirect object—objective case—tells that the map was sent to me (preposition *to* is omitted)

45

Example 2

The teacher brought <u>them</u> some travel posters.

Analysis:

> <u>them</u>—indirect object—objective case—tells that the posters were brought to them (preposition *to* is omitted)

A pronoun (or noun) that follows *than* or *as* can be in the nominative or the objective case, depending on its use. When the rest of the clause has been left out, the clause must be reproduced mentally in order to determine the correct use of the pronoun or noun.

Examples

He knows her as well as <u>I</u> (know her).
He knows her as well as (he knows) <u>me</u>.
He runs faster than <u>I</u> (run).
She sang to him more than <u>I</u> (sang to him).
She sang to him more than (she sang to) <u>me</u>.

In both nominative and objective case, pairs of pronouns can be used in teams. The following is a list of common pairs of pronouns.

Nominative	Objective
he and she	him and her
he and we	him and us
she and I	her and me
she and they	her and them
we and they	us and them
they and I	them and me

Possessive Case

Pronouns denoting ownership are in the *possessive* case. Do not use an apostrophe with the personal pronouns. *Its* (no apostrophe) is the possessive form of the personal pronoun *it*. (See page 56 for more explanation of possessive pronouns.)

Example

Check the dictionary for <u>its</u> pronunciation.

Analysis:

> <u>its</u>—personal pronoun—possessive case—shows ownership to *pronunciation*

Verbs ending in *ing* and used as nouns are called *verbal nouns* or *gerunds*. Pronouns modifying verbal nouns are in the possessive case (*my, his, her, its, our, their, your*).

Example 1

Tom told of <u>his</u> receiving a free plane ride.

Analysis:

> <u>his</u>—personal pronoun—possessive case—modifies verbal noun *receiving*

Example 2

Nancy lost many friends because of <u>her</u> talking.

Analysis:

> <u>her</u>—personal pronoun—possessive case—modifies verbal noun *talking*

TRYOUT EXERCISE

Directions: Complete each of the following sentences by writing in the blank provided at the right the correct pronoun in the parentheses.

1. He and (I, me) listed our Social Security numbers.   1. _____

2. This is (she, her).   2. _____

3. Nicki drove Isabel and (I, me) to work.   3. _____

4. She painted the picture better than (he, him).   4. _____

5. (Me, My) getting the scholarship pleased my parents.   5. _____

Directions: In the sentences below, underline all pronouns in the nominative case once and all pronouns in the objective case twice. Check your answers on page 245 or with your teacher before continuing with your assignment.

1. He bought lunch for him and me at the new cafeteria.

2. We wanted him to go with us rather than with them.

Complete Application Practices 27-28, pages 47-48, at this time.

Pronoun Practice for Person, Number, and Case

application practice **27**

27 Practice Procedure Complete each of the following sentences by writing in the blank provided at the right the correct pronoun in the parentheses. Remember that the pronoun must agree in person and number with its antecedent. Score one point for each correct response.

Answers

1. Marie and Luisa of the Latin American Club showed the class (her, their) film.   1. _____

2. Marie and (we, us) visited some Latin American countries.   2. _____

3. Mrs. Romero gave (he, him) a book about Brazil.   3. _____

4. Mike and Sandra told Gene and (I, me) about the weather there.   4. _____

5. The students and (her, she) listened attentively.   5. _____

6. Instead of (him, his) going, Pam went.   6. _____

7. She and (them, they) traveled through Argentina, Brazil, and Chile.   7. _____

8. Were your parents pleased about (you, your) arriving on time?   8. _____

9. On the plane ride to Brazil, Fred sat between Monica and (I, me).   9. _____

10. The local guide explained the beauty of the country to Theresa and (he, him).   10. _____

11. The tour guide and (we, us) then flew to Paraguay.   11. _____

12. (Me, My) paying attention made the trip enjoyable.   12. _____

13. Later, Gloria told (them, they) about the trip.   13. _____

14. Francisca and Bart wrote an interesting account of (his, their) adventures.   14. _____

15. Was it really (she, her)?   15. _____

16. Wendy and Gerald enjoyed Caracas, the capital of Venezuela, where (she, they) interviewed Mr. Perez.   16. _____

17. Mr. Perez, a successful statesman, explained (his, their) success as a politician.   17. _____

18. We and (they, them) had a wonderful time shopping.   18. _____

19. (He, His) going with the group made our trip fun.   19. _____

20. The speeding bus narrowly missed her and (we, us).   20. _____

21. That was a splendid report by Carlotta and (her, she).   21. _____

22. She was helped by (them, they) with the research.   22. _____

23. Barbara Silva showed him and (I, me) pictures of life in Buenos Aires.   23. _____

24. My parents enjoyed Uruguay better than (he, him).   24. _____

25. (Us, We) students enjoyed our visit through Latin America.   25. _____

Your Total Score _____ /25

If your score was 19 or less, review Sections 7-A and 7-B, pages 43-46, before continuing.

/23

Score

28-A Practice Procedure In the sentences listed below, underline all pronouns in the nominative case (subjects or predicate pronouns). Score one point for each correct response.

Your Score

1. Members of the Constitutional Convention and he discussed many ideas with them.

    1. _____

2. They framed the Constitution for us in 100 days.

    2. _____

3. I learned from them the difference between the Declaration of Independence and the Constitution.

    3. _____

4. We learned about the signers of the Declaration of Independence from her.

    4. _____

5. It was a document carefully prepared by them.

    5. _____

6. The Liberty Bell rang out the note of freedom for us while she sang.

    6. _____

7. They heard it ring at exactly 2 p.m. on July 4, 1776.

    7. _____

8. The patriots and he discussed their various plans.

    8. _____

9. Mrs. Adams and she were proud of their husbands' work.

    9. _____

10. Her husband and they were willing to fight for them and their beliefs.

    10. _____

Your Total Score _____ /10

If your score was 7 or less, review Section 7-B, pages 44-46, before continuing.

28-B Practice Procedure In the sentences below, underline all pronouns in the objective case (objects of verbs, objects of prepositions, and indirect objects). Score one point for each correct response.

1. They taught us that the Constitution is the supreme law of our country.

    1. _____

2. She took the seat between Dale and me to hear the lecture about our early patriots.

    2. _____

3. When the bell rang, we went with Terry and her to the cafeteria for lunch.

    3. _____

4. The teacher thanked us as we left the room.

    4. _____

5. One of us had a report to do for the next day.

    5. _____

6. Dottie and I handed in our assignment to her when it was finished.

    6. _____

7. She gave me a good grade for my preparation.

    7. _____

8. They handed us a copy of the Constitution as we left the room.

    8. _____

9. Dr. Ian Bailey, a famous historian, taught them the value of democracy and liberty.

    9. _____

10. They really helped all of us in understanding the American Revolution.

    10. _____

11. We left his office after he graded me on my work.

    11. _____

12. The class and she thanked them for the information.

    12. _____

13. All the delegates, along with Madison's wisdom and Jefferson's tact, made us a true democracy.

    13. _____

Your Total Score _____ /13

If your score was 9 or less, review Section 7-B, pages 44-46, before continuing.

Date

Name

Indefinite Pronouns

An *indefinite pronoun* is a pronoun that does not define or stand for a particular person or thing. Some common indefinite pronouns are *all, each, either, one, everyone, several, some, other, another, both, none, many.* Indefinite pronouns are often used as adjectives.

Example 1

Many try for office, but few succeed in being elected.

Analysis:

Many—indefinite pronoun used as subject of the verb *try*—refers to no particular person

few—indefinite pronoun used as subject of the verb *succeed*—refers to no particular person

Example 2

Several friends entered the race, and all runners received a ribbon.

Analysis:

Several—indefinite pronoun used as an adjective—modifies the noun *friends*

all—indefinite pronoun used as an adjective—modifies the noun *runners*

Example 3

Each student in class has a secret dream.

Analysis:

Each—indefinite pronoun used as an adjective—modifies the noun *student*

Pronouns must agree in number with their antecedents. (Remember that the antecedent is the word for which the pronoun stands.) When an indefinite pronoun is used as an antecedent, the personal pronoun must agree in number with the indefinite pronoun. Use a singular pronoun with the following pronoun antecedents.

another	either	nobody
anybody	everybody	one
anyone	everyone	somebody
each	neither	someone

Example 1

Either Debra or Grace will get her job.

Analysis:

her—singular personal pronoun—refers to singular antecedent *Either*

Example 2

Each of the men wants his share of fame.

Analysis:

his—singular personal pronoun—refers to singular antecedent *Each*

Example 3

Everybody knows her lesson today.

Analysis:

her—singular personal pronoun—refers to singular antecedent *Everybody* (*His* could be used in place of *her* since the antecedent *Everybody* does not indicate gender.)

Use a plural pronoun with the following indefinite pronoun antecedents: *both, few, many, others,* and *several.* Be careful of the indefinite pronouns *all, any, most, none,* and *some.* These indefinite pronouns can take a singular or plural verb, depending on the antecedent. (See page 79 for verb agreement.)

Example 1

Many teenagers do their work regularly.

Analysis:

their—plural personal pronoun—refers to plural antecedent *Many*

Example 2

Several of them did their reports early.

Analysis:

their—plural personal pronoun—refers to plural antecedent *Several*

Directions: Complete each of the following sentences by writing in the blank provided at the right the correct pronoun in the parentheses. Check your answers on page 245 or with your teacher before continuing with your assignment.

1. Nobody brought (his, their) lunch today.

2. Several of the students left (her, their) work at home.

3. Neither the dog nor the cat liked (his, their) new food.

4. Few of the judges forgot (her, their) instructions.

5. Did anyone bring (his, their) car to school?

6. Many of the students got (her, their) pets from the animal shelter.

1. _____

2. _____

3. _____

4. _____

5. _____

6. _____

Complete Application Practices 29-32, pages 51-54, at this time.

29 Practice Procedure Complete each of the following sentences by writing in the blank provided at the right the correct pronoun in the parentheses. Remember that the pronoun must agree in number with its antecedent. Refer to the lists of singular and plural indefinite pronoun antecedents (page 49) before you decide on your answers. Score one point for each correct response.

Answers

1. Each of our friends will visit (his, their) favorite national park.   1. _____

2. Both David and Jack visited Carlsbad Caverns and (he, they) reported to the group.   2. _____

3. If anyone has ever seen volcanoes, (she, they) will remember them.   3. _____

4. One of the teachers left (his, their) camera in Hawaii.   4. _____

5. Someone told the students about (his, their) watching whales in Alaska.   5. _____

6. If either Esther or Denise enjoys hiking, (she, they) will like our national parks.   6. _____

7. Somebody showed the tourists (his, their) pictures of the Everglades.   7. _____

8. All of the visitors were awed when (she, they) saw the Grand Tetons.   8. _____

9. Before anyone goes to a national park, (she, they) should read about it.   9. _____

10. Several of the employees lost (her, their) work badges.   10. _____

11. Two of our friends shared (her, their) experiences in climbing Mt. Whitney.   11. _____

12. Mammoth Cave is famous for (its, their) numerous limestone deposits and fossils.   12. _____

13. Neither Carrie nor Sara won awards for (her, their) photos.   13. _____

14. Some were impressed when (he, they) saw Niagara Falls.   14. _____

15. Each of the park rangers had (his, their) own special expertise.   15. _____

16. Both of the rangers spoke, and (she, they) did it interestingly.   16. _____

17. If anyone knows what caused the Badlands, (he, they) should tell us.   17. _____

18. All of our national parks have (its, their) unusual attractions.   18. _____

19. Many of the hikers wore (her, their) most comfortable shoes.   19. _____

20. Has everyone enjoyed (his, their) experiences in the parks?   20. _____

21. Will someone give (her, their) notes to the guides?   21. _____

22. Few of the tourists didn't enjoy (his, their) visits through our national parks.   22. _____

23. Andy or Seth will not start work at Yellowstone until (he, they) fills out application forms.   23. _____

24. Others have already finished (his, their) forms.   24. _____

25. Before anyone enters the park system, (she, they) should read about the requirements.   25. _____

Your Total Score _____ /25

If your score was 19 or less, review Section 8, pages 49-50, before continuing.

30 Practice Procedure Complete each of the following sentences by writing in the blank provided at the right the correct pronoun in the parentheses. Remember that the pronoun must agree in number with its antecedent. Refer to the lists of singular and plural indefinite pronoun antecedents (page 49) before you decide on your answers. Score one point for each correct response.

Answers

1. Each of the students had (her, their) favorite hobby. 1. _____

2. Both of the new teachers collected stamps, and (he, they) told us about them. 2. _____

3. If anyone collects coins, could (she, they) bring them to class? 3. _____

4. Few of the senior citizens painted in (his, their) leisure time. 4. _____

5. Neither the English teacher nor the science teacher thought (she, they) would be interested in scuba diving. 5. _____

6. One of them spent (her, their) free time surfing. 6. _____

7. One of the two enjoyed skiing with other skiers whenever (she, they) had the opportunity. 7. _____

8. Some of my aunts who travel with friends collect (her, their) old clocks from different nations. 8. _____

9. Nobody in my family ever lost (his, their) seashells. 9. _____

10. Neither of the women saves music boxes though (she, they) enjoys music. 10. _____

11. Few of the political club members exhibited (her, their) campaign buttons. 11. _____

12. If somebody would like to buy baseball cards, give us (his, their) name. 12. _____

13. Many of the store owners did not start (his, their) antique furniture collections for profit. 13. _____

14. Not everyone realizes the value of (his, their) rare buttons and bows. 14. _____

15. Does someone remember when (she, they) collected autographs? 15. _____

16. Before anyone in school begins a new hobby, (she, they) should read about it. 16. _____

17. Several of our neighbors raced (his, their) cars last week. 17. _____

18. Each of the members of the airplane club brought (his, their) model airplanes to the hobby fair. 18. _____

19. One of our famous Presidents enjoyed stamps and (he, they) had more than 100,000 stamps. 19. _____

20. Neither of my cousins saved labels when (she, they) told us about them. 20. _____

21. Most of the artists who became famous have (his, their) masterpieces in museums. 21. _____

22. Nobody liked to use (her, their) articles. 22. _____

23. Many in the school had (his, their) baseball cards displayed in a show. 23. _____

24. Either of the two art collectors donated (his, their) famous paintings to the art museums. 24. _____

25. Will someone post (her, their) list of do-it-yourself hobbies? 25. _____

Your Total Score _____ /25

If your score was 19 or less, review Section 8, pages 49-50, before continuing.

Pronoun Practice for Person, Number, and Case

31 Practice Procedure Complete each of the following sentences by writing in the blank provided at the right the correct pronoun in the parentheses. Remember that the pronoun must agree in person and number with its antecedent. Score one point for each correct response.

Answers

1. The instructor showed him and (I, me) a film about Mexico. 1. _____

2. Penny and (I, me) learned how to apply for a passport. 2. _____

3. Neither Sandra nor Joan filled out (her, their) papers. 3. _____

4. Joan is not as careful as (I, me). 4. _____

5. Dr. Herrera showed pictures of Mexico City to Gloria and (he, him). 5. _____

6. Many of the pictures featured Hector and (they, them). 6. _____

7. (Him, His) speaking Spanish made it easier for us all. 7. _____

8. If you were (he, him), would you ever have left there? 8. _____

9. The author had traveled more than (she, her). 9. _____

10. Ferdie and Jorge told us of (his, their) experiences. 10. _____

11. It is interesting for (we, us) students to learn more about Mexico. 11. _____

12. Joy, Dan, and (them, they) once went to Guadalajara. 12. _____

13. (Them, Their) talking about the Mexican War was interesting. 13. _____

14. It is a wise person who can understand (her, their) own people. 14. _____

15. Special air fares are available for tourists who buy (his, their) tickets early. 15. _____

16. If anyone knows the capital city of Mexico, (he, they) can tell us. 16. _____

17. Emigrants are people who leave (her, their) country for another country. 17. _____

18. Many of us students couldn't buy (his, our) own tickets. 18. _____

19. My mother related the story of General Huerta to John and (they, them). 19. _____

20. One of my friends has (her, their) home in Monterrey. 20. _____

21. Rosa and Juan taught Spanish to Stacy and (I, me). 21. _____

22. When do (we, us) tourists leave for the trip? 22. _____

23. The lecture about the Mexican revolution was attended by Jason and (she, her). 23. _____

24. When did you first realize it was (he, him)? 24. _____

25. Enrique and (they, them) are related to my sister-in-law. 25. _____

Your Total Score _____ /25

If your score was 19 or less, review Sections 7 and 8, pages 43-46 and 49-50, before continuing.

32 Practice Procedure Complete each of the following sentences by writing in the blank provided at the right the correct pronoun in the parentheses. Remember that the pronoun must agree in person and number with its antecedent. Score one point for each correct response.

Answers

1. Dedi, Kareem, and (her, she) attended the marketing meeting.   1. _____

2. Do Kate and Sandra know to fill out (her, their) registration forms?   2. _____

3. The sponsors ran out of forms without (their, them) realizing it.   3. _____

4. (We, Us) employers realize the importance of good work habits.   4. _____

5. Alison and (he, him) worked together often.   5. _____

6. Neither Gail nor Maxine finished until (she, they) handed in the papers.   6. _____

7. If you were (he, him) what would you do?   7. _____

8. Did Mr. Arroyo say anything about (you, your) leaving early?   8. _____

9. Everybody does (her, their) work better.   9. _____

10. Ingrid sells more merchandise than (he, him).   10. _____

11. She and (I, me) started work last Monday.   11. _____

12. If you were Tara or (I, me), would you take the training course?   12. _____

13. Matt and Scott enjoyed (his, their) new office.   13. _____

14. All of the people worked hard on (her, their) first jobs.   14. _____

15. If Javier wants a good job, (he, they) should prepare for it.   15. _____

16. Marina and Sophie can do (her, their) work on the calculators.   16. _____

17. (He, His) having the right attitude helped his career.   17. _____

18. (Their, Them) speaking carefully worked to their advantage.   18. _____

19. It is a wise person who can understand (her, their) abilities and talents.   19. _____

20. She and (I, me) were eager to start the new course.   20. _____

21. Everybody shares (his, their) experiences.   21. _____

22. Liz works the computer better than (he, him).   22. _____

23. Has anybody here saved (her, their) first paycheck?   23. _____

24. Inez got paid more than (I, me).   24. _____

25. There was no sense in (him, his) reading that book.   25. _____

Your Total Score _____ /25

If your score was 19 or less, review Sections 7 and 8, pages 43-46 and 49-50, before continuing.

Relative Pronouns

Relative pronouns relate or refer to nouns or other pronouns in a sentence. The nouns or pronouns referred to are antecedents. The relative pronouns are *who, whom, whose, which,* and *that.*

Who and *whom* refer to persons. *Who* is used as the subject or predicate pronoun of a sentence and is in the nominative case. *Whom* is used as the object of a verb or the object of a preposition and is in the objective case. (See pages 57-60 for further explanations of *who* and *whom.*)

Example 1

Sandra O'Connor, <u>who</u> became the first woman U.S. Supreme Court Justice, was appointed in 1981.

Analysis:

<u>who</u>—subject of the verb *became*—refers to *O'Connor*, person

Example 2

She is a woman <u>whom</u> the people respect.

Analysis:

<u>whom</u>—object of the verb *respect*—refers to *woman*, person

Which refers to animals or things. *That* and *whose* refer to persons, animals, or things.

Example 1

The dog, <u>which</u> kept me awake, had a loud bark.

Analysis:

<u>which</u>—refers to *dog*, animal

Example 2

The lion paced around his cage, <u>which</u> was secured and locked.

Analysis:

<u>which</u>—refers to *cage*, thing

Example 3

My uncle is a small man <u>that</u> feeds the large animals.

Analysis:

<u>that</u>—refers to *uncle*, particular person

Example 4

We met the woman <u>whose</u> horse won the Kentucky Derby.

Analysis:

<u>whose</u>—refers to *woman*, person

TRAINER (WHO)

WHO—REFERS TO PEOPLE

SADDLE (WHICH)

HORSE (WHICH)

WHICH—REFERS TO ANIMALS AND THINGS

section 10

Demonstrative Pronouns

Demonstrative pronouns are used to point out, to designate, or to demonstrate the particular antecedent to which they refer. The singular demonstrative pronouns are *this* and *that*. The plural demonstrative pronouns are *these* and *those*. When demonstrative pronouns are used as adjectives, they are called *demonstrative adjectives*.

Example 1

This is my country, and I am proud to be a citizen.

Analysis:

This—demonstrative pronoun—designates *country*

Example 2

Is that the roar of the lion?

Analysis:

that—demonstrative pronoun—designates *roar*

Example 3

Those animals are the ones that were donated.

Analysis:

Those—demonstrative adjective—tells which animals

section 11

Possessive Pronouns

Possessive pronouns are pronouns used to denote ownership or possession. They are often used as adjectives, and when so used are called *possessive adjectives*. (See page 128 for more on possessive adjectives.)

	Singular	Plural
1st person	my, mine	our, ours
2nd person	your, yours	your, yours
3rd person	his, her, hers, its	their, theirs

Example 1

Mine is the nicest car on the block.

Analysis:

Mine—possessive pronoun—denotes ownership

Example 2

Yours is the oldest car in the neighborhood.

Analysis:

Yours—possessive pronoun—denotes ownership

Example 3

Theirs was a foreign-made automobile.

Analysis:

Theirs—possessive pronoun—denotes ownership

Example 4

My neighbor likes motorcycles and bicycles.

Analysis:

My—possessive pronoun used as an adjective—tells whose *neighbor*

Example 5

Our cars and his motorcycle were kept in perfect condition.

Analysis:

Our—possessive pronoun—used as an adjective—tells whose *cars*

his—possessive pronoun used as an adjective—tells whose *motorcycle*

Interrogative Pronouns

The *interrogative pronouns* are used in asking questions. They are *who* (nominative), *whom* (objective, referring to persons), *which* (referring to persons or things and telling one object from another), *what* (referring to things), and *whose* (referring to persons or things).

Example 1

Who likes a free airplane ticket to Hawaii?

Analysis:

Who—asks question—refers to person—subject of the verb *likes*

Example 2

Whom do you call for information?

Analysis:

Whom—asks question—refers to people—object of verb *call*

Example 3

Which is safer—an airplane or a ship?

Analysis:

Which—asks question—refers to things and tells one object from another

Example 4

What do you know about the various cruises?

Analysis:

What—asks question—refers to things

Example 5

What are the advantages of jet travel and cruises?

Analysis:

What—asks question—refers to things

Example 6

A traveler left his ticket on the counter. Whose is it?

Analysis:

Whose—asks question—refers to people

TRYOUT EXERCISE **Directions:** Complete each of the following sentences by writing in the blank provided at the right the correct pronoun in the parentheses. Check your answers on page 245 or with your teacher before continuing with your assignment.

1. (Who, Whom) knows the importance of justice? 1. _____

2. (Who, Whom) left this sweater in the cafeteria? 2. _____

3. (What, Which) would you rather have—money or health? 3. _____

4. (Who, Whom) wouldn't like a good job right now? 4. _____

5. (What, Which) is more important—high wages or average wages with health benefits? 5. _____

6. (Who, Whom) do you see if you want a scholarship? 6. _____

Complete Application Practices 33-34, pages 61-62, at this time.

Who and Whom

Perhaps the two pronouns that cause the most confusion are *who* and *whom*. Although the pronoun *who* is used most frequently in daily conversation, it is worthwhile knowing when it should be used and when it is better to use *whom*.

Most of the difficulty lies in the sentences of inverted order like this one:

Who do the people think will become president in the next election?

If you rearrange the sentence as a statement, it is easier to see that *who* is correct.

The people think *who* will become president in the next election.

Remember that *who* is used as the subject or the predicate pronoun of the sentence and is in the nominative case. *Whom* is used as the object of a verb or the object of a preposition and is in the objective case. Look at the clause in this sentence:

The president whom he respected lost the election.

Again, change the order of the clause to see whether *whom* is correct.

he respected *whom*

Whom is the object of the verb *respected* and is therefore correct.

Example 1

Who witnessed the accident near the theater?

Analysis:

Who—subject of verb *witnessed*—nominative case

Example 2

Thomas Edison, who had little formal schooling, invented the electric bulb.

Analysis:

who—subject of verb *had*—nominative case

Example 3

Was it who I thought it was?

Analysis:

who—predicate pronoun—nominative case

Example 4

From <u>whom</u> did he buy the new stereo?

Analysis:

<u>whom</u>—object of preposition *from*—objective case

Example 5

To <u>whom</u> do you give your paycheck?

Analysis:

<u>whom</u>—object of preposition *to*—objective case

Example 6

With <u>whom</u> did his parents travel?

Analysis:

<u>whom</u>—object of preposition *with*—His parents did travel with whom—objective case

Example 7

<u>Whom</u> did he represent?

Analysis:

<u>Whom</u>—object of verb *did represent*—He did represent whom—objective case

Example 8

The man <u>whom</u> I saw at the meeting was my cousin.

Analysis:

<u>whom</u>—object of verb *saw*—I saw whom at the meeting—objective case

Common Mistakes with Who and Whom

A number of mistakes are usually made with *who* and *whom* when they are used in sentences with unrelated clauses or parenthetical expressions such as *I know, in my judgment, in my opinion, we believe, we hope*. To determine whether *who* or *whom* is correct, drop the unrelated or parenthetical expression from the sentence. The meaning or construction of the sentence will not change.

Example 1

Loretta Castille, <u>who</u>, in my judgment, deserves the promotion, lives near my aunt.

Analysis:

<u>who</u>—subject of verb *deserves*—nominative case. Remove the unrelated expression *in my judgment* and the meaning of the sentence is not changed. With the expression *in my judgment* omitted, the sentence reads as follows: Loretta Castille, who deserves the promotion, lives near my aunt.

Example 2

Betty, <u>who</u>, we hope, selects the winning ticket, has planned her trip.

Analysis:

<u>who</u>—subject of verb *selects*—nominative case. Remove the unrelated expression *we hope* and the sentence reads as follows: Betty, who selects the winning ticket, has planned her trip.

Example 3

The clerk, <u>who</u>, in my opinion, knows the merchandise, works carefully with customers.

Analysis:

<u>who</u>—subject of verb *knows*—nominative case. Remove the unrelated expression *in my opinion* and the meaning of the sentence is not changed. With the expression *in my opinion* omitted, the sentence reads as follows: The clerk, who knows the merchandise, works carefully with customers.

Example 4

Karl Kaiser, <u>whom</u>, I know, you met recently, can speak several languages.

Analysis:

<u>whom</u>—object of verb *met*—objective case. Remove the unrelated expression *I know* and the meaning of the sentence is not changed. With the expression *I know* omitted, the sentence reads as follows: Karl Kaiser, whom you met recently, can speak several languages.

Example 5

It was she <u>who</u>, I suppose, was the best singer in the Glee Club.

Analysis:

<u>who</u>—subject of verb *was*—nominative case. Remove the parenthetical expression *I suppose* and the sentence reads as follows: It was she who was the best singer in the Glee Club.

Who-Whom, Whoever-Whomever in Noun Clauses

A common mistake is often made with *who-whom* in noun clauses (see pages 152-154). When you use a noun clause as an object of a verb or preposition, remember *who-whom* is not the object of the main clause but is used as either the subject or object of the noun clause.

Example 1

Do you understand <u>who</u> owns the company?

Analysis:

<u>who owns the company</u>—dependent clause used as a noun—object of verb *do understand. Who* is used as the subject of the clause *who owns the company.*

Example 2

The owner promoted <u>whom</u> you wanted.

Analysis:

<u>whom you wanted</u>—dependent clause used as a noun—object of verb *promoted. Whom* is the object of the verb *wanted* in the clause *whom you wanted.*

Example 3

<u>Who</u> do you believe deserved the job?

Analysis:

<u>Who deserved the job</u>—dependent clause used as a noun—object of verb *do believe. Who* is used as subject of the clause *Who deserved the job.*

Remember to use *whoever* or *whomever* the way it is used in the noun clause, not as the object of the preposition.

Example 1

The teachers will be hired by the principal or by <u>whoever</u> is in charge.

Analysis:

<u>whoever</u>—nominative case—subject of the noun clause *whoever is in charge.* (The entire clause *whoever is in charge* is the object of the preposition *by.*)

Example 2

The singer will be hired by me or by <u>whomever</u> I appoint.

Analysis:

<u>whomever</u>—objective case—object of the verb *appoint* in the noun clause *whomever I appoint.* (The entire clause *whomever I appoint* is the object of the preposition *by.*)

TRYOUT EXERCISE **Directions:** Complete each of the following sentences by writing in the blank provided at the right the correct pronoun in the parentheses. Check your answers on page 245 or with your teacher before continuing with your assignment.

1. Ann Helms is the person (who, whom), in my opinion, has the easiest assignment.   1. _____

2. The last applicant was the one to (who, whom) the job was given.   2. _____

3. Did you know (who, whom) played the villain?   3. _____

4. Mr. Van Stine will present the award to (whoever, whomever) scores highest.   4. _____

5. Smiley Kaii, not Lin, will go with (whoever, whomever) you select.   5. _____

Complete Application Practices 35-42, pages 63-70, at this time.

Relative, Demonstrative, Possessive, and Interrogative Pronouns

33 Practice Procedure Complete each of the following sentences by writing in the blank provided at the right the correct pronoun in the parentheses. Make sure the pronoun agrees with its antecedent. Score one point for each correct response.

Answers

1. Dr. Pierce, (who, whom) is a historian, told us about the different U.S. Presidents.

    1. _____

2. His wife and (he, him) told many humorous stories.

    2. _____

3. With (who, whom) did you go to the lecture?

    3. _____

4. Richard Nixon, (who, whom), I believe, was the only President that ever resigned, left office August 9, 1974.

    4. _____

5. Many of our Presidents did (his, their) best for our country.

    5. _____

6. Everyone voted for (her, their) favorite candidate.

    6. _____

7. Few listed (his, their) qualifications for office.

    7. _____

8. (Me, My) knowing the history lesson helped me get a passing grade.

    8. _____

9. The results surprised Lucy and (I, me).

    9. _____

10. If anyone takes the time to study the candidates' qualifications, (she, they) will vote better.

    10. _____

11. The chairperson told him and (she, her) about the process.

    11. _____

12. Both of the women worked (her, their) hardest in the campaign.

    12. _____

13. Aggie, Eric, and (they, them) were glad when their candidate was elected.

    13. _____

14. Did anyone save (her, their) sample ballot?

    14. _____

15. Maud told my friend and (I, me) about the age requirement for a U.S. Senator.

    15. _____

16. Vera knew the candidates better than (he, him).

    16. _____

17. A wise student was (she, her).

    17. _____

18. Her family and (he, him) went to the mayor's rally.

    18. _____

19. Our congressional representative mailed (his, their) voters a form letter.

    19. _____

20. Jim, Bob, and Sharon did (her, their) best to elect Debra.

    20. _____

21. Tracy, Hilda, and (I, me) were glad the results were final.

    21. _____

22. Either Boyce or Blake will do (his, their) best to clean up after the party.

    22. _____

23. Many losing candidates wrote to Jennie and (she, her).

    23. _____

24. Andy and his dog, (who, which) is a beagle, greeted the committee.

    24. _____

25. (Who, Which) is a smarter animal—a dog or a cat?

    25. _____

Your Total Score _____ /25

If your score was 19 or less, review Sections 9-12, pages 55-57 before continuing.

Interrogative Pronouns and Pronoun Review

34-A Practice Procedure Complete each of the following sentences by writing in the blank space provided at the left the correct interrogative pronoun (*who, whom, which, what, whose*). Score one point for each correct response.

Your Score

1. (   ) candidate has the best chance to win?   1. _____

2. (   ) do you call when you see a robbery?   2. _____

3. (   ) knows the emergency telephone number?   3. _____

4. (   ) is good citizenship?   4. _____

5. (   ) of the three teachers is the best?   5. _____

6. (   ) is interested in our welfare?   6. _____

7. (   ) do you know at the State Department?   7. _____

8. (   ) of the two reporters printed the story?   8. _____

9. (   ) respects his elected officials?   9. _____

10. (   ) are some of your immediate concerns?   10. _____

34-B Practice Procedure Complete each of the following sentences by writing in the blank provided at the right the correct pronoun in the parentheses. Score one point for each correct response.

Answers

1. Mrs. Maki and (he, him) read the biography of Columbus.   1. _____

2. The story was believable to Sergio and (she, her).   2. _____

3. Ms. Morales, our teacher, showed a film about Puerto Rico to Sybil and (I, me).   3. _____

4. The new student, (who, whom), in my judgment, is very smart, had been to El Salvador.   4. _____

5. From Justin and (she, her) we learned about the people of Central America.   5. _____

6. The new students knew geography better than (I, me).   6. _____

7. Miss Sasa, the science teacher, explained Japan's climate to Amy and (we, us).   7. _____

8. Between Ernie and (he, him) sat Darcie and Kim.   8. _____

9. Most of her classes were popular with her and (they, them).   9. _____

10. The history teacher listed the major cultures of South America for (we, us) and him.   10. _____

Your Total Score _____ /20

If your score was 15 or less, review pages 44-46 and 55-57 before continuing.

35 Practice Procedure Complete each of the following sentences by writing in the blank provided at the right the correct form of *who-whom*. Score one point for each correct answer.

Answers

1. (Who, whom) knows the name of the smallest state in the Union?
1. _____

2. Rick Cook, (who, whom) was born there, said it was Rhode Island.
2. _____

3. It was ''Tex'' Cashion (who, whom) told us about Texas.
3. _____

4. They will invite (whoever, whomever) she wants.
4. _____

5. Wasn't it ''Tex'' (who, whom) I saw at the state fair?
5. _____

6. Was it she (who, whom) you chose to lead the delegation?
6. _____

7. Terry Richards is the one (who, whom), I hope, gets the award.
7. _____

8. (Who, Whom) have you asked for a speaker next week?
8. _____

9. Lulu doesn't know (who, whom) is the guest.
9. _____

10. It could be Madge (who, whom) you heard before.
10. _____

11. Monica Medina, (who, whom), I suppose, is talented, will sing our anthem.
11. _____

12. Singers will audition for the music director or for (whoever, whomever) he decides.
12. _____

13. With (who, whom) did you travel to California?
13. _____

14. (Who, Whom) have you asked for information about Oregon?
14. _____

15. We read that there is a home available for (whoever, whomever) wants to settle in Idaho.
15. _____

16. Is there anyone in the office (who, whom), you hope, has the material?
16. _____

17. Do you have friends (who, whom) have lived in the Badger State?
17. _____

18. (Who, Whom) can you depend on for advice about Wisconsin?
18. _____

19. Was it Vida or Reiko (who, whom) knew the Senator from Maine?
19. _____

20. She doesn't know (who, whom) told you the story about the California gold rush.
20. _____

21. (Whoever, Whomever) we ask mentions the gorgeous scenery in Arizona.
21. _____

22. The Swiss settlers are the ones (who, whom) developed the Wisconsin dairy industry.
22. _____

23. Here are Gina and Sal (who, whom), we believe, will be fascinated with the Old West.
23. _____

24. From (who, whom) have you heard tales of the mining camps?
24. _____

25. Wasn't it she (who, whom) arranged the New England tour?
25. _____

Your Total Score _____ /25

If your score was 19 or less, review pages 55 and 57-60 before continuing.

Name

Date

Score

/25

/25

Score

Date

Name

36 Practice Procedure Complete each of the following sentences by writing in the blank provided at the right the correct pronoun in the parentheses. Score one point for each correct answer.

Answers

1. Mr. Brinks and Miss Pitts spoke to (us, we) students about money.

1. _____

2. (Him, His) speaking about the different kinds of U.S. currency was fascinating.

2. _____

3. The presentation was given by Mr. Brinks and (her, she).

3. _____

4. You and (I, me) learned that Washington's portrait was on the $1 bill.

4. _____

5. Vic, Bella, and (us, we) were surprised to hear that Grant's picture was on the $50 bill.

5. _____

6. An argument developed between Natalie and (them, they).

6. _____

7. Did Megan and (he, him) know anything about the U.S. Mint?

7. _____

8. (Their, Them) receiving a book on money surprised me.

8. _____

9. Miss Pitts showed a film about currency to Evan and (her, she).

9. _____

10. Several pupils and (he, him) wanted to look at the $1,000 bill.

10. _____

11. (Me, My) handling the different coins gave me the feeling of being rich.

11. _____

12. He and (she, her) joked about people printing play money.

12. _____

13. Michael, Lana, and (them, they) read about forgers.

13. _____

14. The teacher asked Linda and (I, me) what bill had the White House on its back.

14. _____

15. Both Tara and (he, him) knew the franc was the monetary unit of France.

15. _____

16. (Her, She) knowing the peso was Mexico's monetary unit pleased them.

16. _____

17. The accountant and (us, we) looked carefully at the rare coins.

17. _____

18. They gave us and (she, her) a better understanding of money.

18. _____

19. She presented him and (I, me) a book about the history of coins.

19. _____

20. It was a funny speech given by them and (he, him).

20. _____

21. I thanked (they, them) as they left.

21. _____

22. We went with him and (she, her) to the exit.

22. _____

23. Sandy had more money than (I, me).

23. _____

24. The teacher really liked Sandy better than (I, me).

24. _____

25. Can Jim and (she, her) find another fine speaker?

25. _____

Your Total Score _____ /25

If your score was 19 or less, review pages 44-46 before continuing.

37 Practice Procedure Complete each of the following sentences by writing in the blank provided at the right the correct pronoun in the parentheses. Score one point for each correct answer.

Answers

1. (Who, Whom) gave the talk about the different countries' flags? 1. _____

2. Ms. Leonard showed slides of our flag to Gerry and (I, me). 2. _____

3. Dolores and (he, him) liked the discussion that followed. 3. _____

4. I enjoyed the talk more than (her, she). 4. _____

5. (Me, My) reading about the flag's symbol led to a greater appreciation. 5. _____

6. The speaker and (us, we) students pledged allegiance to the flag. 6. _____

7. Mr. Sawyer from the State Department explained to us and (them, they) about Flag Day. 7. _____

8. (Him, His) telling us when the flag was first raised was interesting. 8. _____

9. Miss Long, (who, whom), as I understand, you invited, had factual information. 9. _____

10. (Their, Them) utilizing slides and film made it easier to understand the lecture. 10. _____

11. Zola, Inez, and (he, him) were happy to salute the flag. 11. _____

12. Did Chin and (she, her) enjoy the Betsy Ross legend? 12. _____

13. Millie and Brad showed (us, we) flags from the other countries. 13. _____

14. They presented pictures of the early flags to (whoever, whomever) you mentioned. 14. _____

15. Mr. Paulson told his story, (what, which) was patriotic. 15. _____

16. Neither Sam nor (she, her) knew what the flag's 50 stars meant. 16. _____

17. They were surprised by (her, she) singing "The Star Spangled Banner." 17. _____

18. (Who, Whom) knows what the white and red stripes on our flag mean? 18. _____

19. Mr. Driver told his version of "Old Glory" to (whoever, whomever) would listen. 19. _____

20. (What, Which) is the prettier flag—United States' or Mexico's? 20. _____

21. We and (them, they) looked at the flags from Canada and Chile. 21. _____

22. Mrs. Ross and Miss Holmes were two of the finest experts in (her, their) field. 22. _____

23. (Who, Whom) do you see for a ticket to the lecture? 23. _____

24. (What, Which) one is Miss Holmes? 24. _____

25. Their presentation was popular with Sharon and (he, him). 25. _____

Your Total Score _____ /25

If your score was 19 or less, review pages 43-46 and 55-60 before continuing.

Name ___ Date ___ Score ___ /25

Drill on Pronouns

38 Practice Procedure Complete each of the following sentences by writing in the blank provided at the right the correct pronoun in the parentheses. Score one point for each correct answer.

/22

Score

Date

Name

Answers

1. Two counselors from the Labor Bureau told (us, we) about job areas.

1. _____

2. We were appreciative of (them, their) sharing their information.

2. _____

3. Ms. Coe, (who, whom), I believe, is the office manager, knew about statistics.

3. _____

4. She gave Chris and (I, me) many helpful hints about different jobs.

4. _____

5. The instructor and (she, her) passed out sample employment forms.

5. _____

6. Jack Fette, (who, whom) you met, impressed the speakers.

6. _____

7. (Me, My) seeing the occupational areas for jobs was valuable.

7. _____

8. Did Diana and (he, him) understand about entry-level employment?

8. _____

9. We agreed with Mr. Hinds and (she, her) about the new job-seekers.

9. _____

10. There should be a good understanding between the employer and (he, him).

10. _____

11. After they left, the class set up mock interviews with (she, her) and them.

11. _____

12. From (who, whom) did you hear about the job?

12. _____

13. Bill is better prepared for that job than (I, me).

13. _____

14. (What, Which) is more important—luck or ability?

14. _____

15. (She, Her) knowing the owner of the company helped.

15. _____

16. Ingrid, Holly, and (he, him) applied for the same position.

16. _____

17. Self-assessment is important for you and (we, us) applicants.

17. _____

18. My sister and (them, they) had interviews arranged.

18. _____

19. Derek and (she, her) applied to several firms.

19. _____

20. The owner had to choose between Eva and (he, him).

20. _____

21. The teacher's assurances meant a great deal to Allen and (I, me).

21. _____

22. An entry-level job may be the first employment for him and (them, they).

22. _____

Your Total Score _____ /22

If your score was 17 or less, review pages 43-46 and 55-60 before continuing.

39 Practice Procedure Complete each of the following sentences by writing in the blank provided at the right the correct pronoun in the parentheses. Score one point for each correct answer.

Answers

1. Carol Dent, (who, whom), I believe, is a talented writer, is our book critic.　　1. _____

2. To (who, whom) does she appeal?　　2. _____

3. (She, Her) reviewing different books helped many readers.　　3. _____

4. (What, Which) books does she prefer—fiction or nonfiction?　　4. _____

5. Some authors (who, whom) she mentioned were mystery writers.　　5. _____

6. The teacher, the guest, and (I, me) discussed the popular writers.　　6. _____

7. Mr. Dunne was willing to donate a popular novel to (whoever, whomever) wanted it.　　7. _____

8. Leona, Blake, and (them, they) had several extra copies to present.　　8. _____

9. Why don't you and (her, she) share the book with us?　　9. _____

10. The librarian gave (us, we) pupils a reading assignment.　　10. _____

11. Mrs. Steele told Cicely and (he, him) to report on their favorite comedies.　　11. _____

12. My sister is a faster reader than (I, me).　　12. _____

13. The clerk placed several books between Geneva and (he, him).　　13. _____

14. Do you know (who, whom) sells more books than Shakespeare ever did?　　14. _____

15. Mr. and Mrs. Magnante will give a prize to (whoever, whomever) writes the best story.　　15. _____

16. The author, the publisher, and (her, she) sat at the head table.　　16. _____

17. (Him, His) writing humorous stories gave him financial success.　　17. _____

18. Either the publisher or the writer will donate (his, their) books.　　18. _____

19. Neither Charlotte nor (us, we) can read more than one book a week.　　19. _____

20. (Who, Whom) do you think will read two books a week?　　20. _____

21. We did not know of (you, your) editing the book reviews.　　21. _____

22. It was (them, they) who formed the school's book club.　　22. _____

Your Total Score _____ /22

If your score was 17 or less, review pages 43-46, 49-50, and 55-60 before continuing.

Drill on Pronouns

40 Practice Procedure Complete each of the following sentences by writing in the blank provided at the right the correct pronoun in the parentheses. Score one point for each correct answer.

Answers

1. Some of his stories are valuable for (its, their) entertainment value.

   1. _____

2. (Us, We) pupils have read four books this semester.

   2. _____

3. (Him, His) telling us about Poe's horror stories was scary.

   3. _____

4. Anybody (who, what) reads Poe's stories will like them.

   4. _____

5. (Who, Whom) do you know has read Poe's poem, *The Raven*?

   5. _____

6. Each one of the writers told us (his, their) early problems.

   6. _____

7. Ruth Rendell, (who, whom) writes under her own name, is a successful author.

   7. _____

8. From (who, whom) did you borrow this book?

   8. _____

9. Arden showed an original manuscript to the teacher and (she, her).

   9. _____

10. She, her sister, and (I, me) enjoyed reading *Romeo and Juliet*.

    10. _____

11. (Who, Whom) wrote that play?

    11. _____

12. Our puppy, (who, which) is very young, chewed the pages.

    12. _____

13. Literature has influenced human behavior and (my, mine) understanding of people.

    13. _____

14. Three experts on children's literature discussed (his, their) theories.

    14. _____

15. If anyone of them knew how we felt, (she, they) would be more factual.

    15. _____

16. One of the writers told us the facts, and (he, they) was interesting.

    16. _____

17. Each of the writers gave us copies of (her, their) books.

    17. _____

18. The editor, (who, whom) we met previously, returned for the second time.

    18. _____

19. Was it she (who, whom) dedicated her book to Miss Roe?

    19. _____

20. Miss Roe, (who, whom), I understand, wrote children's books, was pleased.

    20. _____

21. Mrs. Curtis explained it very well to us and (them, they).

    21. _____

22. I approve of (him, his) writing that kind of book.

    22. _____

Your Total Score _____ /22

If your score was 17 or less, review pages 43-46, 49-50, and 55-60 before continuing.

Matching Exercise and Drill on Nouns and Pronouns

application practice **41**

41-A Practice Procedure Match each item in Column A with the item it describes in Column B. Write the identifying letter from Column A in the blank provided at the right. Score one point for each correct answer.

Column A	Column B	Answers
a. indefinite pronouns	1. George Bush, Dan Quayle	1. _____
b. plural nouns	2. me, they, us	2. _____
c. collective nouns	3. woman's	3. _____
d. personal pronouns	4. who, whom	4. _____
e. common nouns	5. anybody, each, few	5. _____
f. proper nouns	6. this, that, these, those	6. _____
g. possessive form of noun	7. feet, men, oxen	7. _____
h. possessive pronouns	8. ocean, mirror	8. _____
i. demonstrative pronouns	9. mob, team, club	9. _____
j. relative pronouns	10. my, his, their	10. _____

41-B Practice Procedure Underline each noun and tell whether it is a proper, a common, or a collective noun. Place the abbreviation *P* for proper, *C* for common, or *Col* for collective above each noun. Score one point for each correct response.

Your Score

1. Miss Burns helped the singers of the chorus prepare for the performance.   1. _____

2. The club traveled to Washington, D.C., and performed for the President and his family.   2. _____

3. Three members of our faculty accompanied the group.   3. _____

4. Mr. Whelan, the sponsor of the trip, had the good fortune to meet with the President.   4. _____

5. The students performed their songs in Lincoln Center.   5. _____

6. Miss Stevens, who worked hard on the plans for the tour, made all the arrangements.   6. _____

7. The school received a great deal of praise from the writers and from committees in Congress.   7. _____

8. Mr. Curtis, the editor of our paper, gave the band a tour through the White House.   8. _____

9. The audience really enjoyed the chorus in their singing of patriotic songs.   9. _____

10. Senator Watson helped the club prepare for the show.   10. _____

Your Total Score _____ /53

If your score was 41 or less, review Units 2 and 3 before continuing.

69

Pronouns Substituted for Nouns

42 Practice Procedure Read the story below and then go back and substitute the proper pronoun above each of the underlined nouns or phrases. Refer to your lists of pronouns in Sections 7-12, pages 43-60, to determine the proper pronoun to replace the underlined word or phrase. Make certain that the pronouns agree with their antecedents. A pronoun may be used more than once in the story. If more than one word is underlined together, see whether more than one person is mentioned and then use the plural form. Score one point for each correct answer.

Example: Mr. and Mrs. Coe *They* treated my sister *her*, my brother *him*, and me to dinner.

Your Score

My father and mother took the three children on a fishing trip in Alaska.   1. _____

Kathy, Fred, and I set up our tents with help from mother. Our father went to   2. _____

meet the guide at the lodge. Father and the guide then returned to the camp and   3. _____

talked to the family about the guide's seeing bears in the area. Mother noticed   4. _____

that Fred, Kathy, and I weren't paying attention to the warning about the bears.   5. _____

The guide suggested that Kathy, Fred, and I not wander off alone. Foolishly, Fred   6. _____

and Kathy wandered away from camp to a cave nearby to investigate the cave.   7. _____

Fred unexpectedly came face to face with a bear cub. The cub, raising straight   8. _____

up on his back feet, started to growl. The bear's growling frightened Fred and   9. _____

Kathy.   10. _____

Fred ran into the cave as Kathy started to climb a tree. The bear cub sat   11. _____

down between the tree and the cave. Suddenly, Fred bolted from the cave and   12. _____

saw the baby bear sitting on the ground. Fred turned quickly and ran back into   13. _____

the cave. Kathy and Fred started to scream for the guide and our parents. A few   14. _____

seconds later, Fred again ran out of the cave.   15. _____

My sister shouted to Fred, "Why don't you stay in the cave?"   16. _____

"No way," yelled Fred to my sister, "the mother bear is inside the cave."   17. _____

Your Total Score _____ /42

If your score was 33 or less, review Unit 3 before continuing.

Uses of Verbs

OBJECTIVES
1. To recognize and use verbs correctly when making statements, asking questions, or giving commands.
2. To identify principal helping verbs and linking verbs.
3. To use a verb so that it agrees with the subject of the sentence.

A *verb* tells what the subject does or is, or what happens to it. A verb can make a statement, ask a question, or give a command.

The verb is one of the two required words in every sentence. The other required word is the subject. All sentences must have a subject and a verb. When you use verbs properly, your speech will be improved, your writing skills good, and your sentences correct. The proper use of verbs requires great care. Watch your use of verbs, and you will be amazed at how much more your sentences will communicate.

13-A VERBS MAKE STATEMENTS

Example 1

George bought a new calculator.

Analysis:

bought—a verb. It tells what the subject *George* does. It makes a statement.

Example 2

Ms. Perez completed a computer class.

Analysis:

completed—a verb. It tells what the subject *Ms. Perez* did. It makes a statement.

13-B VERBS ASK QUESTIONS

Example 1

Who brought a pencil to class?

Analysis:

brought—a verb. It asks a question of the subject *Who*.

Example 2

Are the computers new?

Analysis:

Are—a verb. It asks a question about the subject *computer*.

13-C VERBS GIVE COMMANDS

Example 1

Bring the book to me.

Analysis:

Bring—a verb. It gives a command to the subject *you* (understood).

Example 2

Answer the question, please.

Analysis:

Answer—a verb. It gives a command to the subject *you* (understood).

Helping Verbs and Linking Verbs

14-A USES OF HELPING VERBS

Helping verbs are well named because they help the main verbs tell what the subjects are doing by asking a question, giving a command, or making a statement. (Helping verbs are also known as *auxiliary verbs*.) Remember them as words that help connect the subject and the main verb.

Principal helping verbs include *is, be, am, are, was, were, have, has, had, may, must, ought, can, might, could, would, should, shall, will, do, does,* and *did*.

Example 1

That word processor <u>was</u> purchased yesterday.

Analysis:

> <u>was</u>—helping verb. It helps the main verb *purchased* tell about the subject *word processor*.

Example 2

Lessons <u>are</u> taught on the computer.

Analysis:

> <u>are</u>—helping verb. It helps the main verb *taught* tell about the subject *Lessons*.

Example 3

The author of this computer program <u>will</u> speak in class tomorrow.

Analysis:

> <u>will</u>—helping verb. It helps the main verb *speak* tell about the subject *author*.

Example 4

Computers <u>can</u> manage our home accounts too.

Analysis:

> <u>can</u>—helping verb. It helps the main verb *manage* tell about the subject *Computers*.

Example 5

Subway riders <u>may</u> purchase tickets from a computer vending machine.

Analysis:

> <u>may</u>—helping verb. It helps the main verb *purchase* tell about the subject *riders*.

Example 6

New machines <u>have</u> improved office efficiency.

Analysis:

> <u>have</u>—helping verb. It helps the main verb *improved* tell about the subject *machines*.

14-B VERB SEPARATIONS

Often the helping verb is separated from the main verb by a *modifier* (a word used to describe another word). You can find the main verb because it still tells what the subject is doing or what is being done to the subject.

Example 1

Computer language is usually displayed in a manual.

Analysis:

is usually displayed—verb separation. Helping verb *is* and the main verb *displayed* are separated by the modifier *usually*.

Example 2

Electronic equipment has really changed the appearance of today's offices.

Analysis:

has really changed—verb separation.

Helping verb *has* and the main verb *changed* are separated by the modifier *really*.

Example 3

In what ways have computers adjusted inventory records in stores?

Analysis:

have computers adjusted—verb separation. Helping verb *have* and the main verb *adjusted* are separated by the subject *computers*.

Example 4

Lost children are often found through computer fingerprint searches.

Analysis:

are often found—verb separation. Helping verb *are* and the main verb *found* are separated by the modifier *often*.

TRYOUT EXERCISE

Directions: Identify the helping verbs in the following sentences by underlining them once. Identify the main verbs by underlining them twice. In the blank provided at the right, write *S* if the verb makes a statement, *Q* if it asks a question, or *C* if it gives a command. Check your answers on page 245 or with your teacher before continuing with your assignment.

1. The large computer is often used.   1. _____

2. Can you operate that computer?   2. _____

3. The tour of the computer room will begin soon.   3. _____

4. A computer program can write checks.   4. _____

5. Computers can help students in the classroom.   5. _____

6. Can computers store all kinds of data?   6. _____

7. Will computers reduce the work force?   7. _____

8. Can word processors improve office efficiency?   8. _____

9. You must teach this computer program to me.   9. _____

10. You will learn this computer program, or else!   10. _____

Complete Application Practices 43-44, pages 75-76, at this time.

14-C USE OF LINKING VERBS WITH PREDICATE NOUNS, PRONOUNS, AND ADJECTIVES

When a form of the verb *be* (*be, am, is, are, was, were, have been, has been, had been, shall be, will be*) is used alone, the word used to complete the meaning of the verb is called a *predicate noun,* a *predicate pronoun,* or a *predicate adjective.* These forms of the verb *be* are called *linking verbs.*

The predicate noun or pronoun is in the nominative case, as it refers to and describes the subject of the sentence. Other linking verbs that take predicate adjectives or predicate nouns or pronouns in the nominative case are *become, seem, appear, taste, smell, feel, sound,* and *look.* (See page 44 for a review of the nominative case and linking verbs.)

Predicate Nouns

Example 1

The computer will be an important business tool in our office.

Analysis:

tool—a noun. It completes the meaning of the verb *will be.* It is a predicate noun because it refers to the subject *computer.*

Example 2

A word processor is an important business machine.

Analysis:

machine—a noun. It completes the meaning of the verb *is.* It is a predicate noun because it refers to the subject *word processor.*

Predicate Pronouns

Example 1

It was she on the phone.

Analysis:

she—a pronoun. It completes the meaning of the verb *was.* It is a predicate pronoun because it refers to the subject *It.*

Example 2

The best computer programmer is he.

Analysis:

he—a pronoun. It completes the meaning of the verb *is.* It is a predicate pronoun because it refers to the subject *programmer.*

Predicate Adjectives

Example 1

The first computers were massive.

Analysis:

massive—an adjective. It completes the meaning of the verb *were.* It is a predicate adjective because it describes the subject *computers.*

Example 2

Computer printouts are long.

Analysis:

long—an adjective. It completes the meaning of the verb *are.* It is a predicate adjective because it describes the subject *printouts.*

TRYOUT EXERCISE **Directions:** Identify the predicate noun, predicate pronoun, or predicate adjective in each of the following sentences by underlining it once. In the space provided, tell whether it is a predicate noun (*N*), a pronoun (*P*), or an adjective (*A*). Check your answers on page 245 or with your teacher before continuing with your assignment.

1. The computer looked old. 1. _____

2. The operator of the word processor was he. 2. _____

3. The teacher was an expert in computers. 3. _____

Complete Application Practices 45-46, pages 77-78, at this time.

Find the Verb

43-A Practice Procedure Identify the verbs in the following sentences by underlining them once. In the answer column at the right, write *S* if the verb makes a statement, *Q* if it asks a question, or *C* if it gives a command. Score one point for each correct verb and one point for each correct sentence type identified.

Answers

1. Many people enjoy ship travel.

1. _____

2. On our last trip, we sailed from New York City.

2. _____

3. A tugboat pulled our ship from the pier.

3. _____

4. On leaving, passengers threw serpentine over the rails.

4. _____

5. A band played music on the pier as we left.

5. _____

6. Look at the lights of Manhattan!

6. _____

7. Who steers a large ocean liner?

7. _____

8. We passed the Statue of Liberty at night.

8. _____

9. We also saw Ellis Island.

9. _____

10. The Staten Island Ferry saluted us with its horn.

10. _____

43-B Practice Procedure Follow the procedure given for 43-A.

1. The bells sounded for dinner in the dining room.

1. _____

2. Passengers located their tables by number.

2. _____

3. Some passengers sat at the wrong tables.

3. _____

4. Who misread his table designation?

4. _____

5. We ordered our food from a large menu.

5. _____

6. Select an appetizer and a salad too.

6. _____

7. Order the steak, not the fish, tonight.

7. _____

8. Fill my water glass, please.

8. _____

9. For dessert, we ate cheesecake.

9. _____

10. Everyone enjoyed the first meal at sea.

10. _____

Your Total Score _____ /40

If your score was 31 or less for 43-A and 43-B, review Section 13, page 71, before continuing.

43-C Practice Procedure Demonstrate your understanding of verbs by writing five sentences on a separate sheet of paper. Underline the verb in each sentence once. Score one point for each correct sentence and one point for each correctly identified verb.

Your Total Score _____ /10

Helping Verbs

44-A Practice Procedure Identify the helping verbs in the following sentences by underlining them once. Identify the main verbs by underlining them twice. Score one point for each correct helping verb and one point for each correct main verb.

Your Score

1. Often, interviews for a job are taken for experience.   1. _____
2. Mary will enjoy a career in office technology.   2. _____
3. When will you finish the interview?   3. _____
4. The interview was ended on a positive note.   4. _____
5. Sean did apply for the position.   5. _____
6. Carol and Loren were also interested in the job.   6. _____
7. Applications for the job will probably close on Tuesday.   7. _____
8. The salary range is determined by the board of directors.   8. _____
9. All interviewees were given interview appointments.   9. _____
10. Sean was selected for the position.   10. _____

44-B Practice Procedure Follow the procedure given for 44-A.

1. Sean will start his new job next week.   1. _____
2. He must report to the sales manager, Mrs. Aitken.   2. _____
3. Mrs. Aitken had started with the company two years ago.   3. _____
4. Did she ever explain her job to you?   4. _____
5. When was she first considered for a promotion?   5. _____
6. Sean must work hard in his new job.   6. _____
7. His co-workers were pleased by his selection.   7. _____
8. Carol and Loren were chosen by Sean for his department.   8. _____
9. Sean and his team must prove themselves to the company.   9. _____
10. The new team can definitely increase sales.   10. _____

Your Total Score _____ /40

If your score was 31 or less for 44-A and 44-B, review Sections 14-A and 14-B, pages 72-73, before continuing.

44-C Practice Procedure On a separate sheet of paper write five sentences, each containing a helping verb and a main verb. Underline helping verbs once and main verbs twice. Score one point for each correct sentence, one point for each correctly identified helping verb, and one point for each correctly identified main verb.

Your Total Score _____ /15

Score   Date   Name

Predicate Nouns, Pronouns, and Adjectives

45-A Practice Procedure Identify the predicate noun, predicate pronoun, or predicate adjective in each of the following sentences by underlining it once. In the answer column, tell whether it is a predicate noun (*N*), pronoun (*P*), or adjective (*A*). Score one point for each correct word and one point for each correct identification.

Answers

1. Fred Astaire was a celebrated dancer.

1. _____

2. It was he who held audiences enthralled by his skills.

2. _____

3. Mr. Astaire was once the best dancer in the world.

3. _____

4. His act was always wonderful.

4. _____

5. Those dancing shoes in the museum are his.

5. _____

6. His collection of shoes was enormous.

6. _____

7. Adele Astaire, Fred's sister, became a dancer too.

7. _____

8. The best dancer in the show was he.

8. _____

9. The show was spectacular.

9. _____

10. Tickets to their shows were expensive.

10. _____

45-B Practice Procedure Identify the predicate nouns, predicate pronouns, and predicate adjectives in the following paragraph by underlining them once. In the spaces provided, write the word you have underlined and indicate whether it is a predicate noun (*N*), pronoun (*P*), or adjective (*A*). Score one point for every correct word and one point for each correct identification.

The circus is a wonderland to the spectator with imagination. All the world becomes a tipsy carousel, and the lights and music are tempting lures to those outside the big top. The cotton candy smells warm and sweet, the lemonade and cola drinks taste refreshingly cool, and the hot dogs are a delightful treat. Circus magic is apparent everywhere, as elephants become dancers, monkeys become bareback riders, and performers in sparkling costumes appear suspended in the air. Tales of dancers and clowns sound enchanting to the stranger in this paradise of fantasy. The happiest onlooker is one who can believe that magic and sorcery are real and present in this starry world of glitter.

_____ _____ _____ _____

_____ _____ _____ _____

_____ _____ _____ _____

_____ _____ _____ _____

Your Total Score _____ /50

If your score was 39 or less for 45-A and 45-B, review Section 14-C, page 74, before continuing.

/60

Score

Date

Name

46-A Practice Procedure Identify the helping verbs by underlining them once and the main verbs by underlining them twice. In the answer column, write *S* if the verb makes a statement, *Q* if it asks a question, or *C* if it gives a command. Score one point for each underlined helping verb and one point for each underlined main verb. Score one point for each sentence type identified correctly.

Answers

1. The airplane flight to Hong Kong was boarding at Gate 7.　　1. _____

2. We had left Seattle early in the morning.　　2. _____

3. We were scheduled for Hong Kong twelve hours later.　　3. _____

4. Mary and Al were booked on the flight.　　4. _____

5. Did all passengers arrive on time for the flight?　　5. _____

6. The attendants should serve lunch after takeoff.　　6. _____

7. The tray tables had been lowered.　　7. _____

8. Will the lunch arrive hot?　　8. _____

9. My special lunch was brought first.　　9. _____

10. In the air you must drink a lot of water.　　10. _____

46-B Practice Procedure Identify the linking verbs by underlining them once. Indicate the predicate nouns, predicate pronouns, and predicate adjectives by underlining them twice. In the answer column, write *S* if the verb makes a statement, *Q* if it asks a question, or *C* if it gives a command. Score one point for each underlined linking verb and one point for each predicate noun, predicate pronoun, or predicate adjective. Score one point for each sentence type identified correctly.

1. The in-flight movie looked exciting.　　1. _____

2. Were they the stars of the movie?　　2. _____

3. The movie was quite long.　　3. _____

4. Space between seats on the plane is narrow.　　4. _____

5. Chuck is a passenger on our flight.　　5. _____

6. Was it he on our tour?　　6. _____

7. The plane looked full.　　7. _____

8. Bette will be a tour leader.　　8. _____

9. It was she on the loudspeaker just now.　　9. _____

10. You will be a member of Bette's tour group.　　10. _____

Your Total Score _____ /60

If your score was 47 or less, review Sections 13 and 14-C, pages 71 and 74, before continuing.

Verb Agreement with Subject

A verb should agree with its subject in person and number. A *singular* (one) *subject* takes a singular form of a verb. A *plural* (more than one) *subject* takes a plural form of a verb. An exception is the pronoun *you* which takes the plural form of the verb in both singular and plural.

Example 1

Mr. Ito <u>is</u> from Japan.

Analysis:

<u>is</u>—singular form of the verb agrees with the singular subject *Mr. Ito*. A singular subject takes a singular verb.

Example 2

He <u>was</u> very young when he arrived in the United States.

Analysis:

<u>was</u>—singular form of the verb agrees with the singular subject *He*. A singular subject takes a singular verb.

Example 3

They <u>are</u> from Kobe, Japan.

Analysis:

<u>are</u>—plural form of the verb agrees with the plural subject *They*. A plural subject takes a plural verb.

Example 4

You <u>are</u> a citizen of California.

Analysis:

<u>are</u>—plural form of the verb. The subject *You* always takes the plural form of the verb.

15-A FORMS OF THE VERB *BE*

Am, is, and *was* are the singular forms of the verb *be* and require singular subjects. *Are* and *were* are the plural forms and require plural subjects. Study the verb forms of *be* so they will become a strong part of your speech. These verb forms are so common that by learning them thoroughly, your language skills will be greatly improved.

SHE IS THE FIRST PLACE WINNER.

THEY ARE THE SECOND AND THIRD PLACE WINNERS.

AGREEMENT of SUBJECT AND VERB

Example 1

She <u>was</u> a tourist in China.

Analysis:

> <u>was</u>—singular form of the verb agrees in number with the singular subject *She*

Example 2

He <u>is</u> the Chinese tour guide.

Analysis:

> <u>is</u>—singular form of the verb agrees in number with the singular subject *He*

Example 3

I <u>am</u> a friend of the tour guide.

Analysis:

> <u>am</u>—singular form of the verb agrees in number with the singular subject *I*

Example 4

He <u>is</u> a graduate of Beijing University.

Analysis:

> <u>is</u>—singular form of the verb agrees in number with the singular subject *He*

Example 5

Those tour members <u>were</u> from New York City.

Analysis:

> <u>were</u>—plural form of the verb agrees in number with the plural subject *members*

Example 6

Emma <u>is</u> the youngest person on the tour.

Analysis:

> <u>is</u>—singular form of the verb agrees in number with the singular subject *Emma*

Example 7

They <u>were</u> acquainted with Emma.

Analysis:

> <u>were</u>—plural form of the verb agrees in number with the plural subject *They*

Example 8

We <u>were</u> late arriving in Shanghai.

Analysis:

> <u>were</u>—plural form of the verb agrees in number with the plural subject *We*

Example 9

Friends <u>were</u> at the airport to say goodbye.

Analysis:

> <u>were</u>—plural form of the verb agrees in number with the plural subject *Friends*

Example 10

My suitcases <u>are</u> heavy.

Analysis:

> <u>are</u>—plural form of the verb agrees in number with the plural subject *suitcases*

Example 11

The airplane attendants <u>are</u> helpful.

Analysis:

> <u>are</u>—plural form of the verb agrees in number with the plural subject *attendants*

Contrary-to-Fact Conditions

When stating a *condition contrary to fact*, use *were* with all subjects, singular or plural. Such a condition does not presently exist, but the speaker plans it or wishes it to be true.

Example 1

She acts as if she <u>were</u> the tour leader.

Analysis:

> <u>were</u>—plural form of the verb is used with a singular subject when stating a condition contrary to fact

Example 2

If she <u>were</u> the leader, I'd be happy.

Analysis:

> <u>were</u>—plural form of the verb is used with a singular subject when stating a condition contrary to fact

Example 3

If they <u>were</u> on the plane, we would have more fun.

Analysis:

> <u>were</u>—plural form of the verb is used with a plural subject when stating a condition contrary to fact

15-B FORMS OF THE VERB *HAVE*

The second most-used verb is *have*. To express something which is happening at the present time, use *have* with all singular and plural subjects. The exception is the third person singular nouns and pronouns (he, she, it). Third person singular requires the use of *has*.

To express something which has happened in the past, use *had* with all subjects, both singular and plural.

I <u>HAVE</u> AN APPLE.

SHE <u>HAS</u> AN ORANGE.

WE <u>HAD</u> BANANAS YESTERDAY.

Example 1

Some travelers <u>have</u> difficulty sleeping on a plane.

Analysis:

have—plural verb agrees with the plural subject *travelers*

Example 2

She is one of those travelers who <u>has</u> difficulty sleeping.

Analysis:

has—singular verb agrees with the subject *She*—third person singular pronoun

Example 3

He <u>has</u> the movie to be shown on the flight.

Analysis:

has—singular verb agrees with the subject *He*—third person singular pronoun

Example 4

The attendants <u>have</u> a hard job.

Analysis:

have—plural verb agrees with the plural subject *attendants*

Example 5

They <u>had</u> a vegetarian dinner.

Analysis:

had—verb expressing past time agrees with the subject *They*—third person plural

Example 6

She <u>had</u> chicken instead.

Analysis:

had—verb expressing past time agrees with the subject *She*—third person singular

Example 7

It <u>had</u> a bitter taste to it.

Analysis:

had—verb expressing past time agrees with the subject *It*—third person singular

15-C PLURAL FORM WITH COMPOUND SUBJECTS

Compound subjects (more than one subject) take the plural form of the verb.

Example 1

Craig and Debbie <u>are</u> Emma's parents.

Analysis:

are—plural verb agrees with the compound subject *Craig and Debbie*

Example 2

The chairs, desks, and tables <u>were</u> to arrive today.

Analysis:

were—plural verb agrees with the compound subject *chairs, desks, and tables*

15-D SINGULAR SUBJECTS AND PLURAL MODIFIERS

Sometimes the singular subject is separated from the verb by a *plural modifier,* which is often a phrase. (Remember that modifiers are words which describe.) Look for the subject and make the verb agree with it. Do not make the mistake of making the verb agree with the modifier.

Example 1

Sean, not Cory and Tyler, <u>is</u> on the trip.

Analysis:

is—singular verb agrees with the singular subject *Sean*

Example 2

The plane, with its many seats, <u>was</u> huge.

Analysis:

was—singular verb agrees with the singular subject *plane*

Example 3

Gary, as well as his seat mates, <u>is</u> asleep.

Analysis:

is—singular verb agrees with the singular subject *Gary*

Example 4

The pilot, together with the flight attendants, <u>was</u> highly professional.

Analysis:

was—singular verb agrees with the singular subject *pilot*

Example 5

My sister, not my parents, <u>is</u> on the plane with me.

Analysis:

is—singular verb agrees with the singular subject *sister*

TRYOUT EXERCISE **Directions:** Complete each of the following sentences by writing in the blank provided at the right the correct form of the verb in the parentheses. Check your answers on page 245 or with your teacher before continuing with your assignment.

1. They (is, are) friends of his.   1. _____

2. The travelers (was, were) eager to leave.   2. _____

3. If she (was, were) going on a trip, I wouldn't.   3. _____

4. Pam (has, have) lost a suitcase.   4. _____

5. My seat, with its several adjustments, (was, were) very comfortable.   5. _____

Complete Application Practices 47-48, pages 83-84, at this time.

Verb and Subject Agreement

47-A Practice Procedure Complete each of the following sentences by writing in the blank provided at the right the correct form of the verb in the parentheses. Make the verb agree in person and in number with the subject. Score one point for every correct verb.

Answers

1. Zion National Park (is, are) in Utah.   1. _____

2. Red sandstone cliffs (is, are) a feature of the park.   2. _____

3. Jade green water (was, were) on the valley floor.   3. _____

4. Zion—the promised land—(was, were) named by the first white settlers.   4. _____

5. Zion Canyon (is, are) the heart of the park.   5. _____

6. Cliffs, 2,000 feet high, (was, were) carved by creeks and rivers.   6. _____

7. Scrub oak and prickly pear cactus (is, are) found there.   7. _____

8. Huge mesas (was, were) part of the park's geologic history.   8. _____

9. The park's water (is, are) from rain and snow.   9. _____

10. Flash floods (is, are) possible from summer storms.   10. _____

47-B Practice Procedure Follow the procedure given for 47-A.

1. The Altar of Sacrifice (was, were) a famous park wall.   1. _____

2. The sandy canyon floor (was, were) often dry.   2. _____

3. Canyon tree frogs (is, are) abundant.   3. _____

4. Pocket gophers and lizards (is, are) also plentiful.   4. _____

5. Floating downstream on rafts (was, were) fun.   5. _____

6. One of the deepest canyons (was, were) Refrigerator Canyon.   6. _____

7. For rock climbers, footholds (was, were) carved in the rocks.   7. _____

8. Indians (was, were) in Zion as early as 500 A.D.   8. _____

9. The Anasazi (is, are) the Indians who built the pueblos there.   9. _____

10. Wall paintings (is, are) our heritage from the Anasazi.   10. _____

Your Total Score _____ /20

If your score was 15 or less for 47-A and 47-B, review pages 79-81 before continuing.

Name ____ Date ____ Score ____ /20

48-A Practice Procedure Complete each of the following sentences by writing in the blank provided at the right the correct form of the verb in the parentheses. Make the verb agree in number with the subject. Score one point for every correct verb.

Answers

1. San Francisco (is, are) one of California's major cities.   1. _____

2. A fort (was, were) built there in 1776 by the Spanish.   2. _____

3. San Franciscans (is, are) loyal to their city.   3. _____

4. The city (was, were) built on 40 hills.   4. _____

5. The ocean and a bay (was, were) on three sides of the city.   5. _____

6. The original town (is, are) known as Yerba Buena.   6. _____

7. The discovery of gold (was, were) the cause of rapid growth.   7. _____

8. People from many countries (was, were) drawn to the city.   8. _____

9. Many ethnic groups (is, are) found in the city today.   9. _____

10. The United Nations Organization (was, were) born there in 1945.   10. _____

48-B Practice Procedure Follow the procedure given for 48-A.

1. Today, San Francisco (is, are) known as the "Wall Street of the West."   1. _____

2. Newspapers (is, are) printed in several foreign languages.   2. _____

3. The city's famous cable cars (was, were) first operated in 1873.   3. _____

4. Alcatraz, once a federal penitentiary, (is, are) on an island in the bay.   4. _____

5. Chinatown (is, are) home to more Chinese than any city outside of Asia.   5. _____

6. The bridge across the entrance to the bay (was, were) named the Golden
Gate Bridge.   6. _____

7. When constructed, it (was, were) one of the longest single-span suspension
bridges ever built.   7. _____

8. The old U.S. Mint (was, were) a survivor of the 1906 earthquake.   8. _____

9. The Mission Dolores (was, were) founded in 1776.   9. _____

10. One of the oldest military stations in the U.S. (is, are) the Presidio.   10. _____

Your Total Score _____ /20

If your score was 15 or less for 48-A and 48-B, review pages 79-82 before continuing.

48-C Practice Procedure On a separate sheet of paper demonstrate your understanding of verb and subject agreement in five well-written sentences. Score one point for each correct sentence.

Your Total Score _____ /5

15-E VERB AGREEMENT WITH INDEFINITE PRONOUNS

Whenever you use an indefinite pronoun as the subject of a sentence, the verb must agree in number with the subject. (Refer to pages 49-50 for a review of indefinite pronouns.) The following indefinite pronouns are used with singular verbs:

another	either	nobody
anybody	everybody	one
anyone	everyone	somebody
each	neither	someone

Example 1

Neither of those films is worth seeing.

Analysis:

is—singular verb agrees in number with the singular subject *Neither*

Example 2

Each was a terrible film.

Analysis:

was—singular verb agrees in number with the singular subject *Each*

The following indefinite pronouns are used with plural verbs:

both	many	several
few	others	

Example 1

Several of the new films are excellent.

Analysis:

are—plural verb agrees in number with the plural subject *Several*

Example 2

Many of the Canadian films were excellent too.

Analysis:

were—plural verb agrees in number with the plural subject *Many*

The following indefinite pronouns may be used with either singular or plural verbs:

all	most	some
any	none	

When indicating *how much*, use a singular verb. When indicating *how many*, use a plural verb.

Example 1

Some of the film was good.

Analysis:

was—singular verb indicates *how much*

Example 2

None of the films were hits.

Analysis:

were—plural verb indicates *how many*

INDEFINITE PRONOUNS

SOMEBODY ANYBODY NEITHER EACH

SEVERAL OTHERS MANY SOME FEW

15-F VERB AGREEMENT WITH *THERE*

There is an *expletive* (meaning to fill out) which introduces a sentence. The verb agrees with the subject that follows the verb when *there* is used to start the sentence. Ignore the word *there* when looking for the subject. It is never used as the subject of a sentence.

Example 1

There <u>is</u> a new movie theater in town.

Analysis:

<u>is</u>—singular verb agrees in number with the singular subject *theater*

Example 2

There <u>are</u> lines of people waiting to get in the new theater.

Analysis:

<u>are</u>—plural verb agrees in number with the plural subject *lines*

Example 3

There <u>is</u> a good film showing tonight.

Analysis:

<u>is</u>—singular verb agrees in number with the singular subject *film*

Example 4

There <u>are</u> refreshment stands in the theater lobby.

Analysis:

<u>are</u>—plural verb agrees in number with the plural subject *stands*

THERE IS THE CAR!

15-G VERB AGREEMENT WITH *OR*

Singular Use of Verb with *Or*

Or, when used to combine two or more subjects, takes a singular verb if the subject nearest the verb is singular.

Example 1

Candies or popcorn <u>is</u> available at the stand.

Analysis:

<u>is</u>—singular verb agrees in number with the nearest subject *popcorn* which is singular

Example 2

The actors, the writers, or the director <u>was</u> to be present at the opening.

Analysis:

<u>was</u>—singular verb agrees in number with the nearest subject *director*

Plural Use of Verb with *Or*

Or, when used to combine two or more subjects, takes a plural verb if the subject nearest the verb is plural.

Example 1

Popcorn or candies <u>are</u> available at the stand.

Analysis:

<u>are</u>—plural verb agrees in number with the nearest subject *candies* which is plural

Example 2

The mayor or two councilpersons <u>are</u> to be present too.

Analysis:

<u>are</u>—plural verb agrees in number with the nearest subject *councilpersons*

15-H VERB AGREEMENT WITH COLLECTIVE NOUNS

A *collective noun* that refers to a group acting as a whole requires a singular verb. A collective noun that refers to a group in which the members act individually requires a plural verb. In most sentences, the collective noun is a unit requiring a singular verb. (See pages 26-27 for a review of collective nouns.)

Example 1

The company is new.

Analysis:

is—singular verb. The collective noun *company* is thought of as one.

Example 2

The school is named for an American Indian leader.

Analysis:

is—singular verb. The collective noun *school* is thought of as one.

Example 3

The chorus is to perform tonight.

Analysis:

is—singular verb. The collective noun *chorus* is thought of as one.

Example 4

The congregation was late for the service.

Analysis:

was—singular verb. The collective noun *congregation* is thought of as one.

Example 5

The trio is composed of students.

Analysis:

is—singular verb. The collective noun *trio* is thought of as one.

Example 6

The audience were applauding wildly.

Analysis:

were—plural verb. The collective noun *audience* is thought of as individuals acting independently of the group.

Example 7

The orchestra is playing an encore.

Analysis:

is—singular verb. The collective noun *orchestra* is thought of as one.

Example 8

The audience was attentive to the performers.

Analysis:

was—singular verb. The collective noun *audience* is thought of as one.

Example 9

The crowd was angry.

Analysis:

was—singular verb. The collective noun *crowd* is thought of as one.

Example 10

The office force are supportive of the management.

Analysis:

are—plural verb. The collective noun *office force* is thought of as individuals acting independently of the group.

Directions: Complete each of the following sentences by writing in the blank provided at the right the correct form of the verb in the parentheses. Check your answers on page 245 or with your teacher before continuing with your assignment.

1. The jury (was, were) called back to court.

1. _____

2. The committee (was, were) composed of men and women.

2. _____

3. Neither (is, are) present in court today.

3. _____

4. There (is, are) a judge in the courtroom.

4. _____

5. The judge or the bailiffs (is, are) attentive to the proceedings.

5. _____

6. The TV camera operator or the reporters (was, were) in the hall.

6. _____

7. Everyone (is, are) ready for the trial to begin.

7. _____

8. Many of the audience (is, are) friends of the defendant.

8. _____

9. Both of the attorneys (was, were) young.

9. _____

10. Some of the testimony (was, were) challenged.

10. _____

Complete Application Practices 49-54, pages 89-94, at this time.

Verb and Subject Agreement

49-A Practice Procedure Complete each of the following sentences by writing in the blank provided at the right the correct form of the verb in the parentheses. Make the verb agree in number with the subject. Score one point for each correct verb.

Answers

1. This voyage to Antarctica (was, were) my first.   1. _____

2. Roald Amundsen and Robert Scott (was, were) early explorers.   2. _____

3. The Chilean city of Punta Arenas (is, are) the starting point for our voyage.   3. _____

4. The city (is, are) the southernmost city on the globe.   4. _____

5. All of us (was, were) looking forward to the trip.   5. _____

6. Antarctica (is, are) one of the coldest places on earth.   6. _____

7. Sometimes it (is, are) colder than Mars.   7. _____

8. Inflatable rafts called *Zodiacs* (was, were) useful.   8. _____

9. We used Zodiacs when the sea (was, were) calm.   9. _____

10. Gale winds (is, are) heading toward us from Cape Horn.   10. _____

49-B Practice Procedure Follow the procedure given for 49-A.

1. Huge albatrosses (was, were) flying overhead.   1. _____

2. Poets claim that the albatross (is, are) bad luck.   2. _____

3. Huge icebergs (is, are) soon floating past our ship.   3. _____

4. Thousands of penguins (was, were) our welcoming party.   4. _____

5. Penguins (is, are) right at home here.   5. _____

6. It seemed to us as if every square foot of ground (was, were) covered with penguins.   6. _____

7. The endangered fur seal (is, are) protected here.   7. _____

8. Whaling once (was, were) a major industry in Antarctica.   8. _____

9. In the past, volcanic action (was, were) frequent.   9. _____

10. Steam (is, are) seen rising from the wet sand of some islands. 10. _____

Your Total Score _____ /20

If your score was 15 or less for 49-A and 49-B, review pages 79-82 before continuing.

Name _____ Date _____ Score _____ /20

Verb Agreement with Indefinite Pronouns, *There*, and *Or*

50-A Practice Procedure Complete each of the following sentences by writing in the blank provided at the right the correct word in the parentheses. Score one point for each correct answer.

Answers

1. An ornate building on Ellis Island or the sights of New York City (was, were) impressive to the new immigrants.

1. _____

2. There (was, were) many tales immigrants told about Ellis Island.

2. _____

3. Everybody (has, have) something to say.

3. _____

4. There (is, are) a record of 900,000 immigrants having come through Ellis Island in 1907.

4. _____

5. Each of the immigrants (is, are) a newcomer to the U.S.

5. _____

6. There (was, were) some immigrants who arrived with illnesses.

6. _____

7. The sick immigrants or the doctor who treated them (is, are) to be interviewed.

7. _____

8. Johan's mother or his aunts (was, were) sent to Ellis Island's hospital.

8. _____

9. Neither of Dixie's parents (was, were) processed at Ellis Island.

9. _____

10. Some earlier immigrants (was, were) processed at Castle Garden in New York City.

10. _____

50-B Practice Procedure Follow the procedure given for 50-A.

1. There (is, are) a new tourist interest in Ellis Island today.

1. _____

2. My wife or her sisters (is, are) to tour Ellis Island soon.

2. _____

3. Photographs or a recorded message about the past (is, are) available for visitors.

3. _____

4. Most of the photographs (was, were) nicely displayed.

4. _____

5. There (is, are) many families who visit Ellis Island as a group.

5. _____

6. Neither of the historical films shown (was, were) long.

6. _____

7. The visitor center or the picnic grounds (was, were) popular.

7. _____

8. There (is, are) many families whose American origins began at Ellis Island.

8. _____

9. Everyone who visits the visitor center (is, are) impressed by its size and its ornateness.

9. _____

10. Each restored building (has, have) a story to tell.

10. _____

Your Total Score _____ /20

If your score was 15 or less for 50-A and 50-B, review pages 85-86 before continuing.

51-A Practice Procedure Complete each of the following sentences by writing in the blank provided at the right the correct word in the parentheses. Score one point for each correct answer.

Answers

1. That grove of trees (is, are) in Washington state.　　1. _____

2. The spotted owl population (is, are) endangered.　　2. _____

3. The committee of environmentalists (is, are) of many viewpoints.　　3. _____

4. The crowd outside the meeting hall (was, were) unruly.　　4. _____

5. The faculty (was, were) unanimous in its support of the plan.　　5. _____

6. The majority of citizens (is, are) in support of the faculty vote.　　6. _____

7. The audience (is, are) leaving their seats.　　7. _____

8. My family (is, are) speaking their minds to the media.　　8. _____

9. The environmental club (is, are) against cutting more trees.　　9. _____

10. The logging crew (is, are) getting out of their cars now.　　10. _____

51-B Practice Procedure Follow the procedure given for 51-A.

1. The team of investigators (was, were) expected today.　　1. _____

2. The majority of animals in the forest (is, are) endangered.　　2. _____

3. That herd of sheep (is, are) not endangered.　　3. _____

4. The team of investigators (was, were) preparing their speeches.　　4. _____

5. The class of students (is, are) arriving slowly.　　5. _____

6. The audience (was, were) quarreling as usual.　　6. _____

7. That flock of birds (is, are) late coming from the north.　　7. _____

8. That stand of sequoias (is, are) magnificent.　　8. _____

9. The team of firefighters (was, were) changing into their uniforms.　　9. _____

10. The large herd of buffaloes (was, were) exciting to watch.　　10. _____

Your Total Score _____ /20

If your score was 15 or less, review Section 15-H, pages 87-88, before continuing.

Name ___ Date ___ Score ___ /20

52-A Practice Procedure Complete each of the following sentences by writing in the blank provided at the right the correct word in the parentheses. Score one point for each correct answer.

Answers

1. Each of the memorandums (was, were) regarding new employees.   1. _____

2. Both memorandums (was, were) signed by the manager.   2. _____

3. There (is, are) company standards for written messages.   3. _____

4. My business associates or my business teacher (is, are) available to help me.   4. _____

5. There (was, were) some rules of writing I found difficult.   5. _____

6. Flip or his friends (was, were) to answer the letter.   6. _____

7. Management (is, are) interested in the quality of its written communications.   7. _____

8. Kathie or her secretaries (is, are) ready to proofread the letter.   8. _____

9. Both inquiries and replies (is, are) related.   9. _____

10. Each inquiry (was, were) seeking information in a reply.   10. _____

52-B Practice Procedure Follow the procedure given for 52-A.

1. There (is, are) good reasons for stating the subject of your written inquiry first.   1. _____

2. The writers or the preparer of that reply (is, are) new at the job.   2. _____

3. Several of the office staff (was, were) just out of school.   3. _____

4. The company (is, are) revising its hiring policy.   4. _____

5. There (is, are) a need for brief written communications.   5. _____

6. The hiring committee (was, were) selected from the management staff.   6. _____

7. The boss or her appointees (is, are) serving on the committee.   7. _____

8. There (is, are) replies that need to be written.   8. _____

9. Neither reply (was, were) judged to be acceptable.   9. _____

10. The office procedures panel (is, are) rewriting its guidelines.   10. _____

Your Total Score _____ /20

If your score was 15 or less for 52-A and 52-B, review pages 85-88 before continuing.

Noun, Verb, and Pronoun Review

53-A Practice Procedure Complete each of the following sentences by writing in the blank provided at the right the correct word in the parentheses. Score one point for each correct answer.

Answers

1. China's capital (is, are) Beijing.

   1. _____

2. The Great Wall of China (was, were) visible to the naked eye by U.S. astronauts on the moon.

   2. _____

3. Beijing's Imperial Palace (was, were) built in the fifteenth century.

   3. _____

4. Giant pandas (is, are) displayed in the Beijing zoo.

   4. _____

5. A boat trip down the Li River (was, were) very exciting.

   5. _____

6. Beautiful limestone mountains (is, are) seen along the Li River.

   6. _____

7. Tourists (has, have) enjoyed visiting China's West Lake.

   7. _____

8. The bicycle (is, are) used for transportation in China.

   8. _____

9. Chopsticks (is, are) used for eating utensils.

   9. _____

10. Each of our meals (was, were) served family style.

    10. _____

53-B Practice Procedure Follow the procedure given for 53-A.

1. (We, us) visited the beautiful West Lake area in Hangzhou.

   1. _____

2. Foreign visitors (is, are) welcome in China.

   2. _____

3. A number of Chinese (was, were) using the parks each morning.

   3. _____

4. Thurman or the tour guides (was, were) in the parks too.

   4. _____

5. (Who, Whom) is leading the dancers in the park?

   5. _____

6. The dancers (is, are) dancing as a form of exercise.

   6. _____

7. Everybody in the park (was, were) exercising in some way.

   7. _____

8. The leader of the dancers invited (we, us) to join the group.

   8. _____

9. The large group of children (was, were) ready to perform.

   9. _____

10. The public (has, have) been asked to express their thoughts about adding food stands to the parks.

    10. _____

Your Total Score _____ /20

If your score was 15 or less, review Units 2, 3, and 4 before continuing.

Noun, Verb, and Pronoun Review

application practice **54**

54-A Practice Procedure Complete each of the following sentences by writing in the blank provided at the right the correct word in the parentheses. Score one point for each correct answer.

Answers

1. Orders, remittances, and acknowledgments (is, are) important business communications.

1. _____

2. (They, Them) can make or break a business.

2. _____

3. The orders (was, were) requests for goods and/or services.

3. _____

4. An order (is, are) placed using an order blank or a letter.

4. _____

5. It is important for (we, us) to know ordering procedure.

5. _____

6. (Who, Whom) is ready to learn the procedure now?

6. _____

7. (We, Us) can learn the procedure quickly.

7. _____

8. (Was, Were) that order blank filled in properly?

8. _____

9. (Is, Are) order blanks preferred over letter orders?

9. _____

10. Order blanks were preferred by (she, her).

10. _____

54-B Practice Procedure Follow the procedure given for 54-A.

1. Remittances (is, are) money payments for goods and/or services.

1. _____

2. His remittance (was, were) enclosed with a letter.

2. _____

3. Acknowledgments (is, are) used in many business operations.

3. _____

4. New customers are among those (who, whom) receive acknowledgments.

4. _____

5. Often, a routine acknowledgment (is, are) a printed form.

5. _____

6. Most acknowledgments, however, (is, are) in letter form.

6. _____

7. (They, Them) received an acknowledgment with the order.

7. _____

8. (She, Her) and the order department worked closely together.

8. _____

9. A simple request type of letter (is, are) frequently used in business.

9. _____

10. There (is, are) easy rules for writing simple requests.

10. _____

Your Total Score _____ /20

If your score was 15 or less for 54-A and 54-B, review Units 2, 3, and 4 before continuing.

OBJECTIVES
1. To recognize and use the present, past, and future tenses of verbs.
2. To recognize and use the perfect tenses of verbs.
3. To recognize and use verbs according to person, number, tense, and voice.

Verbs are used to express the time at which events occur. Some events take place in the present, some took place in the past, and others will take place in the future.

The form of the verb that is used to indicate the time of an event is called *tense*. There are three primary tenses: the *present*, the *past*, and the *future*.

PAST   PRESENT   FUTURE

TENSES

16-A PRESENT TENSE FORM OF VERBS

The *present tense* tells what is happening now. It is also used to express a general truth and to indicate habitual action.

To form the present tense of most verbs, use the verb in its original form for all persons except third person singular. In the third person singular, add the letter *s* to the verb.

Example 1

Eileen <u>teaches</u> office procedures.

Analysis:

<u>teaches</u>—present tense because the subject *Eileen* is doing it now

	Singular	Plural
1st person	I walk	we walk
2nd person	you walk	you walk
3rd person	he, she, it walks	they walk

Study the verbs *sit* and *run*, for example, to see how they are formed in the present tense.

Example 2

She <u>tells</u> her students to study hard.

Analysis:

<u>tells</u>—present tense because it expresses habitual action

I sit	we sit
you sit	you sit
he, she, it sits	they sit

I run	we run
you run	you run
he, she, it runs	they run

16-B PRESENT TENSE FORMS OF THE VERB *BE*

Perhaps the most commonly used verb in the English language is the verb *be*. Unlike the verbs mentioned on the preceding page, this verb changes forms in the first, second, and third person singular. Study these forms of the verb *be* to improve your use of this verb.

	Singular	Plural
1st person	I am	we are
2nd person	you are	you are
3rd person	he, she, it is	they are

(See pages 79-80 for agreement of subjects with the forms of the verb *be*.)

16-C PRESENT TENSE FORMS OF THE VERB *HAVE*

Have is the next most-used verb. This verb is easy to learn because it is the same in almost all forms. The only change takes place in the third person singular when the form *has* is used. *Have* is used with all other singular and plural subjects.

	Singular	Plural
1st person	I have	we have
2nd person	you have	you have
3rd person	he, she, it has	they have

(See page 81 for agreement of subjects with forms of the verb *have*.)

16-D PRESENT TENSE FORMS OF THE VERB *DO*

A common mistake is using the wrong form of the verb *do* in the third person singular. Always be sure to use *does* with third person singular subjects. Do not use *he don't*. Use the correct form *he doesn't*.

	Singular	Plural
1st person	I do	we do
2nd person	you do	you do
3rd person	he, she, it does	they do

Example 1

Incorrect: She <u>don't</u> like chicken.
Correct: She <u>doesn't</u> like chicken.

Analysis:

<u>doesn't</u>—singular verb agrees with the subject *She*—third person singular

Example 2

Incorrect: He <u>don't</u> know her.
Correct: He <u>doesn't</u> know her.

Analysis:

<u>doesn't</u>—singular verb agrees with the subject *He*—third person singular

Example 3

Incorrect: It <u>don't</u> look finished.
Correct: It <u>doesn't</u> look finished.

Analysis:

<u>doesn't</u>—singular verb agrees with the subject *It*—third person singular

---

TRYOUT EXERCISE **Directions:** Complete each of the following sentences by writing in the blank provided at the right the correct form of the verb in the parentheses. Check your answers on page 245 or with your teacher before continuing with your assignment.

1. Our school (buy, buys) textbooks from that company. 1. _____
2. The girls (practice, practices) baseball after school. 2. _____
3. He (has, have) the most home runs on the team. 3. _____
4. Class (don't, doesn't) start until 10:00 a.m. 4. _____

Past Tense

17-A PAST TENSE FORM OF VERBS

The *past tense* tells what has already happened. The past tense of regular verbs is formed by adding *ed* to the verb regardless of number (singular or plural) or person. If the verb ends with the letter *e*, just add *d* to form the past tense. Be careful of the irregular verbs listed on pages 107-108. They are different in form.

Example 1

We <u>visited</u> the school yesterday.

Analysis:

visited—past tense of the verb *visit*—tells that the subject *We* has already completed the act of visiting

Example 2

Ronnie <u>graduated</u> from college.

Analysis:

graduated—past tense of the verb *graduate*—tells that the subject *Ronnie* has already completed the act of graduating

Example 3

Marcia <u>answered</u> the telephone.

Analysis:

answered—past tense of the verb *answer*—tells that the subject *Marcia* has already completed the act of answering

Example 4

I <u>lost</u> my bus ticket.

Analysis:

lost—past tense of the verb *lose*—tells that the subject *I* has already completed the act of losing the ticket. (Note that the verb *lose* is irregular, and the past tense does not add *d*.)

Example 5

This morning we <u>ate</u> pancakes.

Analysis:

ate—past tense of the verb *eat*—tells that the subject *we* has already completed the act of eating. (Note that the verb *eat* is irregular, and the past tense does not add *d*.)

17-B PAST TENSE FORMS OF THE VERB *BE*

The verb form *was* is used with all singular subjects except *you*. Always say and write *you were*. The verb form *were* is used with all plural subjects.

	Singular	Plural
1st person	I was	we were
2nd person	you were	you were
3rd person	he, she, it was	they were

17-C PAST TENSE FORMS OF THE VERB *HAVE*

The past tense of *have* has only one form. It is *had*. Use *had* with all subjects, singular and plural, in the past tense.

	Singular	Plural
1st person	I had	we had
2nd person	you had	you had
3rd person	he, she, it had	they had

Directions: Complete each of the following sentences by writing in the blank provided at the right the past tense of the verb in the parentheses. Check your answers on page 245 or with your teacher before continuing with your assignment.

1. We (live) in Chicago until last year.   1. _____
2. Our family (travel) to Canada on vacation.   2. _____
3. You (be) on time for once.   3. _____
4. Sharon (drive) us to the railroad station.   4. _____

section 18

Future Tense

The *future tense* tells what will happen in the time to come.

Example

Pam will marry Marius tonight.

Analysis:

will marry—future tense because the subject *Pam* will marry Marius in the time to come

To express the future, use *will* before the verb in all persons, except in questions. For the first person (I, we) in questions, use *shall* before the verb.

Examples

Shall we sing?
Shall I leave?
Will you speak tomorrow?

	Singular	Plural
1st person	I will try	we will try
(questions)	Shall I try?	Shall we try?
2nd person	you will try	you will try
3rd person	he, she, it will try	they will try

Note: Some persons use *shall* in the first person singular and plural in declarative sentences (I shall try. We shall try.). This usage, however, is seldom heard today in speech and is considered formal rather than general English usage.

Directions: Complete each of the following sentences by writing in the blank provided at the right the correct future tense helping verb. Check your answers on page 245 or with your teacher before continuing with your assignment.

1. (Shall, Will) we go to the play together?   1. _____
2. I (shall, will) pay for the tickets this time.   2. _____
3. (Shall, Will) I tell Pete we'll be there?   3. _____
4. (Shall, Will) he sit near us?   4. _____

Complete Application Practices 55-56, pages 99-100, at this time.

55-A Practice Procedure Complete each of the following sentences by writing in the blank provided at the right the correct form of the verb in the parentheses. Score one point for each correct answer.

Answers

1. Marion (walk, walks) downtown daily.   1. _____

2. She (live, lives) two blocks from the high school.   2. _____

3. Donna (work, works) at the school too.   3. _____

4. Marion and Donna (teach, teaches) geography.   4. _____

5. (Does, Do) they teach the same grade level?   5. _____

6. They (doesn't, don't) use the same textbooks.   6. _____

7. They (provide, provides) each student with an inflatable globe.   7. _____

8. The students (learn, learns) place geography using the globe.   8. _____

9. All students (doesn't, don't) learn geography easily.   9. _____

10. They (deflate, deflates) their globes at the end of each day.   10. _____

Your Total Score _____ /10

If your score was 7 or less, review Section 16-A, page 95, before continuing.

55-B Practice Procedure Complete each of the following sentences by writing in the blank provided at the right the past tense of the verb in the parentheses. Score one point for each correct answer.

Answers

1. The weather (turn) cold.   1. _____

2. It (rain) hard last night.   2. _____

3. In a nearby town it (snow).   3. _____

4. The weather bureau (predict) the storm.   4. _____

5. The bureau (issue) an advisory at midnight.   5. _____

6. Our family (discuss) the weather at breakfast.   6. _____

7. Mother (tell) the young children to stay inside.   7. _____

8. She (get) them books to read.   8. _____

9. Jimmy (choose) a book about the sea.   9. _____

10. Clara (read) the book to him.   10. _____

Your Total Score _____ /10

If your score was 7 or less, review Section 17, page 97, before continuing.

Future and Present, Past, and Future Tenses

56-A Practice Procedure Complete each of the following sentences by writing in the blank provided at the right the correct future tense helping verb in the parentheses. Score one point for each correct answer.

Answers

1. From December to April, gray whales (shall, will) migrate to Mexican waters.   1. _____

2. Female whales (shall, will) have their calves there.   2. _____

3. Tourists (shall, will) visit these waters to see the whales.   3. _____

4. (Shall, Will) I join a whale-watching group?   4. _____

5. If I do, (shall, will) you come also?   5. _____

6. Some whales (shall, will) surface near small boats.   6. _____

7. If a whale surfaces near my boat, I (shall, will) stroke it.   7. _____

8. (Shall, Will) we go on the same boat?   8. _____

9. We (shall, will) enjoy our outing with the whales.   9. _____

10. (Shall, Will) we call such whales "friendlies"?   10. _____

Your Total Score _____ /10

If your score was 7 or less for 56-A, review Section 18, page 98, before continuing.

56-B Practice Procedure Complete each of the following sentences by writing in the blank provided at the right the correct verb tense or helping verb in the parentheses. Score one point for each correct answer.

Answers

1. Brianne's team (play, plays) softball at school.   1. _____

2. They (practice, practices) every afternoon.   2. _____

3. Brianne (doesn't, don't) ever miss a practice.   3. _____

4. (Shall, Will) I congratulate her for her attendance?   4. _____

5. She (plays, played) pitcher for the past two weeks.   5. _____

6. The team (scores, scored) four runs last night.   6. _____

7. They (shall, will) win the championship.   7. _____

8. (Doesn't, Don't) it make you proud to win?   8. _____

9. The team believes they (shall, will) win the league title.   9. _____

10. They (win, won) the game tonight and the title too.   10. _____

Your Total Score _____ /10

If your score was 7 or less for 56-B, review Sections 16, 17, and 18, pages 95-98, before continuing.

/20

Score

Date

Name

The Perfect Tenses

All the perfect tenses show action that is completed in relation to a later action, circumstance, or time. Although we use the perfect tenses less often, an understanding of them is essential to good English. As you study this text, you will find that the perfect tenses are easy to learn.

19-A PRESENT PERFECT TENSE

The *present perfect tense* is formed by using the present tense of the verb *have* before the past participle of the main verb. With regular verbs, the *past participle* of the verb is formed by adding *ed* to the verb or just *d* if the verb ends in *e*. (Most of the irregular past participles can be found on pages 107-108.) Be careful to have subject and verb agreement. Use *has* only when the subject is third person singular. Use *have* with all other singular and plural subjects.

The present perfect tense is used to show that something has started in the past and has continued to the present. It is also used to show that an action has been completed at some indefinite time in the past.

Present Perfect Tense

	Singular	Plural
1st person	I have talked	we have talked
2nd person	you have talked	you have talked
3rd person	he has talked	they have talked

Example 1

I have ordered business cards.

Analysis:

have ordered—singular verb agrees in number with the subject *I*—first person singular

Example 2

He has replied to my letter.

Analysis:

has replied—singular verb agrees in number with the subject *He*—third person singular

Example 3

They have rented more office space.

Analysis:

have rented—plural verb agrees in number with the subject *They*—third person plural

Example 4

We have brought our equipment with us.

Analysis:

have brought—irregular plural verb agrees in number with the subject *We*—first person plural

---

19-B PAST PERFECT TENSE

The *past perfect tense* is formed in all numbers and persons by using *had* with the past participle of the main verb. The past perfect tense refers to something that was completed in the past before another past action or event.

Past Perfect Tense

	Singular	Plural
1st person	I had hoped	we had hoped
2nd person	you had hoped	you had hoped
3rd person	she had hoped	they had hoped

Example 1

Bob <u>had walked</u> to school before the bus came.

Analysis:

had walked—past perfect tense. The action was completed before another past action. *Had* is always used to form the past perfect tense, regardless of singular or plural subjects.

Example 2

They <u>had listened</u> to hear the school bell, but it rang late.

Analysis:

had listened—past perfect tense. The action was completed in the past before another past action.

19-C FUTURE PERFECT TENSE

The *future perfect tense* is formed by using *will have* with the past participle of the main verb. Use *shall have* instead of *will have* for the first person in questions. The future perfect tense is used when an action begun at any time will be completed by some time in the future.

Future Perfect Tense

	Singular	Plural
1st person	I will have polished	we will have polished
2nd person	you will have polished	you will have polished
3rd person	he will have polished	they will have polished

Example 1

By tomorrow they <u>will have completed</u> the battery of tests.

Analysis:

will have completed—future perfect tense. The action will be completed by tomorrow.

Example 2

<u>Shall</u> we <u>have arrived</u> at school before the tardy bell rings?

Analysis:

Shall have arrived—future perfect tense in a first person question. The action will be completed before the tardy bell rings or later.

TRYOUT EXERCISE **Directions:** Complete each of the following sentences by writing in the blank provided at the right the correct form of the verb in the parentheses. Check your answers on page 246 or with your teacher before continuing with your assignment.

1. They (present perfect of start) their engines. 1. _____

2. By the weekend, we (future perfect of selected) the winner. 2. _____

3. You (past perfect of practiced) the violin. 3. _____

4. I (future perfect of know) you a year today. 4. _____

5. She (present perfect of reply) to your letter already. 5. _____

Complete Application Practices 57-58, pages 103-104, at this time.

57-A Practice Procedure Complete each of the following sentences by writing in the blank provided at the right the correct perfect tense of the verb in the parentheses. Watch the past participle in irregular verbs. See the chart of irregular verbs on pages 107-108 when necessary. Score one point for each correct answer.

Answers

1. Scientists (present perfect of study) salmon species.   1. _____
2. There (present perfect of be) seven species identified.   2. _____
3. Salmon (past perfect of hatch) in rivers.   3. _____
4. They (future perfect of travel) to the sea.   4. _____
5. Salmon (future perfect of die) after laying their eggs.   5. _____
6. On occasion, Atlantic salmon (present perfect of live) to spawn again.   6. _____
7. The Japanese (present perfect of eat) 300,000 tons of salmon annually.   7. _____
8. Pacific fisheries (past perfect of hope) to increase sales.   8. _____
9. Early Alaskans (past perfect of worship) salmon in their ceremonies.   9. _____
10. They (past perfect of record) their ceremonies in journals.   10. _____
11. In the future, salmon farms (future perfect of replace) present fishing methods.   11. _____
12. The Japanese (present perfect of prefer) wild salmon.   12. _____
13. Wild salmon soon (future perfect of disappear) from some rivers.   13. _____
14. The lives of coastal Indians and salmon (present perfect of mingle) for some time.   14. _____
15. Indians (past perfect of hope) that their lives would not change.   15. _____

57-B Practice Procedure Complete the following sentences using the correct perfect tense form of the verb in parentheses. Score one point for each correct sentence.

1. Priscilla (present perfect of see) _____

2. The salmon (past perfect of swim) _____

3. The fishing season (future perfect of end) _____

4. Helen (future perfect of achieve) _____

Your Total Score _____ /19

If your score was 14 or less for 57-A and 57-B, review Section 19, pages 101-102, before continuing.

Tense Review

application practice **58**

58-A Practice Procedure Complete the sentences below by writing in the blank at the right the correct form of the verb in the parentheses. Remember that *present tense* tells what is happening now, *past tense* tells what has already happened, and *future tense* tells what will happen later. Score one point for each correct answer.

Answers

1. Carole (reports, reported, will report) to her new job last month.

1. _____

2. She (teaches, taught, will teach) classes to the new docent volunteers next week.

2. _____

3. Docents (learn, learned, will learn) about zoo services.

3. _____

4. After the classes, the docents (take, took, will take) children on tours of the zoo.

4. _____

5. They especially (like, liked, will like) the elephant class earlier this morning.

5. _____

6. Nancy, the elephant, (likes, liked, will like) being praised every day.

6. _____

7. She and her hippo friends (inhabit, inhabited, will inhabit) their new enclosure next winter.

7. _____

8. Zoo visitors (see, saw, will see) a new elephant show after today.

8. _____

9. Before they were captured, elephants (walk, walked, will walk) many miles a day.

9. _____

10. The docents (spend, spent, will spend) last week at the elephant exhibit.

10. _____

58-B Practice Procedure Follow the procedure given for 58-A.

1. The docents (spend, spent, will spend) their time tomorrow observing the pandas.

1. _____

2. The two pandas in our zoo (arrive, arrived, will arrive) from China last year.

2. _____

3. The Chinese government (loans, loaned, will loan) these pandas to us for two years.

3. _____

4. Immediately, visitors (throng, thronged, will throng) to the panda exhibit.

4. _____

5. Visitors always (enjoy, enjoyed, will enjoy) the playful pandas.

5. _____

6. Daily, they (laugh, laughed, will laugh) at the antics of these animals.

6. _____

7. The Chinese (share, shared, will share) scientific data about the pandas before the animals arrived.

7. _____

8. The docents (enjoy, enjoyed, will enjoy) their study of the pandas yesterday.

8. _____

9. Next week Carole (talks, talked, will talk) to school children.

9. _____

10. She (doesn't, don't) know their teacher.

10. _____

11. The talk (has, have) aroused interest in the zoo.

11. _____

Your Total Score _____ /21

If your score was 16 or less for 58-A and 58-B, review Sections 16-18, pages 95-98, before continuing.

/21

Score

Date

Name

Conjugation of Verbs

Conjugation means breaking the verb down into its different forms to show person, number, tense, and voice. All verbs have these forms called *principal parts*. By knowing which part of the verb to use, your sentences will be correct.

Remember that the main tenses of any verb are the present, past, and future. From these three forms, you can make up the tense of any verb. The present tense is formed by using the verb as it is, except in the third person singular when you add *s* to the verb. The past tense of regular verbs is formed by adding *ed* or *d*, and the same is true in forming the *past participle*. The *present participle* is formed by adding *ing* to the verb. Page 106 shows the complete conjugation of a regular verb.

The irregular verbs have unusual parts. They are, however, the most-used verbs in the English language. Learning them involves practice and memorization. Pages 107 and 108 list irregular verbs and their variations. The charts on pages 106-108 will simplify conjugation as much as possible, but the only way to learn how to conjugate verbs is to use them repeatedly.

Verbs may be in either the *active voice* or the *passive voice*. A verb is in the active voice when the subject does the action. A verb is in the passive voice when the action is done to the subject by something or someone else. Some form of the helping verb *be* and a past participle are necessary with the passive voice.

Example 1

The dishwasher broke a plate.

Analysis:

broke—active voice—action is done by the subject *dishwasher*

Example 2

The cafe manager saw it happen.

Analysis:

saw—active voice—action is done by the subject *manager*

Example 3

The menu was prepared by the chef.

Analysis:

was prepared—passive voice—action is done to the subject *menu*

Example 4

The food was eaten by the customers.

Analysis:

was eaten—passive voice—action is done to the subject *food* by the customers

Example 5

I went to the cafe regularly.

Analysis:

went—active voice—action is done by the subject *I*

THE LIFEGUARD THROWS THE FLOAT.

PASSIVE

THE SWIMMER IS SAVED FROM DROWNING.

ACTIVE

20-A CONJUGATION OF THE VERB *MOVE*

The active voice (action done by the subject) is on the left-hand side of this page. The passive voice (action done to the subject) is on the right-hand side of this page. The verbs are used in the singular and the plural forms, with the subject *he* used to illustrate the third person singular.

This chart can be used as a guide and check in deciding how a verb is broken down into its different parts. Use and refer to this chart often.

Verb	Present Participle	Past Tense	Past Participle
move	moving	moved	moved

Active Voice
(Action done by subject)

Singular	Plural

Present Tense

Singular	Plural
I move	we move
you move	you move
he moves	they move

Past Tense

Singular	Plural
I moved	we moved
you moved	you moved
he moved	they moved

Future Tense

Singular	Plural
I will (shall) move	we will (shall) move
you will move	you will move
he will move	they will move

Present Perfect Tense

Singular	Plural
I have moved	we have moved
you have moved	you have moved
he has moved	they have moved

Past Perfect Tense

Singular	Plural
I had moved	we had moved
you had moved	you had moved
he had moved	they had moved

Future Perfect Tense

Singular	Plural
I will have moved	we will have moved
you will have moved	you will have moved
he will have moved	they will have moved

Passive Voice
(Action done to subject)

Singular	Plural

Present Tense

Singular	Plural
I am moved	we are moved
you are moved	you are moved
he is moved	they are moved

Past Tense

Singular	Plural
I was moved	we were moved
you were moved	you were moved
he was moved	they were moved

Future Tense

Singular	Plural
I will (shall) be moved	we will (shall) be moved
you will be moved	you will be moved
he will be moved	they will be moved

Present Perfect Tense

Singular	Plural
I have been moved	we have been moved
you have been moved	you have been moved
he has been moved	they have been moved

Past Perfect Tense

Singular	Plural
I had been moved	we had been moved
you had been moved	you had been moved
he had been moved	they had been moved

Future Perfect Tense

Singular	Plural
I will have been moved	we will have been moved
you will have been moved	you will have been moved
he will have been moved	they will have been moved

20-B PRINCIPAL PARTS OF IRREGULAR VERBS

These 50 irregular verbs do not follow the rule for forming the past tense and the past participle. Many of them are used in daily speech. Review them now, and study any that are unfamiliar to you.

Commonly Used Irregular Verbs

Irregular Verb	Past Tense	Past Participle
be (am, is, are)	was (were)	been
become	became	become
begin	began	begun
bite	bit	bitten
blow	blew	blown
break	broke	broken
bring	brought	brought
build	built	built
come	came	come
do	did	done
draw	drew	drawn
drink	drank	drunk
drive	drove	driven
eat	ate	eaten
fall	fell	fallen
fight	fought	fought
fly	flew	flown
get	got	gotten or got
give	gave	given
go	went	gone
grow	grew	grown
hear	heard	heard
hit	hit	hit
know	knew	known
lay	laid	laid
lead	led	led
leave	left	left
let	let	let
lie (recline)	lay	lain
lose	lost	lost
put	put	put
ride	rode	ridden
ring	rang	rung
run	ran	run
say	said	said
see	saw	seen
show	showed	shown or showed
sing	sang	sung
sink	sank or sunk	sunk
sit	sat	sat
sleep	slept	slept
speak	spoke	spoken
swim	swam	swum
take	took	taken
teach	taught	taught
tell	told	told
think	thought	thought
throw	threw	thrown
wear	wore	worn
write	wrote	written

The list below contains 29 additional irregular verbs. They are important for you to learn, as well.

Less Frequently Used Irregular Verbs

Irregular Verb	Past Tense	Past Participle
arise	arose	arisen
awake	awaked or awoke	awaked or awoken
bear	bore	borne
beat	beat	beaten
burst	burst or bursted	burst or bursted
catch	caught	caught
choose	chose	chosen
cling	clung	clung
cost	cost	cost
dive	dived or dove	dived
fling	flung	flung
forget	forgot	forgot or forgotten
freeze	froze	frozen
hang	hung	hung
hang (death)	hanged	hanged
hurt	hurt	hurt
keep	kept	kept
pay	paid	paid
read	read	read
rise	rose	risen
set	set	set
shake	shook	shaken
shine	shone	shone
spring	sprang or sprung	sprung
steal	stole	stolen
swear	swore	sworn
swing	swung	swung
tear	tore	torn
wake	waked or woke	waked or woken

TRYOUT EXERCISE   **Directions:** Complete each of the following sentences by writing in the blank provided at the right the correct tense of the verb in the parentheses. Check your answers on page 246 or with your teacher before continuing with your assignment.

1. The puppy (past of fall) off the bed.

1. _____

2. The puppy's owner had (past participle of hear) the fall.

2. _____

3. The owner (future of keep) the puppy close to him.

3. _____

Complete Application Practices 59-60, pages 109-110, at this time.

Irregular Verbs

59-A Practice Procedure Complete each of the following sentences by writing in the blank provided at the right the correct form of the verb in the parentheses. Refer to the lists on pages 107-108 if necessary. Score one point for each correct answer.

Answers

1. To get to Washington, D.C., we (past of drive) across country.   1. _____

2. We (past of know) our trip would take several days.   2. _____

3. To cross the desert, we always (past of leave) at night.   3. _____

4. A severe storm had (past participle of blow) through ahead of us.   4. _____

5. In Arizona the sun (past of shine) brightly.   5. _____

6. Just out of Tucson our car (past of blow) a tire.   6. _____

7. A friendly passerby had (past participle of give) us a hand.   7. _____

8. To pass the time on a trip, we often (present of sing).   8. _____

9. In El Paso we soon had (past participle of lose) our way.   9. _____

10. Along the highway, we had (past participle of see) unusual rock formations.   10. _____

59-B Practice Procedure Follow the procedure given for 59-A.

1. From El Paso we (past of set) our sights for Dallas.   1. _____

2. We (past of keep) on major highways most of the time.   2. _____

3. My mother had (past participle of ride) in the front seat from El Paso to Dallas.   3. _____

4. By Dallas we had (past participle of grow) tired of traveling.   4. _____

5. Our parents (past of say) we would rest in Dallas awhile.   5. _____

6. We (past of be) happy to stay put for the time being.   6. _____

7. In the car all of us (past of wear) loose clothing.   7. _____

8. While in Dallas we (past of write) postcards to friends.   8. _____

9. After a two-day rest we (past of hit) the road again.   9. _____

10. Little Rock and Memphis (past of be) our next large cities.   10. _____

11. After Memphis, Nashville (present of lay) ahead.   11. _____

12. We had (past participle of hear) the mountains of Kentucky were beautiful.   12. _____

13. In Charlottesville, Virginia, a guide (past of show) us Jefferson's home.   13. _____

14. From Charlottesville we (past of go) to Richmond, Virginia's capital.   14. _____

15. From Richmond the road (past of lead) to our nation's capital.   15. _____

Your Total Score _____ /25

If your score was 19 or less for 59-A and 59-B, review pages 107-108 before continuing.

Active and Passive Voices

60-A Practice Procedure Determine whether the underlined verb in each of the following sentences is active or passive. Write *active* or *passive* in the blank provided at the right. Score one point for each correct answer.

Answers

1. Redwood National Park <u>has been photographed</u> many times. 1. _____

2. I <u>took</u> a photograph of a redwood tree 300 feet high. 2. _____

3. The framed photograph <u>hangs</u> on my bedroom wall. 3. _____

4. Heavy bark <u>protects</u> redwood trees from diseases. 4. _____

5. Redwoods <u>tolerate</u> flooding. 5. _____

6. The National Park Service <u>was created</u> by Congress. 6. _____

7. My family <u>enjoys</u> visiting our national parks. 7. _____

8. Redwood trees <u>were restricted</u> to foggy coastal regions by the Ice Age. 8. _____

9. The domain of redwoods <u>has been reduced</u> by logging. 9. _____

10. Shops in the area <u>sell</u> souvenirs made of redwood. 10. _____

60-B Practice Procedure Follow the procedure given for 60-A.

1. Ocean tide pools <u>can be found</u> in the park too. 1. _____

2. Our group <u>walked</u> over sandy beaches to the tide pools. 2. _____

3. We <u>saw</u> a hermit crab living in a seashell. 3. _____

4. An anemone <u>was seen</u> attached to a rock. 4. _____

5. Gulls <u>flew</u> above us in search of food. 5. _____

6. We <u>spotted</u> several large starfish in the pools. 6. _____

7. Sea lions <u>were observed</u> lazing on the rocks. 7. _____

8. Tiny limpets <u>eat</u> seaweed, not grass. 8. _____

9. The incoming tide <u>filled</u> the pools with seawater. 9. _____

10. Our visit to the park <u>was appreciated</u> by all of us. 10. _____

Your Total Score _____ /20

If your score was 15 or less for 60-A and 60-B, review page 106 before continuing.

110

Misused Verbs

A few verbs can be troublesome. Special attention should be given when you use them.

Some of the most troublesome verbs are *lie* and *lay* and *sit* and *set*.

21-A LIE AND LAY

Uses of the Verb *Lie*

The verb *lie* means to rest or recline. With *lie* the subject usually takes a position or is in a position. *Lie* never has an object (a word following the verb which answers the question "what" or "whom").

Present Tense: lie

I lie	we lie
you lie	you lie
he, she, it lies	they lie

Past Tense: lay

I lay	we lay
you lay	you lay
he, she, it lay	they lay

Past Participle: lain

I have lain	we have lain
you have lain	you have lain
he, she, it has lain	they have lain

Hint: If you cannot use *place* or *put* instead of the verb *lie,* you know some form of the verb *lie* is correct.

Example 1

At home I <u>lie</u> on the couch to watch TV.

Analysis:

> <u>lie</u>—present tense—means to rest or recline on the couch—does not have an object

Example 2

Sam <u>lies</u> on the floor to read.

Analysis:

> <u>lies</u>—present tense—means to rest or recline—does not have an object

Example 3

They <u>lay</u> on the grass at the picnic.

Analysis:

> <u>lay</u>—past tense—means to rest or recline—does not have an object

Example 4

They <u>lay</u> under the only palm tree in the park.

Analysis:

> <u>lay</u>—past tense—means to rest or recline—does not have an object

Example 5

You <u>have lain</u> in bed all morning.

Analysis:

> <u>have lain</u>—past participle—means to rest or recline—does not have an object

LIE — REST OR RECLINE (NO OBJECT)

I LIE ON THE BEACH.

LAY — PLACE OR PUT (TAKES OBJECT)

I LAY THE TOWEL ON THE SAND.

Uses of the Verb *Lay*

The verb *lay* is often misused for the verb *lie*. *Lay* means to place or put something down. It always takes an object (a word following the verb which answers the question "what" or "whom").

Present Tense: lay

I lay	we lay
you lay	you lay
he, she, it lays	they lay

Past Tense: laid

I laid	we laid
you laid	you laid
he, she, it laid	they laid

Past Participle: laid

I have laid	we have laid
you have laid	you have laid
he, she, it has laid	they have laid

Hint: If you can use *place* or *put* instead of the verb *lay*, you know some form of the verb *lay* is correct.

Example 1

I <u>lay</u> the paper on the desk.

Analysis:

lay—present tense—means to place or put something down—has an object *paper*

Example 2

She <u>lays</u> the silverware on the table.

Analysis:

lays—present tense—means to place or put something down—has an object *silverware*

Example 3

The students <u>laid</u> their pens down.

Analysis:

laid—past tense—means to place or put something down—has an object *pens*

Example 4

We <u>laid</u> the bricks in the patio.

Analysis:

laid—past tense—means to place or put something down—has an object *bricks*

Example 5

They <u>have laid</u> their jackets over there.

Analysis:

have laid—past participle—means to place or put something down—has an object *jackets*

REVIEW

lie (to rest or recline)	lying	lay	lain	(no object)
lay (to put or place)	laying	laid	laid	(always an object)

112

21-B SIT AND SET

The verbs *sit* and *set* are also troublesome verbs. Having learned the use of *lie* and *lay*, *sit* and *set* will be easy. *Sit* and *lie* are governed by the same rules while *set* and *lay* have the same rules.

Uses of the Verb *Sit*

Sit means to have a seat or occupy a position. It never has an object (a word following the verb which answers the question "what" or "whom").

Present Tense: sit

I sit	we sit
you sit	you sit
he, she, it sits	they sit

Past Tense: sat

I sat	we sat
you sat	you sat
he, she, it sat	they sat

Past Participle: sat

I have sat	we have sat
you have sat	you have sat
he, she, it has sat	they have sat

Example 1

On the school bus, I <u>sit</u> by the window.

Analysis:

> <u>sit</u>—present tense—means to have a seat or occupy a position—does not have an object

Example 2

Marcia usually <u>sits</u> near me.

Analysis:

> <u>sits</u>—present tense—means to have a seat or occupy a position—does not have an object

Example 3

They always <u>sat</u> together if they could.

Analysis:

> <u>sat</u>—past tense—means to have a seat or occupy a position—does not have an object

Example 4

They <u>have sat</u> near the emergency door.

Analysis:

> <u>have sat</u>—past participle—means to have sat or occupied a position—does not have an object

Example 5

You <u>have sat</u> near the side before.

Analysis:

> <u>have sat</u>—past participle—means to have sat or occupied a position—does not have an object

SIT TO RECLINE OR REST

SET TO PLACE OR PUT

113

Uses of the Verb *Set*

Set means to put or place. It always has an object. Remember the hint: If you can substitute *place* or *put* for the verb *set*, you know some form of *set* is correct.

Present Tense: set

I set	we set
you set	you set
he, she, it sets	they set

Past Tense: set

I set	we set
you set	you set
he, she, it set	they set

Past Participle: set

I have set	we have set
you have set	you have set
he, she, it has set	they have set

Example 1

We <u>set</u> the dishes on the table early.

Analysis:

set—present tense—means to place or put something down—has an object *dishes*

Example 2

He <u>sets</u> his skis on the porch.

Analysis:

<u>sets</u>—present tense—means to place or put something down—has an object *skis*

Example 3

They <u>set</u> the trash barrels by the curb.

Analysis:

<u>set</u>—past tense—means to place or put something down—has an object *barrels*

Example 4

Yesterday you <u>set</u> the plants in the ground.

Analysis:

<u>set</u>—past tense—means to place or put something down—has an object *plants*

Example 5

She <u>has set</u> the library books on the desk.

Analysis:

<u>has set</u>—past participle—means to have placed or put something down—has an object *books*

REVIEW

sit (rest or occupy a position)	sitting	sat	sat	(no object)
set (place or put)	setting	set	set	(always an object)

TRYOUT EXERCISE **Directions:** Complete each of the following sentences by writing in the blank provided at the right the correct form of the verb in the parentheses. Check your answers on page 246 or with your teacher before continuing with your assignment.

1. He (sit, set) the newspaper by the door.   1. _____

2. She (lies, lays) on the beach to get a tan.   2. _____

3. I (lay, laid) my coat on the chair.   3. _____

4. They (sat, set) together on the train.   4. _____

Complete Application Practices 61-62, pages 115-116, at this time.

61-A Practice Procedure Complete each of the following sentences by writing in the blank provided at the right the correct form of the verb indicated in the parentheses. Score one point for each correct answer.

Answers

1. The nurse (past of lay) her keys on the desk.   1. _____
2. She (past of lie) on the bed to get a quick rest.   2. _____
3. Busy nurses (present of lie) down whenever they can.   3. _____
4. A tired nurse's aide (past participle of lie) down on another cot.   4. _____
5. An orderly (present of lay) prescription slips on the nurse's desk.   5. _____
6. He (past of lay) other reports beside the slips.   6. _____
7. The head nurse (past participle of lay) new patient charts beside the current charts.   7. _____
8. One patient was told to (present of lie) flat on his back in bed.   8. _____
9. After lunch, an ambulatory patient (past of lie) on a lounge in the sun.   9. _____
10. The patient (past of lay) his book on a nearby chair.   10. _____

61-B Practice Procedure Follow the procedure given for 61-A.

1. Jodie, a puppy, has learned to (lie, lay) down on command.   1. _____
2. Kringle, our Siamese cat, (has lain, has laid) in the sun all morning.   2. _____
3. Last night, Tim (lay, laid) awake for hours.   3. _____
4. This morning our dog (lay, laid) the newspaper at Tim's door.   4. _____
5. Now, Tim (lies, lays) in bed reading the newspaper.   5. _____
6. Our dogs and cats (have lain, have laid) on the outdoor lounge.   6. _____
7. At obedience school, the instructor (lay, laid) his manual on the floor. 7. _____
8. A large dog (lay, laid) down on the manual.   8. _____
9. The instructor (lies, lays) on the floor to examine each dog.   9. _____
10. Our dog, Zuma, (has lain, has laid) there quietly for some time.   10. _____
11. Owners always (lie, lay) their dog's leases by the door.   11. _____
12. One owner (has lain, has laid) down to take a nap.   12. _____
13. John (lay, laid) a check on the counter for the trainer.   13. _____
14. Debbie (lies, lays) her dog's enrollment card next to John's check.   14. _____
15. At the end of the session, almost all dogs (lay, laid) beside their owners. 15. _____

Your Total Score _____ /25

If your score was 19 or less for 61-A and 61-B, review Section 21-A, pages 111-112, before continuing.

/25

Score

Date

Name

62-A Practice Procedure Complete each of the following sentences by writing in the blank provided at the right the correct form of the verb indicated in the parentheses. Score one point for each correct answer.

Answers

1. Dan (past participle of set) his luggage by the door.

1. _____

2. His cat, Kris, quickly (past of sit) on the luggage.

2. _____

3. Dan (present of set) his airline tickets by the luggage.

3. _____

4. On the plane, Dan usually (present of sit) in a coach seat.

4. _____

5. Today, however, he (past of sit) in first class.

5. _____

6. His wife, Priscilla, (present of sit) there too.

6. _____

7. Before takeoff, Dan (past of set) his book on the seat.

7. _____

8. Dan urged Priscilla to (present of sit) by the window.

8. _____

9. At takeoff, the attendants (past of sit) on jump seats.

9. _____

10. The attendants (past participle of set) the beverage cart in the aisle.

10. _____

62-B Practice Procedure Follow the procedure given for 62-A.

1. At Don and Kim's wedding, guests (sat, set) on folding chairs.

1. _____

2. Her friends (sat, set) to the left of the center aisle.

2. _____

3. Don's friends will (sit, set) on the right.

3. _____

4. Each guest (sat, set) his or her invitation on a plate at the door.

4. _____

5. They (sat, set) their gifts on a special table in the rear.

5. _____

6. Kim's grandmother (sits, sets) in a wheelchair to the side.

6. _____

7. The florist (sit, set) a flower basket by the altar.

7. _____

8. Kim's mother (sits, sets) to the left of the center aisle.

8. _____

9. Don's mother (has sat, has set) down already.

9. _____

10. The ushers (have sat, have set) extra chairs in back.

10. _____

11. Kim's friends from her office (sat, set) together.

11. _____

12. Because of his poor eyesight, Don's uncle (sits, sets) in front.

12. _____

13. After the ceremony, the guests (sat, set) at the luncheon tables.

13. _____

14. The wedding party will (sit, set) at a special table.

14. _____

15. The wedding cake (sits, sets) on a small table.

15. _____

Your Total Score _____ /25

If your score was 19 or less for 62-A and 62-B, review Section 21-B, pages 113-114, before continuing.

Less Troublesome Verbs

Now that you understand *lie, lay* and *sit, set,* we'll look at some less troublesome verbs. Most of these verbs you already know; however, all of us misuse them occasionally.

22-A SHALL, SHOULD, WILL, AND WOULD

You have already learned to use the verb forms of *shall* and *will* in the future tense. If necessary refer to page 98 for a review.

Should and *would* are used in conditional sentences. These sentences contain some doubt or uncertainty about the statement being made. *Should* is used with the subjects *I* and *we. Would* is used with all other subjects.

Examples

We <u>should</u> leave as soon as possible.
Do you think <u>she would</u> leave anyway?

Should is used with all subjects to indicate obligation. In such sentences *should* is used in the sense of *ought.*

Examples

<u>I should</u> pay the bill now.
<u>He should</u> remember me.

Exceptions: Use *will* and *would* with the subjects *I* and *we* to show determination or emphasis. Determination is a strong and definite feeling. *Shall* is used with all other subjects in sentences that show determination.

Examples

<u>We will</u> fire her tonight.
<u>She shall</u> be in school, or else!

Would is used in polite or unemphatic requests.

Examples

<u>Would you</u> respond to this letter please?
<u>She would</u> reply if he asked.

22-B MAY, MIGHT, CAN, AND COULD

May and *might* are used to express permission, possibility, or probability.

Examples

<u>You might</u> be surprised by his answer.
<u>I may</u> like it when I'm older.

Can and *could* are used to express abilty or power to do something.

Examples

<u>Can you</u> hear the baby if he cries?
<u>She could</u> be kinder if she tried.

22-C LEAVE AND LET

Leave is often confused with *let*. *Leave* means to depart from one place to another. It also means to allow to remain.

Let means to permit or allow. Only with *alone* meaning "stop from disturbing" can either verb be used.

Examples

Did he <u>leave</u> his books with you?

Will she <u>leave</u> early in the morning?

Examples

Will you <u>let</u> me enroll in that class?

Her mother <u>let</u> her go with us on vacation.

We will be happy to <u>leave</u> (or <u>let</u>) you alone!

Jon <u>let</u> his little sister watch television.

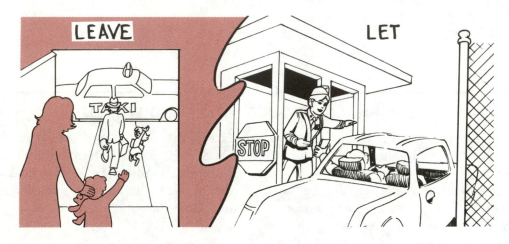

22-D TEACH AND LEARN

Teach mans to instruct or to show someone how something is done.

Examples

I <u>teach</u> science at the high school.

He will <u>teach</u> at the police academy.

Learn means to acquire or obtain knowledge and information.

Examples

She will <u>learn</u> to play golf this summer.

We <u>learn</u> much from our parents.

22-E BORROW AND LEND

Borrow means to take or to obtain something from someone else on loan. You do not have it so you borrow it.

Lend means to let someone use something of yours for a period of time. You have it, and you allow the other person to use it.

Examples

May I <u>borrow</u> your class notes?

Will she <u>borrow</u> your luggage for the trip?

Examples

Will you <u>lend</u> me your bicycle?

Tim will <u>lend</u> you his camera.

22-F BRING, TAKE, AND FETCH

Bring means to carry something toward a person, place, or thing or to *come* carrying something.

Examples

Jean will <u>bring</u> the birthday cake to the party.
Please <u>bring</u> me your guest list for the party.

Take means to carry something away from a person, place, or thing, or to *go* carrying something.

Examples

Please <u>take</u> my groceries to the car.
Will you <u>take</u> the dog home for me?

Fetch means to go after and bring back.

Examples

Vince will be pleased to <u>fetch</u> your mail if you like.
Spot, <u>fetch</u> the ball!

22-G RISE AND RAISE

Rise means to get up, arise, or ascend. It never has an object.

Examples

Please <u>rise</u> for the school song.
When the full moon <u>rises</u> over the ocean, the water shimmers.

Raise means to lift something. It may have an object.

Examples

Please <u>raise</u> those windows.
When I call your name, <u>raise</u> your hand.
The honor guard <u>raised</u> the flag.

Directions: Complete each of the following sentences by writing in the blank provided at the right the correct form of the verb in the parentheses. Check your answers on page 246 or with your teacher before continuing with your assignment.

1. If we (would, should) go, will you go too?   1. _____
2. (May, Can) I leave now?   2. _____
3. (Leave, Let) me see her.   3. _____
4. My brother will (teach, learn) us to skate.   4. _____
5. Will you (borrow, lend) me a pen?   5. _____
6. Please (bring, take) this note home.   6. _____
7. (Rise, Raise) you little finger if you can.   7. _____

Complete Application Practices 63-68, pages 121-126, at this time.

63-A Practice Procedure Complete each of the following sentences by writing *shall* or *will* in the blank provided at the right. Score one point for each correct answer.

Answers

1. When we visit Vancouver, (?) we see Stanley Park?   1. _____
2. Jim (?) meet us at the Vancouver airport.   2. _____
3. He (?) show us some Indian artwork.   3. _____
4. (?) I see some totem poles too?   4. _____
5. I (?) buy an Indian necklace for my mother.   5. _____
6. (?) I buy a matching bracelet too?   6. _____
7. In Gastown she (?) photograph the steam clock.   7. _____
8. They (?) eat smoked salmon at a pier restaurant.   8. _____
9. (?) I make a reservation at the restaurant?   9. _____
10. (?) you eat dinner with us too?   10. _____

63-B Practice Procedure Complete each of the following sentences by writing *should* or *would* in the blank provided at the right. Score one point for each correct answer.

1. At the fish hatchery, you (?) see salmon jumping the ladder.   1. _____
2. (?) you take my picture at the hatchery if the sun's out?   2. _____
3. We (?) arrive at the hatchery soon.   3. _____
4. If you (?) hear my name called by the ranger, tell me.   4. _____
5. (?) you pay for my ticket to the hatchery?   5. _____
6. My friends advised me that we (?) visit the bird sanctuary too.   6. _____
7. They (?) like us to go with them.   7. _____
8. (?) you like to go to the bird sanctuary?   8. _____
9. I (?) visit the aquarium while I'm here.   9. _____
10. You (?) need to be here a long time to see everything.   10. _____

Your Total Score _____ /20

If your score was 15 or less for 63-A and 63-B, review Sections 18 and 22-A, pages 98 and 117, before continuing.

63-C Practice Procedure On a separate sheet of paper, write five sentences using *shall* and *will* and five sentences using *should* and *would*. Try to make your writing interesting. Score one point for each correct answer.

Your Total Score _____ /10

64-A Practice Procedure Complete each of the following sentences by writing *may* or *can* in the blank provided at the right. Score one point for each correct answer.

Answers

1. Please, (?) I take my new camera on the trip?   1. _____

2. I (?) carry it in my new camera bag.   2. _____

3. The X-ray machines at some airports (?) ruin highly sensitive film.   3. _____

4. We (?) miss the plane if we don't get started soon.   4. _____

5. (?) we hear the flight number called over the loudspeaker?   5. _____

6. The skycap (?) check our luggage at the curb.   6. _____

7. Mother (?) wish to carry her small bag on the plane.   7. _____

8. We (?) check in at the airline desk now.   8. _____

9. The airline desk attendant (?) give us seat locations.   9. _____

10. We (?) board the plane when our row number is called.   10. _____

64-B Practice Procedure Follow the procedure given for 64-A.

1. On arrival at our destination, we (?) meet at the baggage claim area.   1. _____

2. We (?) get lost if we're not organized.   2. _____

3. (?) I carry the present for grandmother?   3. _____

4. It (?) be some time before our luggage is off the plane.   4. _____

5. (?) you estimate how long it will take?   5. _____

6. (?) you find your small red bag?   6. _____

7. To avoid a back injury, father (?) call a baggage attendant for help.   7. _____

8. Our rental car (?) arrive before we want it.   8. _____

9. With all our luggage we (?) wish we had two cars.   9. _____

10. Now we (?) call grandmother and tell her we've arrived.   10. _____

Your Total Score _____ /20

If your score was 15 or less for 64-A and 64-B, review Section 22-B, page 117, before continuing.

64-C Practice Procedure On a separate sheet of paper, write five sentences using *may* and five sentences using *can*. Try to make your writing interesting. Score one point for each correct answer.

Your Total Score _____ /10

/30

Score

Date

Name

65-A Practice Procedure Complete each of the following sentences by writing in the blank provided at the right the correct tense of the verb in the parentheses. Score one point for each correct answer.

Answers

1. Our company (sell, sells) office supplies.   1. _____

2. We (buy, buys) our paper stock from Acme Corporation.   2. _____

3. I (am, are) a sales representative.   3. _____

4. Aitken Lumber Company (place, placed) a large order yesterday.   4. _____

5. They (shall, will) call on them next month.   5. _____

6. (Shall, Will) we call on them next year too?   6. _____

7. It (don't, doesn't) need to be decided today.   7. _____

8. Barbara (was, were) a buyer for the crafts store.   8. _____

9. I (shall, will) introduce myself to her.   9. _____

10. The crafts store (open, opened) last year.   10. _____

65-B Practice Procedure Follow the procedure given for 65-A.

1. Pete (join, joined) our sales staff last month.   1. _____

2. He (show, showed) great promise from the start.   2. _____

3. His sales message (has, have) a punch to it.   3. _____

4. It (is, are) a pleasure to read.   4. _____

5. He (shall, will) read his latest sales message to the staff.   5. _____

6. Gerry (talk, talked) about written sales messages this morning.   6. _____

7. He (shall, will) repeat his lecture tomorrow.   7. _____

8. (Shall, Will) we go together to Gerry's lecture?   8. _____

9. Attendance (don't, doesn't) require a ticket.   9. _____

10. We (have, had) better leave early to get there.   10. _____

Your Total Score _____ /20

If your score was 15 or less for 65-A and 65-B, review Sections 16, 17, and 18, pages 95-98, before continuing.

Name

Date

Score

/20

66-A Practice Procedure In each of the sentences below identify the perfect tense and verb of the underlined words. Write your answer in the blank provided at the right. Watch the past participle in irregular verbs. See the chart of irregular verbs on pages 107-108 when necessary. Score one point for each correct answer.

Answers

1. Bob has traveled to Costa Rica often.   1. _____
2. He had hoped to live there one day.   2. _____
3. Soon he will have learned the Spanish language.   3. _____
4. He has studied Spanish for about one year.   4. _____
5. He has taught his Costa Rican friends English.   5. _____
6. They will have learned English by the end of the year.   6. _____
7. They had visited Bob in the U.S. in the spring.   7. _____
8. Earlier, they had used a tape recorder to practice their English.   8. _____
9. They will have listened to their tapes frequently.   9. _____
10. Bob and his friends have worked hard to become bilingual tour guides.   10. _____
11. Visitors to Costa Rica have enjoyed the natural riches of the country.   11. _____
12. Before leaving, most visitors will have seen many of the country's 29 national parks.   12. _____
13. They will have driven to the parks to experience the unusual plants and animals.   13. _____
14. Most tours had included visits to the nation's many volcanoes.   14. _____
15. Visitors to Costa Rica have grown in number.   15. _____

66-B Practice Procedure Complete the following sentences using the correct perfect tense form of the verb in parentheses. Score one point for each correct sentence.

1. Kathy (past perfect of decide) _____

_____

2. She (past perfect of hope) _____

_____

3. Before dinner, we (future perfect of finish) _____

_____

4. They (present perfect of enjoy) _____

_____

Your Total Score _____ /19

If your score was 14 or less for 66-A and 66-B, review Section 19, pages 101-102, before continuing.

Verb Review III—Irregular Verbs, Active and Passive

application practice **67**

67-A Practice Procedure Complete each of the following sentences by writing in the blank provided at the right the correct form of the verb in the parentheses. You will need to put some verbs in the passive voice. Score one point for each correct answer.

Answers

1. In June our family (past of drive) to San Francisco, California.
2. After a week we (past of sail) for Alaska.
3. Before sailing, our baggage (past perfect of place) in our cabins.
4. Our ship (past perfect of berth) at Pier 89.
5. At sailing time, the gangway (future of move).
6. The ship's whistle (past of sound) three short blasts.
7. Now the ropes to the pier (present perfect of remove).
8. The ship (past of begin) to move on its own.
9. My parents (present perfect of go) to the bow.
10. The passengers (future of view) the Golden Gate Bridge.

1. _____
2. _____
3. _____
4. _____
5. _____
6. _____
7. _____
8. _____
9. _____
10. _____

67-B Practice Procedure Follow the procedure given for 67-A.

1. We (past perfect of take) many photographs after boarding.
2. The photos (future perfect of develop) in 24 hours.
3. At the stern the sound of the engines (future perfect of grow) louder.
4. In the open sea, the ship (past of roll) somewhat.
5. We (past perfect of give) motion sickness kits in our cabin.
6. I (past of put) my kit in my pocket.
7. All passengers (future of hear) the captain on the loudspeakers.
8. The time for his announcement (present perfect of change).
9. We (past of sit) in the lounge to hear the captain's speech.
10. He (present of speak) in a well-modulated voice.

1. _____
2. _____
3. _____
4. _____
5. _____
6. _____
7. _____
8. _____
9. _____
10. _____

Your Total Score _____ /20

If your score was 15 or less for 67-A and 67-B, review Section 20, pages 105-108, before continuing.

67-C Practice Procedure On a separate sheet of paper, write a short paragraph about any interesting subject. In the paragraph, use and identify as many forms as possible of the tenses in the chart on page 106. The lists of verbs on pages 107-108 will also help.

Name

Date

Score

/20

125

/25

Score

Date

Name

68-A Practice Procedure Complete each of the following sentences by writing in the blank provided at the right the correct form of the verb in the parentheses. See pages 107-108 for the forms of the irregular verbs, if necessary. Score one point for each correct answer.

Answers

1. Americans (present perfect of enjoy) pleasure piers for many years.   1. _____

2. They (past of learn) about them from the British.   2. _____

3. The first pleasure pier in Atlantic City (past of build) by George Howard.   3. _____

4. Everyone (past perfect of hope) the pier would last forever.   4. _____

5. Unfortunately, it (past of destroy) in a huge storm.   5. _____

6. A more successful Atlantic City pier (past of open) in 1884.   6. _____

7. Over the years, thousands (present perfect of visit) the pier.   7. _____

8. Since 1884, many families (future perfect of visit) it.   8. _____

9. They (future of tell) their friends about their experiences.   9. _____

10. The friends (past of ask) about the foods that were available.   10. _____

68-B Practice Procedure Follow the procedure given for 68-A. Refer to Sections 17-19, if necessary.

1. Pleasure pier owners (past perfect of hope) to keep costs down.   1. _____

2. They (future of see) their profits disappear unless expenses are reduced.   2. _____

3. Despite large crowds, profits (present perfect of drop) steadily.   3. _____

4. The number of pier attractions (present perfect passive of increase).   4. _____

5. By now, thrill rides on the pier (future perfect of grow).   5. _____

6. Visitors (past of ride) the roller coaster often.   6. _____

7. To ride, they (future perfect active of wait) in long lines.   7. _____

8. Ballroom dancing (past of become) popular.   8. _____

9. Some pier owners (past perfect active of operate) large ice shows.   9. _____

10. Some of these skaters (present perfect passive of know) as the best in the world.   10. _____

11. Bright colored lights (past of draw) attention to pleasure piers.   11. _____

12. Today, theme parks (future perfect active of replace) pleasure piers.   12. _____

13. At some theme parks, hotels (present perfect passive of build).   13. _____

14. The cleanliness of theme parks (present perfect passive of maintain).   14. _____

15. Theme parks (present perfect active of include) both educational and thrill attractions.   15. _____

Your Total Score _____ /25

If your score was 19 or less for 68-A and 68-B, review Sections 17, 18, 19, and 20 before continuing.

Adjectives

OBJECTIVES
1. To recognize and use the different types of adjectives and adverbs.
2. To learn and use the three degrees of comparison for adjectives.

Adjectives are words used to modify nouns or pronouns. They are the picture words which make sentences more interesting. Adjectives tell color, number, or kind.

23-A DESCRIPTIVE ADJECTIVES

A *descriptive adjective* describes the noun or pronoun it modifies.

Example 1

The expensive dish was dropped by the careless child with the curly hair.

Analysis:

expensive—descriptive adjective—modifies noun *dish*

careless—descriptive adjective—modifies noun *child*

curly—descriptive adjective—modifies noun *hair*

Example 2

The attractive, talented singer with the red hair had a successful career.

Analysis:

attractive, talented—descriptive adjectives —modify noun *singer*

red—descriptive adjective—modifies noun *hair*

successful—descriptive adjective—modifies noun *career*

23-B PROPER ADJECTIVES

When an adjective is derived from a proper noun, it is a *proper adjective* and begins with a capital letter.

Example 1

The Turkish candy was sold in an Egyptian store.

Analysis:

Turkish—proper adjective—derived from proper noun *Turkey*—tells what kind of *candy*

Egyptian—proper adjective—derived from proper noun *Egypt*—tells what kind of *store*

Example 2

The Russian students drove along the Spanish coast in an American car.

Analysis:

Russian—proper adjective—derived from proper noun *Russia*—tells what kind of *students*

Spanish—proper adjective—derived from proper noun *Spain*—tells what kind of *coast*

American—proper adjective—derived from proper noun *America*—tells what kind of *car*

23-C DEFINITE AND INDEFINITE ADJECTIVES

Definite (the) and *indefinite* (a, an) *adjectives* are called *articles*. Definite means a certain person or thing, and indefinite means no one person or thing in particular. Use *a* before words that start with a consonant or with words that start with a long-sounding *u*. Use *an* before words that start with a vowel (*a, e, i, o,* and short-sounding *u*) or with words that sound as if they start with a vowel (*hour*).

A woman can do any job.
We have a cousin in Peoria.
Pete has an engineering degree.
We watched an interesting game.

Example 1

The musician played a beautiful song.

Analysis:

The—definite adjective

a—indefinite adjective—no particular song

Example 2

The boss was an energetic worker and a fair employer.

Analysis:

The—definite adjective
an—indefinite adjective—no particular worker
a—indefinite adjective—no particular employer

23-D POSSESSIVE ADJECTIVES

Possessive pronouns are used as adjectives when they precede and modify nouns. They are *my, his, her, its, our, their, whose,* and *your*.

Example 1

His sister was manager of their offices.

Analysis:

His—possessive adjective—modifies noun *sister*
their—possessive adjective—modifies noun *offices*

Example 2

My aunt and her friends went skiing in Aspen with our neighbors.

Analysis:

My—possessive adjective—modifies noun *aunt*
her—possessive adjective—modifies noun *friends*
our—possessive adjective—modifies noun *neighbors*

23-E DEMONSTRATIVE ADJECTIVES

This, that, these, and *those* are pronouns used as adjectives. They are called *demonstrative adjectives* because they not only modify nouns, but also specify or call attention to them. *This* and *that* are singular and describe singular nouns. *These* and *those* are plural and describe plural nouns. *This* usually refers to something near and *that* refers to something farther away.

Example 1

This dictionary was a gift from my parents.

Analysis:

This—demonstrative adjective—singular—modifies singular noun *dictionary*

Example 2

That dog barks most of the night.

Analysis:

That—demonstrative adjective—singular—modifies singular noun *dog*

Example 3

These doctors work at St. Vincent's Hospital.

Analysis:

These—demonstrative adjective—plural—modifies plural noun *doctors*

Example 4

Those nurses had excellent training.

Analysis:

Those—demonstrative adjective—plural—modifies plural noun *nurses*

Example 5

These books belong to the library.

Analysis:

These—demonstrative adjective—plural—modifies plural noun *books*

Complete Application Practices 69-70, pages 129-130, at this time.

Descriptive, Proper, and Possessive Adjective Identification

application practice **69**

69-A Practice Procedure In the following sentences some adjectives are underlined. Indicate why you think they are descriptive adjectives. Score one point for each correct response.

A <u>funny</u>, <u>enjoyable</u>, and <u>exciting</u> movie starred the <u>capable</u> actress.

1. _____
2. _____
3. _____
4. _____

The <u>scary</u>, <u>thrilling</u>, and <u>shocking</u> mystery occurred during a <u>snowy</u> night.

5. _____
6. _____
7. _____
8. _____

69-B Practice Procedure In the following sentences some adjectives are underlined. Indicate why you think they are proper or possessive adjectives. Score one point for each correct response.

<u>Her</u> uncle wrote about <u>his</u> experiences as a scientist.

1. _____
2. _____

<u>Our</u> friends have <u>their</u> home in Wisconsin.

3. _____
4. _____

My <u>Danish</u> neighbor showed <u>her</u> film about Denmark.

5. _____
6. _____

<u>Whose</u> ancestors lived on the <u>Finnish</u> coast near the <u>Swedish</u> border?

7. _____
8. _____
9. _____

Your Total Score _____ /17

If your score was 13 or less for 69-A and 69-B, review Sections 23-A, 23-B, and 23-D, pages 127-128, before continuing.

Name

Date

Score

/17

129

70-A Practice Procedure Complete each of the following sentences by writing in the blank provided at the right the correct adjective in the parentheses. Remember that *this* and *that* are singular and *these* and *those* are plural. Score one point for each correct response.

Answers

1. (This, These) fog is the worst of the year.   1. _____

2. (That, Those) headlights never helped our driving.   2. _____

3. (That, Those) weather forecaster over there is on Channel 9.   3. _____

4. (This, These) are the people that measure earthquakes.   4. _____

5. (This, These) type of forecaster knows the weather.   5. _____

6. (That, Those) charts of the nation's weather are helpful.   6. _____

7. (This, These) is the woman that they named "Stormy."   7. _____

8. (This, Those) weather forecasters worked for the U.S. Weather Bureau.   8. _____

9. (This, These) are the only weather charts available.   9. _____

10. Ted Castle bought (that, those) weather vanes for his father.   10. _____

11. Of all the deserts, (that, those) is the driest one.   11. _____

12. (This, These) person is called a climatologist.   12. _____

70-B Practice Procedure Complete each of the following sentences by writing *a* or *an* in the blank provided at the right. Score one point for each correct response.

1. It snowed for (a, an) hour during the night.   1. _____

2. (A, An) hurricane caused much damage to the city.   2. _____

3. (A, An) hilarious myth of weather forecasting involves the groundhog.   3. _____

4. (A, An) chirping cricket can act as a living thermometer.   4. _____

5. (A, An) obliging weather service employee answered questions.   5. _____

6. We averted (a, an) imminent disaster by preparation.   6. _____

7. Records indicate that (a, an) heavy rainfall is due.   7. _____

8. (A, An) handy gadget for the house is a thermometer.   8. _____

9. (A, An) hot day sent everybody to the beach.   9. _____

10. (A, An) colossal earthquake destroyed several towns.   10. _____

Your Total Score _____ /22

If your score was 17 or less for 70-A and 70-B, review Sections 23-C and 23-E, pages 127-128, before continuing.

section 24

Degrees of Comparison

The *positive, comparative,* and *superlative* are the three degrees of comparison for adjectives. The *positive degree* is used when the person or thing modified is not being compared with another. An adjective does not change its form in the positive degree. The *comparative degree* is used when comparing two persons or things. In most cases, add *er* to an adjective to form the comparative. The *superlative degree* is used when comparing three or more persons or things. Add *est* to an adjective to form the superlative. If the adjective ends in *e*, just add *r* for the comparative and *st* for the superlative.

Example 1

Tom is a <u>hard</u> worker.

Analysis:

hard—talking of only one worker—positive degree

Example 2

Susan is a <u>harder</u> worker than Tom.

Analysis:

harder—comparison between two people— comparative degree

Example 3

Jim is the <u>hardest</u> worker in our class.

Analysis:

hardest—comparison of more than two people—superlative degree

To form the comparative and superlative degrees of adjectives that end in *y*, change the *y* to *i* before adding *er* or *est*. With some one-syllable adjectives that end in a single consonant, the comparative and superlative degrees are formed by doubling the last consonant before adding *er* or *est*.

Example 1

Grant is <u>happier</u> than Sarah.

Analysis:

happier—comparison between two people —*Grant* and *Sarah*—comparative degree

Example 2

Kauai is the <u>wettest</u> place in the United States.

Analysis:

wettest—comparison of more than two places—superlative degree

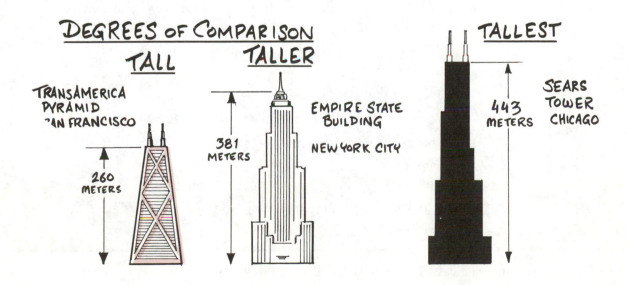

DEGREES OF COMPARISON

TALL — TRANSAMERICA PYRAMID ?AN FRANCISCO — 260 METERS

TALLER — EMPIRE STATE BUILDING NEW YORK CITY — 381 METERS

TALLEST — SEARS TOWER CHICAGO — 443 METERS

Most adjectives that end in *ful, less,* or *some* and all adjectives of more than two syllables form their degrees by adding *more* for the comparative degree (comparison between two things) and *most* for the superlative degree (comparison of more than two things).

Example 1

Della is a <u>more successful</u> lawyer than Roger.

Analysis:

<u>more successful</u>—comparison between two people—add *more* before the adjective—comparative degree

Example 2

Dean is the <u>most successful</u> lawyer in the town.

Analysis:

<u>most successful</u>—comparison of more than two persons—add *most* before the adjective—superlative degree

Exceptions: Some adjectives are different in all three forms. Study these adjectives so that you remember them. You probably already know most of them, as they are often used in speech and writing.

Positive	Comparative	Superlative
good	better	best
much	more	most
bad (ill)	worse	worst
little	less	least

I KNEW MUCH—MORE—MOST!

Example 1

Mr. Kelly is a <u>good</u> executive.

Analysis:

<u>good</u>—talking of only one person—positive degree

Example 2

Miss Dunn is the <u>better</u> executive of the two.

Analysis:

<u>better</u>—comparison betwen two people—comparative degree

Example 3

Mrs. Cook is the <u>best</u> executive in the firm.

Analysis:

<u>best</u>—comparison of more than two people—superlative degree

---

TRYOUT EXERCISE **Directions:** Complete each of the following sentences by writing in the blank provided at the right the correct form of the adjective in the parentheses. Check your answers on page 246 or with your teacher before continuing with your assignment.

1. Dodd had been the (skillfulest, most skillful) of the engineers.   1. _____

2. Tracy is the (better, best) student in her class.   2. _____

3. Which is (smarter, smartest)—a cat or a dog?   3. _____

4. That coach was the (worse, worst) of the previous four.   4. _____

5. Nell is the (happiest, most happy) of the five girls.   5. _____

6. The watchdog was (tamer, more tame) than the puppy.   6. _____

Complete Application Practices 71-72, pages 133-134, at this time.

Degrees of Comparison

application practice **71**

71 Practice Procedure Indicate the comparative degree and the superlative degree of each of the following adjectives. Remember that you usually add *er* to form the comparative (comparison between two things) and *est* to form the superlative (comparison of more than two things). Watch out for the exceptions. Score one point for each correct response.

Positive	Comparative	Superlative
Examples: clear	*clearer*	*clearest*
beautiful	*more beautiful*	*most beautiful*
1. neat		
2. late		
3. little		
4. tall		
5. handsome		
6. fast		
7. bold		
8. much		
9. fearful		
10. good		
11. careful		
12. funny		
13. strong		
14. bad		
15. successful		
16. ruthless		
17. slow		
18. weak		
19. helpful		
20. gracious		
21. tiresome		
22. young		
23. careless		
24. fresh		
25. wise		

Your Total Score _____ /50

If your score was 39 or less, review Section 24, pages 131-132, before continuing.

72 Practice Procedure Complete each of the following sentences by writing in the blank provided at the right the correct form of the adjective in the parentheses. Remember that the comparative degree is used to compare two things and the superlative degree is used to compare more than two things. Score one point for each correct response.

Answers

1. Mr. Sloan is the (most tactful, tactfulest) in the store.

   1. _____

2. Dorrs' Video is one of the (largest, most large) stores in the state.

   2. _____

3. Our employees are (more tactful, tactfuler) than those of our closest competitor.

   3. _____

4. Mr. Lindsey was the (worse, worst) manager of the last three.

   4. _____

5. Mrs. Austin invented the (cheapest, most cheap) machine in the industry.

   5. _____

6. These calculators are the (easiest, most easy) to learn.

   6. _____

7. It is the (safest, most safe) machine we sell.

   7. _____

8. The owner was (more, most) interested in safety than in profit.

   8. _____

9. The store is located (closer, more close) to the airport than to downtown.

   9. _____

10. Our old equipment was the (less, least) safe of the equipment in all the companies.

    10. _____

11. Ms. Marks's merchandising ideas were (sounder, more sound) than Mr. Little's.

    11. _____

12. His workers were the (happiest, most happy) in the industry.

    12. _____

13. Burt is the (worse, worst) salesperson in the company.

    13. _____

14. Miss Orr was the (thoughtfulest, most thoughtful) person in the office.

    14. _____

15. Her cousin is (pleasanter, more pleasant) than she.

    15. _____

16. She is also (more smart, smarter) than Miss Orr.

    16. _____

17. Her brother was the (loudest, most loud) one in the family.

    17. _____

18. Ray was fired because he was the (most forgetful, forgetfulest) worker in the department.

    18. _____

19. Kerry is the (accuratest, most accurate) person in the firm.

    19. _____

20. We are the (largest, most large) store in the country.

    20. _____

21. The closest competitor is (fearfulest, most fearful) of a buy-out.

    21. _____

22. The owner's son is a (handsome, handsomer) man.

    22. _____

23. He looks (taller, more tall) than his father.

    23. _____

24. Tim is the (better, best) salesperson of the five in the office.

    24. _____

25. The company's picnic was held on the (wettest, most wet) day of the month.

    25. _____

Your Total Score _____ /25

If your score was 19 or less, review Section 24, pages 131-132, before continuing.

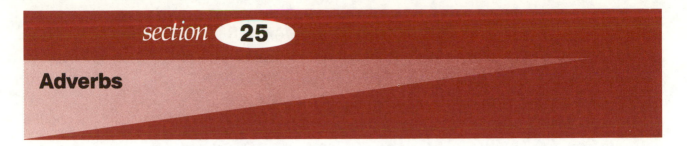

section 25

Adverbs

An *adverb* is a word used to modify a verb, an adjective, or another adverb. It makes these words clearer or more specific. Adverbs answer the questions "when," "where," "how," or "to what extent."

25-A ADVERBS OF TIME

Adverbs of time answer the question "when." *Now, then, soon, often, seldom,* and *finally* are adverbs of time.

Example 1

We <u>often</u> travel to Mexico City.

Analysis:

often—adverb of time—answers the question "when"—modifies the verb *travel*

Example 2

<u>Now</u> my sister <u>finally</u> saw the Aztec ruins.

Analysis:

<u>Now</u>—adverb of time—answers the question "when"—modifies the verb *saw*

<u>finally</u>—adverb of time—answers the question "when"—modifies the verb *saw*

25-B ADVERBS OF PLACE

Adverbs of place answer the question "where." The most common are *here* and *there.* Often *there* is used at the beginning of a sentence and is mistakenly identified as the subject.

When *down* and *up* are not followed by a noun, they are adverbs.

Example 1

The people <u>there</u> speak Spanish.

Analysis:

there—adverb of place—answers the question "where"—modifies the verb *speak*

Example 2

<u>Here</u> in our hotel the restaurant workers understand English.

Analysis:

<u>Here</u>—adverb of place—answers the question "where"—modifies the verb *understand*

Example 3

From the roof of the hotel we peeked <u>down</u>.

Analysis:

<u>down</u>—adverb of place—answers the question "where"—modifies the verb *peeked*

135

25-C ADVERBS OF MANNER

Adverbs of manner answer the question "how." These adverbs usually end in *ly. Lovely, friendly, ugly,* and *lonely* are adjectives, not adverbs.

Example 1

Mr. Rosales walked slowly and cautiously along the path.

Analysis:

slowly, cautiously—adverbs of manner—answer the question "how"—modify the verb *walked*

Example 2

My younger brother talked loudly during the walk.

Analysis:

loudly—adverb of manner—answers the question "how"—modifies the verb *talked*

25-D ADVERBS OF DEGREE

Adverbs of degree answer the question "to what extent." The most common are *too, really, quite,* and *very.* Such adverbs often modify adjectives.

Example

It was very fascinating and quite educational to use Mexican money.

Analysis:

very—adverb of degree—answers the question "to what extent"—modifies adjective *fascinating*

quite—adverb of degree—answers the question "to what extent"—modifies adjective *educational*

25-E INTERROGATIVE ADVERBS

How, when, why, and *where* are *interrogative adverbs.* They introduce questions.

Example 1

Where did you buy that pretty sombrero?

Analysis:

Where—interrogative adverb—introduces a question—modifies the verb *did buy*

Example 2

When will we change our money to pesos?

Analysis:

When—interrogative adverb—introduces a question—modifies the verb *will change*

25-F MOST FREQUENTLY USED ADVERBS

finally	indeed	nevertheless	often	sometimes	there	what
here	later	not	probably	soon	too	when
however	never	now	seldom	still	very	where

TRYOUT EXERCISE

Directions: Identify the adverbs in the following sentences by underlining them once. Check your answers on page 246 or with your teacher before continuing with your assignment.

1. Probably Mr. Delgardo will show his Aztec movie there.

2. Where did he give his recently successful show?

3. Finally Mrs. Delgardo sang a very delightful song.

4. She often sang but seldom played the piano.

Complete Application Practices 73-76, pages 137-140, at this time.

73 Practice Procedure Identify the adverbs in the following sentences by underlining them. Can you tell why they are adverbs? Insert a *P* over adverbs of *place*, an *M* over adverbs of *manner*, a *T* over adverbs of *time*, a *D* over adverbs of *degree*, and an *I* over *interrogative* adverbs. Score one point for each correct adverb and one point for each correct identification.

Your Score

1. The museum recently held a fine exhibit about precious stones.   1. _____

2. We were surely interested in the film about diamonds.   2. _____

3. How did they display the expensive gems?   3. _____

4. Tight security was everywhere with police on guard.   4. _____

5. They showed a fascinating film there.   5. _____

6. Why are you so interested in rare stones?   6. _____

7. I read a book about gems once.   7. _____

8. Surely everyone would like to own a rare diamond.   8. _____

9. Plainclothes detectives stood watch outside.   9. _____

10. People happily left the museum with pleasant dreams.   10. _____

11. We later went to a store and bought a book about gems.   11. _____

12. Where did you hear that famous story?   12. _____

13. It is written there in the brochure.   13. _____

14. The Koh-i-noor is still one of the largest gems.   14. _____

15. Here is a photo of that large stone of 189 carats.   15. _____

16. In 1850 that huge diamond was finally presented to Queen Victoria.   16. _____

17. It really is a spectacular and priceless stone.   17. _____

18. The famous Hope Diamond is frequently exhibited.   18. _____

19. It is closely guarded in the Smithsonian Institute.   19. _____

20. Emi always remembers the story of Kimberley Mines.   20. _____

21. When did you first hear about rubies and pearls?   21. _____

22. Jackie never heard about the lapis blue stones.   22. _____

23. Yesterday we saw several lapis gems.   23. _____

24. Diamonds are generally the valuable prized gems.   24. _____

25. At the factory the cutting of gems was upstairs.   25. _____

Your Total Score _____ /50

Name

Date

Score

/50

If your score was 39 or less, review Section 25, pages 135-136, before continuing.

74 Practice Procedure Identify the adjectives and adverbs in the following sentences. Underline the adjectives once and the adverbs twice. Score one point for each correct identification.

Your Score

1. Many minerals and stones are often used for jewelry.   1. _____

2. Where can I find a good book about priceless stones?   2. _____

3. Different gems are frequently recognized by the shape of the crystals.   3. _____

4. Gorgeous opals are found usually in areas with little rainfall.   4. _____

5. Jewels are generally found in all ornamental jewelry.   5. _____

6. There are many excellent books about unusual stones.   6. _____

7. A real diamond is always the hardest mineral.   7. _____

8. New buyers of gems are easily fooled by artificial jewels.   8. _____

9. How can you determine the value of rare stones?   9. _____

10. The real price of a fine diamond is indeed based on quality.   10. _____

11. Small diamonds are often used in wedding rings.   11. _____

12. Cecil Rhodes finally became the majority owner of Kimberley Mines.   12. _____

13. His company soon became known as Debeers.   13. _____

14. It still is a dominant company in the world.   14. _____

15. Tiffany is generally believed to be an excellent name for jewelry.   15. _____

16. A good diamond is indeed rare and expensive.   16. _____

17. Synthetic gems of good quality have been recently produced.   17. _____

18. Once gems could be produced, fine rubies and sapphires were made.   18. _____

19. Some jewelry occasionally has a reasonable price.   19. _____

20. Turquoise, surprisingly, means "Turkish stone."   20. _____

21. That stone is never found in the Eastern U.S.   21. _____

22. Emerald means "green stone," and emeralds are often transparent.   22. _____

23. Once the desired sapphires came mainly from Kashmir.   23. _____

24. The Cullinan is still the largest diamond found.   24. _____

25. It is now on a king's crown in the Tower of London.   25. _____

Your Total Score _____ /86

If your score was 68 or less, review Sections 23-25, pages 127-136, before continuing.

Adjective Drills

75-A Practice Procedure Complete each of the following sentences by writing in the blank provided at the right the correct adjective in the parentheses. Score one point for each correct answer.

Answers

1. How did you manage to get (this, these) job offers?

1. _____

2. The opportunity for advancement is the greatest in (this, these) type of employment.

2. _____

3. I would like (a, an) career with that company.

3. _____

4. Miss Hornsby is (a, an) pleasant boss to have.

4. _____

5. I went for (a, an) interview last Tuesday.

5. _____

6. (This, These) interviewers knew how to help you relax.

6. _____

7. That firm is the most successful in (this, these) type of business.

7. _____

8. (This, These) computers are used in offices.

8. _____

9. It's not (a, an) unusual dream to want to begin at the top.

9. _____

10. Angie was ready to report for work in (a, an) hour.

10. _____

75-B Practice Procedure Complete each of the following sentences by writing in the blank provided at the right the correct form of the adjective in the parentheses. Score one point for each correct answer.

1. Lindsey is the (better, best) informed student in class.

1. _____

2. Of all the teachers in school, Miss Rios is the (most graceful, gracefulest).

2. _____

3. Ms. Toll is the teacher who is (more, most) concerned about all endangered animals.

3. _____

4. Among the animals the cheetah is the (faster, more fast, fastest) of them all.

4. _____

5. Is the crocodile (prettier, more pretty) than the alligator?

5. _____

6. This animal helper was (worse, worst) than the previous one.

6. _____

7. (Littler, Less, Smaller) space is taken up by the wallaby.

7. _____

8. The zoo director was the (graciousest, most gracious) person we met.

8. _____

9. The new system of feeding the animals is the (better, best) system ever used.

9. _____

10. The old method was (slower, slowest, more slow) than the new system.

10. _____

Your Total Score _____ /20

If your score was 15 or less for 75-A and 75-B, review Section 23 before continuing.

76 Practice Procedure Identify the adjectives and adverbs in the following sentences. Underline the adjectives once and the adverbs twice. Score one point for each correct identification.

Your Score

1. When was tropical Hawaii admitted as the fiftieth state?

1. _____

2. Mr. and Mrs. O'Neal were once tourists and now work there in the college.

2. _____

3. Kind Leilani soon will return to the native area.

3. _____

4. The strongest earthquake ever in North America occurred in our forty-ninth state.

4. _____

5. Yes, I read about the volcano in the paper yesterday.

5. _____

6. Sometimes Leotie dreams of an exciting trip to Alaska.

6. _____

7. The winter months seldom are very warm in Nome.

7. _____

8. Ray Dodez is still a better traveler than Carey.

8. _____

9. Carey, however, is the more cheerful one.

9. _____

10. How did you decide to visit the historic landmarks in Mississippi?

10. _____

11. What were the special points of particular interest?

11. _____

12. Miss Jevons often returns to her old home and her former neighbors in Nebraska.

12. _____

13. The delta is probably the distinguishing feature in Louisiana.

13. _____

14. Where did you visit in the rich and colorful state?

14. _____

15. Skip finally learned that Delaware was the first state admitted to the nation.

15. _____

16. The two smallest states are, indeed, Rhode Island and Delaware.

16. _____

17. The opportunity for a new job and the wonderful climate soon made him move to Arizona.

17. _____

18. Laura gradually became accustomed to the warm weather.

18. _____

19. Sue luckily got a job as an accountant in a large firm.

19. _____

20. She is too smart to feel completely secure.

20. _____

21. Bill eventually took a position as a consultant in public relations.

21. _____

22. Did he learn about the interesting work there?

22. _____

23. Long, solid experience is, however, the best teacher.

23. _____

24. A clever and diligent employee is certainly necessary for success.

24. _____

25. Too many inexperienced employees surely don't insure profits.

25. _____

Your Total Score _____ /102

If your score was 81 or less, review Sections 23-25, pages 127-136, before continuing.

Prepositions

OBJECTIVES
1. To learn the purposes and uses of prepositions and conjunctions.
2. To understand the use of pronouns as objects of prepositions.
3. To learn the use of prepositional phrases.

Pick up your pencil. Hold it in your right hand. Now place your left hand *over* the pencil, *beneath* the pencil, *toward* the pencil, *on* the pencil, *below* the pencil. The italicized words show the relationship between your hand and the pencil. These words are called *prepositions*. A *preposition* is a word which shows a relationship between a noun or pronoun and some other part of the sentence.

Example 1

The neighbor <u>with</u> the beard drove the car.

Analysis:

<u>with</u>—preposition—shows relationship between *neighbor* and *beard*

Example 2

Mr. Timms called my father <u>from</u> the garage.

Analysis:

<u>from</u>—preposition—shows relationship between *father* and *garage*

Every preposition has a noun or pronoun as an object. If a pronoun follows a preposition, it must be in the objective case (*me, him, her, us, them*). Be careful of compound objects when the pronoun is the second object mentioned.

Example 1

My mother drove the car for <u>us</u>.

Analysis:

<u>us</u>—pronoun used as object of the preposition *for*—objective case

Example 2

My cousin went with <u>her</u> and <u>them</u>.

Analysis:

<u>her</u>, <u>them</u>—pronouns used as compound objects of the preposition *with*—objective case

Example 3

The tow truck came towards my mother and <u>me</u>.

Analysis:

<u>me</u>—pronoun used as the second object of the preposition *towards*—objective case

26-A USES OF THE PREPOSITIONAL PHRASE

A phrase is a group of related words that does not contain a subject and a verb in combination. A *prepositional phrase* consists of a preposition, a noun or pronoun that is the object of the preposition, and any modifiers that fall in between. If the prepositional phrase modifies a noun or pronoun, it is an *adjective phrase*. If it modifies a verb, an adjective, or an adverb, it is an *adverbial phrase*. (A more detailed explanation of phrases is given on pages 149-151.)

Example 1

The dog <u>with the loud bark</u> growled.

Analysis:

<u>with the loud bark</u>—adjective phrase as it modifies the noun *dog*

Example 2

A police officer drove <u>across the road</u>.

Analysis:

<u>across the road</u>—adverbial phrase as it modifies the verb *drove*

26-B MOST FREQUENTLY USED PREPOSITIONS

about	around	between	in	round	underneath
above	at	by	into	since	until
across	before	down	of	through	up
after	behind	during	off	till	upon
against	below	except	on	to	with
along	beneath	for	over	toward(s)	within
among	beside	from	past	under	without

TRYOUT EXERCISE

Directions: Identify the prepositions in the following sentences by circling them. Identify the prepositional phrases by underlining them.

Example: They hired a lawyer (with) a good reputation.

1. Mrs. Olson worked with the Legal Aid Foundation.

2. She once worked for the district attorney.

3. The clerk of the court called our name.

Directions: Complete each of the following sentences by writing in the blank provided at the right the correct pronoun in the parentheses. Check your answers on page 246 or with your teacher before continuing with your assignment.

1. Mrs. Olson spoke to the judge and (us, we).   1. _____

2. The bailiff sat between the judge and (I, me).   2. _____

3. The judge listened to my mother and (her, she).   3. _____

Complete Application Practices 77-78, pages 143-144, at this time.

Recognizing Prepositions and Prepositional Phrases

77-A Practice Procedure Identify the prepositions in the following sentences by circling them. Identify the prepositional phrases by underlining them. Score one point for each preposition identified and one point for each phrase correctly identified.

Your Score

Example: The President is elected (for) four years.

1. The President is the chief executive of the federal government.
2. George Washington, our first President, was born in Virginia.
3. During their presidencies four Presidents were assassinated.
4. Only two Presidents graduated from West Point.
5. William Harrison died thirty-one days after his election.
6. Which Presidents' faces are carved on Mount Rushmore?
7. The first elected President born in the twentieth century was John Kennedy.
8. The only President born in California was Richard Nixon.
9. Lincoln was killed at the Ford Theater while watching a show.
10. John Adams was President between Washington and Jefferson.
11. The high point during Nixon's presidency was the Apollo moon landing.
12. President Woodrow Wilson kept sheep at the White House.
13. Candidates with political backing often win the election.
14. Between the two men there was little difference.
15. Next election my sister will vote for the first time.

1. _____
2. _____
3. _____
4. _____
5. _____
6. _____
7. _____
8. _____
9. _____
10. _____
11. _____
12. _____
13. _____
14. _____
15. _____

77-B Practice Procedure Identify the prepositional phrases in each of the following sentences by underlining them. Identify each phrase as an adjective phrase or as an adverbial phrase by writing your answers in the blanks provided at the right. Score one point for each phrase correctly identified and one point for each correct answer as to the type of phrase.

Answers
adjective

Example: The plane with the funny mascot flew nonstop overseas.

1. A country of many attractions is New Zealand.
2. It lies between the equator and the South Pole.
3. Our group flew there from Los Angeles.
4. We went through the sheep country.
5. A native family with a wonderful cook prepared dinner.
6. Later we explored the dazzling grotto of glowworms.
7. The travel agent without pamphlets or film was very informative.
8. She sat between the driver and me.
9. A launch went across Lake Wakatipu.
10. We cruised Milford Sound and went near the falls.

1. _____
2. _____
3. _____
4. _____
5. _____
6. _____
7. _____
8. _____
9. _____
10. _____

Your Total Score _____ /50

If your score was 39 or less for 77-A and 77-B, review Section 26, pages 141-142, before continuing.

78 Practice Procedure Complete each of the following sentences by writing in the blank provided at the right the correct pronoun in the parentheses. Remember that the objective case is used after prepositions. Score one point for each correct answer.

Answers

1. Four people besides Donna and (I, me) got interviews.

1. _____

2. The personnel manager made the choice between Dave and (her, she).

2. _____

3. From the other applicants and (us, we), Miss Drew hired three people.

3. _____

4. The interviewer spoke Japanese to Hirota and (they, them).

4. _____

5. Kwan started work before Stacey and (I, me).

5. _____

6. From (who, whom) did you get your first paycheck?

6. _____

7. The boss was happy with the work of Pete and (her, she).

7. _____

8. Maria came to this country with her and (he, him).

8. _____

9. Joe's desk was near (she, her) and Vicki.

9. _____

10. Mr. Graf explained the firm's policy to Jane and (us, we).

10. _____

11. Miss McBride's desk was located behind Wanda, Brian, and (I, me).

11. _____

12. We took a walk with Eric and (her, she) after lunch.

12. _____

13. Art borrowed business books from Ms. Dorsey and (he, him).

13. _____

14. Later he returned them to Ms. Dorsey, but not to (I, me).

14. _____

15. The boss sent Jerry on a sales trip with Mary Soto and (us, we).

15. _____

16. Some of (us, we) trainees hoped to go on the trip.

16. _____

17. Cody received advice from his uncle and (them, they).

17. _____

18. The cafeteria served excellent food to the employees and (he, him).

18. _____

19. Several of (us, we) went to the corner cafe.

19. _____

20. Music was piped in for him and the rest of (us, we).

20. _____

21. Between Beth and (he, him) there was a storeroom.

21. _____

22. Sales techniques were explained to Ashley and (them, they).

22. _____

23. The owner walked toward Sal and (her, she).

23. _____

24. Linda was hired after Justin and (I, me).

24. _____

25. Tara Stevens discussed the evaluation reports with Ali and (her, she).

25. _____

Your Total Score _____ /25

If your score was 19 or less, review Section 26, pages 141-142, before continuing.

Conjunctions

Conjunctions join words, phrases (groups of related words), or clauses (parts of sentences that contain a subject and a verb). Conjunctions are classified as coordinating, subordinating, or correlative. (See pages 149-151 and 152-154 for further explanations of phrases and clauses.)

27-A COORDINATING CONJUNCTIONS

Coordinating conjunctions join sentence parts of equal rank. Clauses of a compound sentence are connected by coordinating conjunctions. (See pages 207-208 for the compound sentence.) Frequently used coordinating conjunctions are *and, but, or, nor, yet.*

Example 1

Canada <u>and</u> Mexico are neighbors of the United States.

Analysis:

and—coordinating conjunction—joins two words to form a compound subject *Canada* and *Mexico*

Example 2

Jason <u>or</u> Rita visited their aunt in Ottawa.

Analysis:

or—coordinating conjunction—joins two words to form a compound subject *Jason* and *Rita*

Example 3

Many people travel to Mexico City for profitable business <u>or</u> for a relaxing vacation.

Analysis:

or—coordinating conjunction—connects two phrases *for profitable business* and *for a relaxing vacation*

Example 4

A few tourists are rude, <u>but</u> most travelers are considerate.

Analysis:

but—coordinating conjunction—joins two clauses, *A few tourists are rude* with *most travelers are considerate*

27-B SUBORDINATING CONJUNCTIONS

Subordinating conjunctions connect subordinate (dependent) clauses to the main clause. (See pages 152-154 for an explanation of subordinate clauses.) The most frequently used subordinating conjunctions are:

after	for	till
although	if	unless
as	since	until
as if	so that	when
as though	than	where
because	that	wherever
before	though	while

Example 1

<u>When</u> Anne arrived late at the airport, her plane had already departed.

Analysis:

When—subordinating conjunction—connects the subordinate clause *Anne arrived late at the airport* to the main clause *her plane had already departed*

Example 2

You will get lost <u>unless</u> you follow directions.

Analysis:

unless—subordinating conjunction—connects the subordinate clause *you follow directions* to the main clause *You will get lost*

27-C CORRELATIVE CONJUNCTIONS

Correlative conjunctions are conjunctions used in pairs. The main ones are *either . . . or, both . . . and, neither . . . nor, not only . . . but (also), whether . . . or.*

Example 1

Either Sharon or Matt will drive to the theater.

Analysis:

Either, or—correlative conjunctions—connect words *Sharon* and *Matt*. Remember that *either, or* takes a singular verb when the subjects themselves are singular.

Example 2

They bought not only the expensive tickets but also the fancy dinner.

Analysis:

not only, but also—correlative conjunctions —connect words *the expensive tickets* and *the fancy dinner*

Example 3

Whether the show was good or the dinner was expensive didn't matter.

Analysis:

Whether, or—correlative conjunctions— connect clauses

TRYOUT EXERCISE

Directions: Identify the underlined words as coordinating, subordinating, or correlative conjunctions and tell whether they connect words, phrases, or clauses. Write your answers in the blanks provided at the right. Check your answers on page 246 or with your teacher before continuing with your assignment.

1. Neither Barry nor Marcie had ever seen a hockey game.

1. _____

_____

2. Though their uncle had season tickets, he had never invited them.

2. _____

_____

3. Ying or Sue had never heard of a hockey puck.

3. _____

_____

4. Wayne Gretzky and Bobby Hull were great hockey players.

4. _____

_____

5. A hockey puck not only is made of vulcanized rubber but also is one inch thick.

5. _____

_____

Complete Application Practices 79-80, pages 147-148, at this time.

79 Practice Procedure Identify the conjunctions as coordinating, subordinating, or correlative. Tell whether they connect words, phrases, or clauses. Score one point for each conjunction type identified and one point for each connection explained.

Your Score

Example: Neither Jefferson nor Madison was our second President.

Neither, nor — **correlative conjunctions—connect words**

1. President Reagan had once been a governor and a movie actor.

   and _____ 1. _____

2. When Lincoln was assassinated, Andrew Johnson became President.

   When _____ 2. _____

3. Either John Adams or John Quincy Adams was our second President.

   Either, or _____ 3. _____

4. Before you answer the next question, read it carefully.

   Before _____ 4. _____

5. The only President and Vice-President of the U.S. not elected to these offices was Gerald Ford.

   and _____ 5. _____

6. Unless you read about the U.S. Presidents, you will not know much about them.

   Unless _____ 6. _____

7. Not only John Kennedy but also William McKinley was assassinated in office.

   Not only, but also _____ 7. _____

8. If the President and Vice-President die in office, which person is next in line for the presidency?

   If _____ 8. _____

9. Twenty-two Presidents served in our armed forces, but Washington was the first one.

   but _____ 9. _____

10. Teddy Roosevelt was not only a famous Rough Rider but also a fearless President.

    not only, but also _____ 10. _____

11. Neil Armstrong landed on the moon in July 1969, when Richard Nixon was President.

    when _____ 11. _____

12. Both George Bush and Lyndon Johnson were elected Vice-President and later elected President.

    Both, and _____ 12. _____

Your Total Score _____ /24

If your score was 18 or less, review Section 27, pages 145-146, before continuing.

80 Practice Procedure Construct 20 sentences using each of the following conjunctions. Tell whether the conjunctions join words, phrases, or clauses. Score one point for each correct sentence and one point for each connection explained.

Example: <u>Since</u> I started working, I have rented my own apartment. (<u>Since</u>—joins clauses)

1. before	**6.** neither, nor	**11.** but	**16.** until
2. not only, but also	**7.** while	**12.** whether, or	**17.** either, or
3. if	**8.** or	**13.** after	**18.** although
4. and	**9.** unless	**14.** yet	**19.** nor
5. because	**10.** both, and	**15.** when	**20.** since

1. _____

2. _____

3. _____

4. _____

5. _____

6. _____

7. _____

8. _____

9. _____

10. _____

11. _____

12. _____

13. _____

14. _____

15. _____

16. _____

17. _____

18. _____

19. _____

20. _____

Your Total Score _____ /40

If your score was 31 or less, review Section 27, pages 145-146, before continuing.

OBJECTIVES

1. To recognize and use prepositional, infinitive, and participial phrases.
2. To recognize and use independent and dependent (subordinate) clauses.

A *phrase* is a group of related words used as a noun, an adjective, or an adverb. It does not contain a subject and a verb in combination. Most phrases consist of a preposition plus a noun or pronoun (and modifiers). (See page 142 for a list of prepositions.)

Three important types of phrases are:

1. Prepositional phrases
2. Infinitive phrases
3. Participial phrases

28-A PREPOSITIONAL PHRASES

Prepositional phrases are used as adjectives to modify nouns or pronouns (adjective phrases) or as adverbs to modify verbs, adjectives, or other adverbs (adverbial phrases). (See page 141 for a review of prepositional phrases.)

Example 1

He ran to the car.

Analysis:

to the car—prepositional (adverbial) phrase —It contains a preposition *to*, plus a noun *car*, and the modifier *the*. The phrase modifies the verb *ran*.

Example 2

Debbie usually studies for the test.

Analysis:

for the test—prepositional (adverbial) phrase—It contains a preposition *for*, plus a noun *test*, and the modifier *the*. The phrase modifies the verb *studies*.

Example 3

That book on the shelf is a classic.

Analysis:

on the shelf—prepositional (adjective) phrase—It contains a preposition *on*, plus a noun *shelf*, and the modifier *the*. The phrase modifies the noun *book*.

Example 4

They at the school should know my test scores.

Analysis:

at the school—prepositional (adjective) phrase—It contains a preposition *at*, plus a noun *school*, and the modifier *the*. The phrase modifies the pronoun *They*.

Example 5

The plant on the table in my kitchen is expensive.

Analysis:

on the table—prepositional (adjective) phrase—It contains a preposition *on*, plus a noun *table*, and the modifier *the*. The phrase modifies the noun *plant*.

in my kitchen—prepositional (adjective) phrase—It contains a preposition *in*, plus a noun *kitchen*, and the modifier *my*. The phrase modifies the noun *table*.

Example 6

The dog jumped over the fence and into the street.

Analysis:

over the fence—prepositional (adverbial) phrase—It contains a preposition *over*, plus a noun *fence*, and the modifier *the*. The phrase modifies the verb *jumped*.

into the street—prepositional (adverbial) phrase—It contains a preposition *into*, plus a noun *street*, and the modifier *the*. The phrase modifies the verb *jumped*.

Directions: Underline the prepositional phrases in the following sentences. In the answer column at the right indicate whether they are adjective (*adj*) or adverbial (*adv*) phrases. Check your answers on page 246 or with your teacher before continuing with your assignment.

1. The sofa in the living room is new.   1. _____

2. Joan returned to the office.   2. _____

3. That house by the river is huge.   3. _____

28-B INFINITIVE PHRASES

The second most often used phrase is the infinitive phrase. The *infinitive phrase* consists of the preposition *to* plus a verb form. Infinitive phrases may have an object or they may be described by an adverb. (*To write the letter* is my chore—infinitive phrase with object. I will try *to write legibly*—infinitive phrase with adverbial modifier.) Most infinitive phrases are used as nouns either as the subject or the object of the sentence, although the phrases may also be used as adverbs or adjectives.

Example 1

To make the team is Hilda's goal.

Analysis:

To make the team—infinitive phrase containing a preposition *To* plus a verb *make* and its object *team*—It is used as a noun (subject).

Example 2

To give a speech is my next assignment.

Analysis:

To give a speech—infinitive phrase containing a preposition *To* plus a verb *give* and its object *speech*—It is used as a noun (subject).

Example 3

The clerk hoped to promote quickly.

Analysis:

to promote quickly—infinite phrase containing a preposition *to* plus a verb *promote* and its modifier *quickly*—It is used as a noun and is the object of the verb *hoped*.

Example 4

Karen asked to lead the choir.

Analysis:

to lead the choir—infinitive phrase containing a preposition *to* plus a verb *lead* and its object *choir*—It is used as a noun and is the object of the verb *asked*.

The following infinitive phrases are used as adverbs. They modify verbs and answer the questions ''where,'' ''why,'' ''how,'' ''when,'' or ''to what extent.''

Example 1

Henry worked to earn money.

Analysis:

to earn money—infinitive phrase used as an adverb—modifies the verb *worked*

Example 2

Sue ran to catch the bus.

Analysis:

to catch the bus—infinitive phrase used as an adverb—modifies the verb *ran*

The following infinitive phrases are used as adjectives. They modify nouns.

Example 1

His desire to beat Jon was strong.

Analysis:

to beat Jon—infinitive phrase used as an adjective—modifies the noun *desire*

Example 2

Juan's plan <u>to save money</u> was commendable.

Analysis:

to save money—infinitive phrase used as adjective—modifies the noun *plan*

Example 3

Now, that is a steak <u>to enjoy</u>!

Analysis:

to enjoy—infinitive phrase used as an adjective—modifies the noun *steak*

TRYOUT EXERCISE

Directions: Underline the infinitive phrases in the following sentences. In the answer column at the right indicate whether the phrase is used as a noun (*n*), an adjective (*adj*), or an adverb (*adv*). Check your answers on page 246 or with your teacher before continuing with your assignment.

1. Helen went to the game with John.   1. _____

2. Alan's hope to win the scholarship was great.   2. _____

3. To write a composition is easy for Sue.   3. _____

28-C PARTICIPIAL PHRASES

A *participial phrase* begins with the present participle (verb form ending in *ing*—seeing, loving) or the past participle (verb form ending in *ed, t, en*—covered, kept, forgotten). (Irregular past participles may be found in the tables on pages 107-108.) The participle and the rest of the phrase act as an adjective. A participial phrase does not have a subject.

Example 1

<u>Hearing the starting gun</u>, the runners dashed ahead.

Analysis:

Hearing the starting gun—participial phrase formed by adding *ing* to the verb *hear* (present participle)—modifies the noun *runners*

Example 2

<u>Leaving the bus</u>, Dick slipped and fell.

Analysis:

Leaving the bus—participial phrase formed by adding *ing* to the verb *leave* (present participle)—modifies the noun *Dick*

Example 3

<u>Thrown from the horse</u>, Ron hit his head.

Analysis:

Thrown from the horse—participial phrase formed with the irregular past participle of the verb *throw*—modifies the noun *Ron*

Example 4

The class, <u>singing the school song</u>, gave a robust rendition.

Analysis:

singing the school song—participial phrase formed by adding *ing* to the verb *sing* (present participle)—modifies the noun *class*

TRYOUT EXERCISE

Directions: Underline the participial phrases in the following sentences. In the answer column at the right, indicate the noun the phrase modifies. Check your answers on page 246 or with your teacher before continuing with your assignment.

1. Fighting a cold, Pam went to work anyway.   1. _____

2. The house, given a new coat of paint, looked wonderful.   2. _____

3. The girl wearing the red dress is my sister.   3. _____

Complete Application Practices 81-82, pages 155-156, at this time.

Clauses

A *clause* is a part of a sentence that contains a complete subject and a complete predicate. The two types of clauses are listed at the right.

1. Independent clauses
2. Dependent (subordinate) clauses

29-A INDEPENDENT CLAUSES

An *independent clause* expresses a complete thought and has a subject and a verb. It is the main thought of the sentence and can stand alone correctly as a simple sentence without anything attached to it.

Example 1

Jim sang the song at the top of his lungs be-cause he liked it.

Analysis:

Jim sang the song at the top of his lungs— independent clause—It is the main idea of the sentence and can be used alone as a simple sentence.

Example 2

The game will be played tonight even if it rains.

Analysis:

The game will be played tonight—indepen-dent clause—It is the main idea of the sentence and can be used alone as a simple sentence.

Example 3

Although he studied hard for the test, he didn't get a good mark.

Analysis:

he didn't get a good mark—independent clause—It is the main idea of the sen-tence and can be used alone as a simple sentence.

29-B DEPENDENT CLAUSES

The *dependent* (or subordinate) *clause* depends upon the independent (main) clause for under-standing. A dependent clause when standing alone is not a complete sentence. Just as a person needs food in order to live and a plant needs water in order to grow, a dependent clause needs an independent clause to express a complete thought.

Dependent clauses used as adjectives (de-scribing nouns or pronouns) are introduced by relative pronouns (*who, whom, whose, that, which*). (Check page 55 for a review of relative pronouns.)

Example 1

The player who won the game for us was Mark.

Analysis:

who won the game for us—dependent clause introduced by the relative pronoun *who*—It modifies the noun *player* and is an adjective clause.

Example 2

The subject that I like best is English.

Analysis:

that I like best—dependent clause intro-duced by the relative pronoun *that*—It modifies the noun *subject* and is an ad-jective clause.

Example 3

The family <u>whose cat is lost</u> lives on the corner.

Analysis:

<u>whose cat is lost</u>—dependent clause introduced by the relative pronoun *whose*—It modifies the noun *family* and is an adjective clause.

Dependent clauses used as *adverbs* are introduced by subordinating conjunctions. They modify verbs, adjectives, or other adverbs by answering the questions "how," "where," "when," "why," "to what extent," or "under what conditions." (See page 145 for a list of subordinating conjunctions.)

Example 1

<u>Unless I hear otherwise</u>, we'll see you Sunday.

Analysis:

<u>Unless I hear otherwise</u>—dependent clause introduced by the subordinating conjunction *unless*—modifies the verb *see* and is an adverbial clause

Example 2

Bill laughed at the joke <u>until he cried</u>.

Analysis:

<u>until he cried</u>—dependent clause introduced by the subordinating conjunction *until*—modifies the verb *laughed* and is an adverbial clause

Example 3

Wilma earned my respect <u>because she was honest</u>.

Analysis:

<u>because she was honest</u>—dependent clause introduced by the subordinating conjunction *because*—modifies the verb *earned* and is an adverbial clause

Example 4

The ocean was noisier <u>than she had remembered</u>.

Analysis:

<u>than she had remembered</u>—dependent clause introduced by the subordinating conjunction *than*—modifies the adjective *noisier* and is an adverbial clause

Example 5

<u>When the curtain rose</u>, the audience quieted.

Analysis:

<u>When the curtain rose</u>—dependent clause introduced by the subordinating conjunction *When*—modifies the verb *quieted* and is an adverbial clause

Dependent clauses used as *nouns* (subjects, objects, appositives) or predicate nouns are *noun clauses*. Most noun clauses are used either as subjects or objects of sentences. Occasionally they are used as objects of prepositions. Look for the verb first and then determine how the clause is used.

Most noun clauses are introduced by *that, how, why, what, whatever, whoever, whether* and are followed by a group of words that are used as a single noun.

Example 1

<u>Why he came to the party</u> is a mystery to me.

Analysis:

<u>Why he came to the party</u>—dependent clause used as a noun—It is the subject of the verb *is*.

Example 2

<u>Whatever food remained</u> was eaten later.

Analysis:

<u>Whatever food remained</u>—dependent clause used as a noun—It is the subject of the verb *was eaten*.

Example 3

<u>Whoever answered the telephone</u> was a friend of theirs.

Analysis:

<u>Whoever answered the telephone</u>—dependent clause used as a noun—It is the subject of the verb *was*.

Example 4

The teacher explained <u>that voting was a privilege</u>.

Analysis:

<u>that voting was a privilege</u>—dependent clause used as a noun—It is the object of the verb *explained*.

Example 5

It might have been <u>that the telephone was out of order</u>.

Analysis:

<u>that the telephone was out of order</u>—dependent clause used as a noun—It is a predicate noun.

Example 6

I'll speak to <u>whoever is home</u>.

Analysis:

<u>whoever is home</u>—dependent clause used as object of the preposition *to*

Example 7

We'll eat at <u>whatever restaurant has seafood</u>.

Analysis:

<u>whatever restaurant has seafood</u>—dependent clause used as object of the preposition *at*

TRYOUT EXERCISE

Directions: Underline the independent clauses once and the dependent clauses twice in the following sentences. In the answer column at the right, tell whether the dependent clauses are adjective (*adj*) or adverbial (*adv*) clauses.

1. Because the bus was late, we missed the first act.   1. _____

2. The birds that flew overhead were sea gulls.   2. _____

Directions: Underline the noun clauses in the following sentences. In the answer column at the right, tell whether they are used as subjects, objects, objects of prepositions, or predicate nouns. Check your answers on page 246 or with your teacher before continuing with your assignment.

1. What the newscaster said was grim.   1. _____

2. I believe that they will go with us.   2. _____

3. His reason for arriving late was that his watch was broken.   3. _____

4. I will go to whatever school accepts me.   4. _____

Complete Application Practices 83-86, pages 157-160, at this time.

Prepositional and Participial Phrases

81-A Practice Procedure Underline the prepositional phrases in the following sentences. In the answer column at the right indicate whether they are adjective (*adj*) or adverbial (*adv*) phrases. All of these sentences are popular quotations from William Shakespeare's plays. Shakespeare, the most famous of all playwrights, lived in England during the reign of Queen Elizabeth I in the latter part of the sixteenth century. Score one point for each phrase correctly underlined and one point for each phrase correctly described.

Answers

1. The better part of valor is discretion.   1. _____
2. My pride fell with my fortune.   2. _____
3. A merry heart goes through the day.   3. _____
4. Fear of death is worse than death itself.   4. _____
5. I speak in a monstrous little voice.   5. _____
6. Brevity is the soul of wit.   6. _____
7. A rose by any other name would smell as sweet.   7. _____
8. The quality of mercy is not strained.   8. _____
9. Men of few words are the best men.   9. _____
10. Blessed are the peacemakers on earth.   10. _____

81-B Practice Procedure Underline the participial phrases in the following sentences. Score one point for each phrase correctly underlined.

Your Score

1. Studying her lines, the actress prepared for an audition.   1. _____
2. Seeing the play performed, John liked it.   2. _____
3. Kept for a second reading of his part, Bill was encouraged.   3. _____
4. Hearing the actors read their lines, the playwright beamed.   4. _____
5. Julia, meeting the playwright, was impressed by his manner.   5. _____
6. The director, pleased with her actors, ended the rehearsal.   6. _____
7. Hired for the part, Bill was overjoyed.   7. _____
8. Rehearsing for eight weeks, the cast was ready for opening night. 8. _____
9. Seeing long lines at the box office, the producer was delighted. 9. _____
10. Beginning at eight, the play ended at ten.   10. _____

Your Total Score _____ /30

If your score was 23 or less for 81-A and 81-B, review Sections 28-A and 28-C, pages 149 and 151, before continuing.

82-A Practice Procedure Underline the infinitive phrases in the following sentences. In the answer column state if the phrase is used as a noun (*n*), an adjective (*adj*), or an adverb (*adv*). Score one point for each phrase correctly underlined and one point for each phrase correctly described.

Answers

1. To visit China was our goal.   1. _____

2. To see the sights of China is a big undertaking.   2. _____

3. In Beijing we went to see the Great Wall.   3. _____

4. Our hope to walk along the Great Wall was achieved.   4. _____

5. To build the Wall took three hundred thousand workers.   5. _____

6. To finish the Wall took ten years.   6. _____

7. We also went to view the Ming Tombs.   7. _____

8. To view the beautiful jewelry at the Tombs was a treat.   8. _____

9. To experience the huge Imperial Palace was awesome.   9. _____

10. To walk through the entire Palace would take days.   10. _____

82-B Practice Procedure Follow the procedure given for 82-A.

1. Our guide, Bing Chu, wants to become an expert on Chinese art.   1. _____

2. He studies to prepare himself.   2. _____

3. To learn about Chinese art is an enjoyable task.   3. _____

4. Bing's plan to improve his knowledge is commendable.   4. _____

5. We learned to appreciate the art pieces in the Winter Palace.   5. _____

6. Our desire to visit the Summer Palace Park was achieved.   6. _____

7. To purchase gifts at the Friendship Store was everyone's goal.   7. _____

8. We stopped to see the Beijing Zoo also.   8. _____

9. To shop for antiques is a must in Beijing.   9. _____

10. For Chinese, to receive a gift is preferred over a tip.   10. _____

Your Total Score _____ /40

If your score was 31 or less for 82-A and 82-B, review Section 28-B, pages 150-151, before continuing.

82-C Practice Procedure Demonstrate your understanding of infinitive phrases by using them in a short paragraph. Select a topic of your own choosing and use a separate sheet of paper. Underline the phrases and be prepared to explain how each is used.

/40

Score

Date

Name

83-A Practice Procedure Underline the independent clauses once and the dependent clauses twice in the following sentences. In the answer column at the right, tell whether the dependent clauses are adjective (*adj*) or adverbial (*adv*) clauses. Score one point for each correctly underlined clause and one point for each correctly identified clause.

Answers

1. Taos, which is a famous artist's colony, is in New Mexico.   1. _____
2. Although jets don't land there, a half million people visit Taos each year.   2. _____
3. Taos pueblo, which was built over 500 years ago, is a center for the Taos
   Indians.   3. _____
4. The Rio Grande River, which passes near Taos, has cut a spectacular gorge.   4. _____
5. When there is no moon, the night sky is alive with stars.   5. _____
6. Since Taos was established, the town has remained an adobe village.   6. _____
7. After we entered the pueblo grounds, we were guided around by a member
   of the tribe.   7. _____
8. Although a fee is paid to use one's camera, it is improper to photograph
   Indians in the pueblo without permission.   8. _____
9. The pueblo buildings, which were built as forts, reflect a love of nature.   9. _____
10. The pueblo plaza, that serves as a ceremonial ground, is considered sacred.   10. _____

83-B Practice Procedure Follow the procedure given for 83-A.

1. A visitors' center, which provides information, sells Indian arts and crafts.   1. _____
2. A unique eighteenth-century church, that was built from volcanic rock, is a
   favorite of artists.   2. _____
3. Because old Indian and Spanish art is found in Taos, the town attracts artists
   of today.   3. _____
4. When we visited Taos, we saw and enjoyed all kinds of art.   4. _____
5. A first view of Taos, which includes vast mountains and plains, is unforget-
   table.   5. _____
6. Wherever you stay in Taos, you are reminded of its cultural background.   6. _____
7. Famous writers and artists, who were drawn to Taos, are part of the town's
   heritage.   7. _____
8. Kit Carson, who was a famous American frontiersman, once lived in Taos.   8. _____
9. The Rio Grande Gorge Bridge, which crosses the river 650 feet below, is one
   of America's highest bridges.   9. _____
10. Until they visit it, people are unaware of the peace and tranquility Taos affords. 10. _____

Your Total Score _____ /60

If your score was 47 or less, review Section 29, pages 152-154, before continuing.

Noun Clauses

/30

Score

Date

Name

84-A Practice Procedure Underline the noun clauses in the following sentences. In the answer column at the right, tell whether they are used as subjects, objects, objects of prepositions, or predicate nouns. Score one point for each clause correctly underlined and one point for each correct identification.

Answers

1. Whoever visits Colorado's Mesa Verde National Park is impressed by its cliff dwellings.

1. _____

2. That the Anasazi Indians first lived there in the sixth century A.D. has been verified.

2. _____

3. A park ranger told us that the Anasazi left Mesa Verde about 1300 A.D.

3. _____

4. It may have been that enemies chased the Anasazi away from their home.

4. _____

5. There must be good reasons for why they left their cliff dwellings.

5. _____

6. Whatever actually caused them to leave remains a mystery.

6. _____

7. Carefully recovered artifacts reveal why the Anasazi were such a remarkable people.

7. _____

8. We asked how the Anasazi were able to create such a civilization.

8. _____

9. Whoever wants to visit major cliff dwellings in Mesa Verde must be with a park ranger.

9. _____

10. Why the Anasazi created both round and square shaped buildings remains a mystery.

10. _____

84-B Practice Procedure In the spaces below, write sentences using any four of the following noun clauses as subjects, four as objects, and two as objects of prepositions. Identify each in the margin (*S* = subject; *O* = object; *OP* = object of preposition). Score one point for each correct sentence.

1. Whoever calls now
2. What they said
3. Whatever she says
4. How we swim

5. Why my family likes you
6. What we say at school
7. Whether it is true or not
8. Whether it is correct

9. What we have seen
10. What they want to do
11. That people talk about you
12. That I should come to this

1. _____

2. _____

3. _____

4. _____

5. _____

6. _____

7. _____

8. _____

9. _____

10. _____

Your Total Score _____ /30

If your score was 23 or less for 84-A and 84-B, review Section 29-B, pages 152-154, before continuing.

85-A Practice Procedure Match each item in Column A with the item it describes in Column B. Write the identifying letter from Column A in the blank provided at the right. Score one point for each correct answer.

Column A	Column B	Answers
a. noun clause used as a subject	**1.** We rode *over the bridge.*	**1.** _____
b. dependent clause	**2.** Hers is the book *on the left.*	**2.** _____
c. prepositional phrase used as an adjective	**3.** *That she is a great singer* is understood.	**3.** _____
d. infinitive phrase used as an object	**4.** in, from, to, under	**4.** _____
e. infinitive phrase used as a noun	**5.** The signal changed *while we waited.*	**5.** _____
f. prepositional phrase used as an adverb	**6.** *Singing in public* scares her.	**6.** _____
g. independent clause	**7.** Juan asked *to leave early.*	**7.** _____
h. infinitive phrase used as an adverb	**8.** Toby studied *to pass the test.*	**8.** _____
i. participial phrase	**9.** Lee's job is *to answer the phone.*	**9.** _____
j. prepositions	**10.** Sylvia missed the bus.	**10.** _____

85-B Practice Procedure Follow the procedure given for 85-A.

Column A	Column B	
a. prepositions	**1.** Today, everyone agrees *that she was a great dancer.*	**1.** _____
b. participial phrase		
c. noun clause used as an object	**2.** They *on the panel* were well prepared.	**2.** _____
d. prepositional phrase used as an adverb	**3.** *Whoever has tickets to the show* is fortunate.	**3.** _____
e. prepositional phrase used as an adjective	**4.** The book *that Julio wrote* was a best seller.	**4.** _____
f. independent clause	**5.** Because we had reservations, *we didn't wait for a table.*	**5.** _____
g. infinitive phrase used as a noun		
h. infinitive phrase used as an adverb	**6.** Tyrone borrowed a bike *from the school.*	**6.** _____
i. dependent clause	**7.** Hiro, *wanting to win*, ran harder.	**7.** _____
j. noun clause used as a subject	**8.** at, up, of, till	**8.** _____
	9. *To stay up later* was Natasha's hope.	**9.** _____
	10. She worked *to earn money.*	**10.** _____

Your Total Score _____ /20

If your score was 15 or less, review Sections 28-29, pages 149-151 and 152-154, before continuing.

86-A Practice Procedure Underline the phrases in the following sentences and in the answer column identify each as being prepositional, infinitive, or participial. Score one point for each phrase correctly underlined and one point for each phrase correctly identified.

Answers

1. At the office a business report helps management make decisions.

1. _____

2. A business report must be based upon the truth.

2. _____

3. Asked by her manager, Lori prepared a written report.

3. _____

4. To type the report, Lori's secretary stayed late.

4. _____

5. Preparing the business report, Lori dealt only with facts.

5. _____

6. In a report, conclusions must be organized.

6. _____

7. The manager wanted to see the completed report.

7. _____

8. Seeing the report, the manager said he disliked its form.

8. _____

9. The intended reader of a business report is a busy person.

9. _____

10. Lori's desire to prepare a good report impressed her manager.

10. _____

86-B Practice Procedure Underline the independent clauses once and the dependent clauses twice in the following sentences. Score one point for each clause correctly identified.

Your Score

1. Business reports that are short are called information reports.

1. _____

2. Although informal reports are short, they may be several pages in length.

2. _____

3. Memorandum reports, which are for in-house use, are very informal.

3. _____

4. When reports call for recommendations, they are prepared in a more detailed document.

4. _____

5. While reports may differ in style, they do not differ in terms of quality.

5. _____

6. Because they are often sent to people outside the company, formal reports are usually printed.

6. _____

7. Before a report is submitted, it must be carefully read and edited.

7. _____

8. When a business report is requested, the writer must prepare it properly.

8. _____

9. The writer who is selected to prepare a business report must be familiar with the report's topic.

9. _____

10. Because he was familiar with stock accounting, Joe was chosen to prepare the report.

10. _____

Your Total Score _____ /40

If your score was 31 or less for 86-A and 86-B, review Sections 28-29, pages 149-151 and 152-154, before continuing.

Punctuation

1. To recognize and use punctuation marks.
2. To know when to use capital letters.

Punctuation in writing indicates pauses, gestures, and desired changes of expression. Punctuation keeps words from running together so the meaning is clear.

Notice how ridiculous this information sounds without punctuation, capitalization, or paragraph division:

Most people have difficulty with the usage of two too and to and and but both conjunctions are usually easy to use correctly but even those who should know sometimes confuse two too and to two which follows one and comes before three is of course a number too often confused with to usually is an adverb modifying an adjective such as too large too sometimes means also in addition to likewise besides etc in which case it is still an adverb to like in of and at is a preposition although to is also used with the verb form to form an infinitive such as to run everywhere you go you will find those who do not understand the usage of two too and to never never permit youself to confuse the three

Did you understand it? Your own writing can be just as confusing if you do not punctuate correctly:

Most people have difficulty with the usage of "two," "too," and "to." "And" and "but," both conjunctions, are usually easy to use correctly; but even those who should know sometimes confuse "two," "too," and "to."

"Two," which follows "one" and comes before "three," is, of course, a number. "Too," often confused with "to," usually is an adverb modifying an adjective, such as "too large." "Too" sometimes means "also," "in addition to," "likewise," "besides," etc., in which case it is still an adverb. "To," like "in," "of," and "at," is a preposition, although "to" is also used with the verb form to form an infinitive, such as "to run."

Everywhere you go you will find those who do not understand the usage of "two," "too," and "to." Never, never permit youself to confuse the three.

CLEAN UP YOUR SPEECH!

30-A THE PERIOD .

Periods as End Punctuation

The *period* in punctuation serves the same purpose as the stop sign on a highway. It brings you to a halt. *The period marks the end of a declarative sentence* (a statement of fact) *or an imperative sentence* (a command). Every sentence that is a statement should end with a period.

Examples

Sea lions like to laze on the rocks. (declarative sentence)

Beachgoers love to watch the sea lions. (declarative sentence)

Hedy, drop the subject. (imperative sentence)

Open the door as soon as she knocks. (imperative sentence)

Periods Within a Sentence

Use a period after an initial and after most abbreviations. Remember, however, that the use of periods and capitalization in some abbreviations can vary. Several styles may be acceptable, as in *a.m.*, *A.M.*, *am*, and *AM*. Whichever style you select, try to be consistent in your usage.

Examples

Nov. (November)

CA (California)

a.m. (ante meridiem or before noon)

p.m. (post meridiem or after noon)

MOST ABBREVIATIONS REQUIRE PERIODS.

Example

<u>Mr.</u> <u>G.</u> <u>A.</u> Sterns and <u>Ms.</u> <u>M.</u> <u>M.</u> Mullins will enter <u>U.C.L.A.</u> this fall.

Analysis:

<u>Mr.</u>—abbreviation for Mister

<u>G. A.</u>—first and middle initials

<u>Ms.</u>—used instead of Miss or Mrs. when a woman's marital status is unknown

<u>M. M.</u>—first and middle initials

<u>U.C.L.A.</u>—abbreviation for University of California, Los Angeles

---

Chart of Common Abbreviations

Abbreviation	Meaning
ad	advertisement
a.m.	ante meridiem (before noon)
amt.	amount
anon.	anonymous
ans.	answer
atty.	attorney
Ave.	Avenue
B.A.	Bachelor of Arts
Blvd.	Boulevard
Capt.	Captain
cm	centimeter
COD	cash on delivery
dept.	department
doz	dozen
Dr.	Doctor
e.g.	for example
etc.	et cetera (and so forth)
ft	foot
g	gram
in	inch
int.	interest
IQ	Intelligence Quotient
Jr.	Junior
kg	kilogram
l	liter
lit.	literal, literally
Lt.	Lieutenant
m	meter
M.D.	Doctor of Medicine
memo	memorandum
mg	milligram
mm	millimeter
Mr.	Mister
Mrs.	Mistress
Ms.	Miss or Mistress
no.	number
oz	ounce
pd.	paid
p.m.	post meridiem (after noon)
qt	quart
recd.	received
Rev.	Reverend
sec., secy.	secretary
Sr.	Senior
St.	Saint
St.	Street
USA	United States of America
viz.	namely
vol.	volume

30-B THE QUESTION MARK   ?

A question mark is also used as a full stop in punctuation. *A question mark is used after an interrogative sentence.* These sentences ask direct questions.

Examples

How old are you?
Do you know Ned Farmer?
What time is it?

30-C THE EXCLAMATION POINT   !

An exclamation point is used after words, phrases, or sentences to express sudden emotion or feeling (joy, fear, pain, happiness, anger) *and forceful commands.* Use exclamation points sparingly in your writing because they are like a voice raised in a burst of feeling. Reserve them to express truly strong feeling.

Examples

Look out!
I got an A!
Help!
Ouch, that hurts!
Don't leave!

TRYOUT EXERCISE

Directions: Fill in the necessary period (.), question mark (?), and exclamation point (!) in the following sentences.

1. Don't shove me (   )
2. Are you the new teacher (   )
3. Let's take a walk on the beach (   )

Directions: In the first column, write the proper abbreviation for each word given. In the second column, write the proper word for each abbreviation given. Check your answers on page 246 or with your teacher before continuing with your assignment.

1. memorandum _____
2. Street _____
3. Avenue _____

1. qt _____
2. no. _____
3. vol. _____

Complete Application Practices 87-88, pages 167-168, at this time.

30-D THE COMMA   ,

Commas are used as signposts in writing. The comma is similiar to a traffic warning sign on the highway. When you want to make a turn while you are driving a car, you signal and then turn. In writing, if you want to change your thoughts, insert some other ideas, or identify parts, you use the comma. Often, the sound of the spoken sentence with a pause and change of voice pitch will serve as a guide in the placement of commas in writing.

Commas clarify the meaning of your sentences. They show you where one word or group of words ends and the next word or group of words begins.

163

PAM, GARY, DEBBIE, TOM, KARA, AND GRANT WENT DANCING.

COMMAS SEPARATE WORDS IN A SERIES.

Series

A comma separates words and numbers in a series. Notice how these sentences read without the comma, and then see how they sound with a comma.

Example 1

Wrong: Tom Lee and I are here.
Right: Tom, Lee, and I are here.

Example 2

Wrong: The room was small narrow and dark.
Right: The room was small, narrow, and dark.

Example 3

Wrong: Emmy bought a skirt blouse and sweater at the sale.
Right: Emmy bought a skirt, blouse, and sweater at the sale.

Example 4

Wrong: A bell rings at 2:00 a.m. 11:00 a.m. and 6:00 p.m. daily.
Right: A bell rings at 2:00 a.m., 11:00 a.m., and 6:00 p.m. daily.

Example 5

Wrong: The price of our room includes breakfast lunch and dinner.
Right: The price of our room includes breakfast, lunch, and dinner.

Note: It is also correct to omit the comma after a word in a series when it is followed by *and*. If you use this form, be consistent in its use.

Appositives

A comma may be used to set off an appositive. An *appositive* is a word or a group of words that functions as a noun. An appositive explains more about the noun or pronoun that it follows.

Example 1

Sarah, <u>my aunt</u>, is a chemist.

Analysis:

<u>my aunt</u>—appositive—explains who Sarah is

Example 2

Mr. Garcia, <u>our Spanish teacher</u>, is retiring.

Analysis:

<u>our Spanish teacher</u>—appositive—explains who Mr. Garcia is

If the comma is not used in setting off the appositive, the meaning can be changed. Notice how commas change the meaning of these sentences.

Example 1

Koji, our visitor from Japan is here.

Analysis:

You are addressing Koji and describing your visitor from Japan.

Example 2

Koji, our visitor from Japan, is here.

Analysis:

You are describing Koji who actually is your visitor from Japan.

Dependent Clauses

A comma is used after a dependent clause at the beginning of a sentence. The comma sets off the independent (main) clause. The slight pause indicated by the comma prevents reading words together. If the comma is omitted or misplaced, the meaning of the sentence is changed.

Examples

Wrong: When the sun set the sky turned a bright red.

Right: When the sun set, the sky turned a bright red.

Wrong: After the crowd left the python went to sleep.

Right: After the crowd left, the python went to sleep.

Quotations

A quotation (direct speech) *is set off by commas from the rest of the sentence.* (See pages 178-179 for more information on punctuation with quotation marks.)

Examples

Jack shouted, "Look out for that green car!"

Lily asked, "What airline flies directly to Tampa, Florida?"

"The book is due in two weeks," noted the librarian.

Dates and Addresses

The comma is used to set off the second and all following items in complete dates and in addresses.

Examples

His last trip to Mexico was on May 29, 1990.

Send your check for $20 to 1760 Milpas Street, Goleta, California.

His play opened on April 23, 1991, and closed on April 27, 1991.

No comma is needed with incomplete dates.

Examples

In May 1990 my parents bought their first store.

In 1992 she had planned to visit Hawaii for her birthday.

Parenthetical Expressions

Use the comma to set off most parenthetical expressions (unrelated words in a sentence). These expressions interrupt the thought of the sentence. In speaking, you would pause before and after using the expression.

Examples

Larry, you know, is a senior now.

The play, to be honest with you, is a flop.

Jojo, I bet, will win the contest.

Note: When commas are used to set off words or phrases, two of them are needed unless the phrase is at the beginning or the end of the sentence.

Transitional Expressions

Such words as of course, indeed, for instance, moreover, and no doubt are set off by commas from the rest of the sentence.

Examples

Mrs. Hazlewood, of course, is proud of her grandchild.

The test, indeed, was difficult.

Your red sweater, for instance, is warm enough for tonight.

AFTER A DEPENDENT CLAUSE STANDING FIRST IN A SENTENCE, USE A COMMA.

Introductory Words

Introductory words are separated from the rest of the sentence by a comma. A comma is also placed after addressing a person by name. If the person's name is used in the middle of the sentence, two commas are used to set it off.

Examples

Yes, I'll be home on time.

Mr. Silva, repeat your question.

Please, Fred, be on time for the bus.

Okay, I'll clean out the garage tomorrow.

Coordinating Conjunctions

A comma is used before a coordinating conjunction (and, but, or, nor, yet) *in a compound sentence.*

Examples

Pat wants to go to France, but I want to go to Ireland.

The farmers' market opened at 9:00 a.m., and we were sold out of our lettuce by noon.

Teri got good marks on her tests, for she was an attentive student.

She went to work, or she cared for her brother at home.

Note: The comma may be omitted before coordinating conjunctions if the two clauses are short or have the same subjects. For instance: The telephone rang and she got up to answer it. He failed the test and he didn't care.

Common Comma Usage

1. To separate words and numbers in a series.

2. To set off an appositive.

3. After a dependent clause at the beginning of a sentence.

4. To set off quotations.

5. With addresses and complete dates.

6. To set off parenthetical expressions (unrelated words).

7. To set off such words as *of course, indeed, for instance, moreover, no doubt.*

8. After introductory words that are separated from the rest of the sentence.

9. Before a coordinating conjunction in a compound sentence.

TRYOUT EXERCISE **Directions:** Insert the necessary commas in the following sentences. Check your answers on page 246 or with your teacher before continuing with your assignment.

1. Myron my uncle is from Ohio.

2. I bought apples oranges and grapes.

3. Yes I can see you tonight.

4. Bart was born on March 8 1980 in Texas.

5. Her father said "You must be home by midnight."

Complete Application Practices 89-96, pages 169-176, at this time.

87-A Practice Procedure Fill in the necessary periods, question marks, and exclamation points in the following sentences. Remember that a period is placed at the end of a sentence that states a fact or gives a command and after some abbreviations and initials. A question mark is placed after a sentence that asks a direct question. An exclamation point is placed after words or sentences that express sudden feeling or emphasis. Score one point for each correct response.

Your Score

1. Our nation believes in the rule of law 1. _____

2. What is the rule of law 2. _____

3. Why must a nation have laws 3. _____

4. A nation's values are reflected by its laws 4. _____

5. Why do laws change 5. _____

6. A change in values can change laws 6. _____

7. Everyone should obey the law 7. _____

8. If you don't like a law, work with the lawmakers to change it 8. _____

9. Let's repeal that law, or else 9. _____

10. Why do we sometimes have unfair laws 10. _____

87-B Practice Procedure Follow the procedure given for 87-A

1. How are our laws made 1. _____

2. Common law had its origins in England 2. _____

3. Is the common law system still practiced in England 3. _____

4. To understand it you must study the law 4. _____

5. Is common sense really common 5. _____

6. The first great legal system was in Rome 6. _____

7. Roman law was in the form of a code 7. _____

8. Who developed the French Civil Code 8. _____

9. Every civilized state has a code of law 9. _____

10. Civil law is different from military law 10. _____

Your Total Score _____ /20

If your score was 15 or less for 87-A and 87-B, review Sections 30-A, 30-B, and 30-C, pages 161-163, before continuing.

87-C Practice Procedure Using a topic of your own choosing, write a short paragraph demonstrating your ability to properly use the period, the question mark, and the exclamation point as end punctuation. Use a separate sheet of paper.

Abbreviation Practice

application practice **88**

88 Practice Procedure In the first answer column, write the proper abbreviation for each word given. In the second answer column, write the proper word or words for each abbreviation given. If necessary, use your dictionary. Score one point for each correct answer.

Answers   Answers

1. Tuesday	_____	26. memo	_____
2. yard	_____	27. Lt.	_____
3. Friday	_____	28. Capt.	_____
4. postscript	_____	29. Mr.	_____
5. Avenue	_____	30. ft	_____
6. Minnesota	_____	31. p.m.	_____
7. cash on delivery	_____	32. Rev.	_____
8. Doctor of Medicine	_____	33. asst.	_____
9. please reply	_____	34. Wash. (WA)	_____
10. ante meridiem (before noon)	_____	35. amt.	_____
11. millimeter	_____	36. m	_____
12. et cetera (and so forth)	_____	37. anon.	_____
13. Colonel	_____	38. doz	_____
14. Miss or Mistress	_____	39. ans.	_____
15. Private	_____	40. Fla. (FL)	_____
16. volume	_____	41. oz	_____
17. received	_____	42. l	_____
18. department	_____	43. St.	_____
19. Arizona	_____	44. Sun.	_____
20. inch	_____	45. Blvd.	_____
21. West Virginia	_____	46. qt	_____
22. New York	_____	47. Wed.	_____
23. Young Men's Christian Association	_____	48. Apr.	_____
24. advertisement	_____	49. Calif. (CA)	_____
25. paid	_____	50. B.A.	_____

Your Total Score _____ /50

If your score was 39 or less, review Section 30-A, page 162, before continuing.

Comma Usage—Series and Appositives

89-A Practice Procedure Fill in the necessary commas in the following sentences. Score one point for each comma correctly placed.

Your Score

1. John my assistant is a fine dependable and loyal employee.

   1. _____

2. He types keeps the books and manages the office.

   2. _____

3. Letita John's helper takes care of the counter does the filing and answers the phone.

   3. _____

4. Kelly a student helper works on Mondays Wednesdays and Fridays.

   4. _____

5. Our offices which are on Ash Street are near a travel agency a dentist's office a pharmacy and a cafe.

   5. _____

6. Our building on a corner is large old and ugly.

   6. _____

7. It is painted blue white and yellow.

   7. _____

8. John Letita and Kelly work well together.

   8. _____

9. Mr. Jorgensen our oldest customer is tall brown-eyed and gray-headed.

   9. _____

10. Mrs. Everett a company adviser has worked as a teacher a bank teller a writer and a secretary.

    10. _____

89-B Practice Procedure Follow the procedure given for 89-A.

1. Kathy Mrs. Everett's daughter works with her mother.

   1. _____

2. Helen Kathy's friend is a part-time employee.

   2. _____

3. Mrs. Everett Kathy and Helen are good workers.

   3. _____

4. They meet with us each Monday Wednesday and Friday.

   4. _____

5. John my assistant Mrs. Everett Kathy and Helen are a great team.

   5. _____

6. True View our company name was selected by our advisers.

   6. _____

7. The company sells childrens' magazines books and computer software.

   7. _____

8. Thomas Wilson and Yeager our advertising firm will develop a new sales message for us.

   8. _____

9. We sell our materials to independent schools public schools and teacher training institutions.

   9. _____

10. M. M. Mullins our company president is pleased with our efforts.

    10. _____

Your Total Score _____ /60

If your score was 47 or less for 89-A and 89-B, review Section 30-D, pages 163-164, before continuing.

89-C Practice Procedure Write a short paragraph on a separate sheet of paper to demonstrate your understanding of the use of the comma in a series and with appositives.

Comma Usage—Dependent Clauses and Quotations

90-A Practice Procedure In the following sentences, insert a comma in its proper place after dependent clauses at the beginning of sentences and with quotations. Score one point for each comma correctly placed.

Your Score

1. When we decided to join the tour we didn't know anyone else who was going.

1. _____

2. "I want to go on a tour with people I know " Phyllis said.

2. _____

3. "Although we don't know anyone else now we certainly will by the end of the trip " interjected Lisa.

3. _____

4. "Before we go I'll need some new clothes " Mary commented.

4. _____

5. "New England in October could be a little cool " noted Eira.

5. _____

6. Because this trip was in the fall the tour brochure suggested taking warm clothing.

6. _____

7. Since we were leaving in less than two weeks we had to get everything ready in a hurry.

7. _____

8. "I can't believe we're really going to see the trees in their fall colors " commented Phyllis.

8. _____

9. Because we chose the first week in October for our tour the trees would be in full color.

9. _____

10. "Pinch me so I'll know that we're really going " said Lisa.

10. _____

90-B Practice Procedure Follow the procedure given for 90-A.

1. Because we started our land tour in Boston we had to fly there from our home in Texas.

1. _____

2. Before our plane took off friends came to the airport and hollered "Bon Voyage!"

2. _____

3. One friend commented "I sure wish I could go."

3. _____

4. When our flight's departure was announced we all got very excited.

4. _____

5. "Flight 95 for Cincinnati and Boston leaves in ten minutes " announced the attendant.

5. _____

6. As we took our seats a flight attendant passed by and said "Welcome!"

6. _____

7. "Fasten your seat belts " announced a flight attendant over the plane's loudspeaker.

7. _____

8. When the plane started down the runway Mary squealed with joy!

8. _____

9. As we looked down on Dallas at night the view was truly a sight to behold.

9. _____

10. "We're finally on our way " Lisa observed.

10. _____

Your Total Score _____ /24

If your score was 18 or less, review Section 30-D, page 165, before continuing.

Comma Usage—Addresses, Dates, and Unrelated Expressions

91-A Practice Procedure In the following sentences, insert commas when needed around addresses, complete dates, and unrelated expressions. Score one point for each comma correctly placed.

Your Score

1. On August 5 1775 you know Europeans discovered San Francisco Bay.

   1. _____

2. It was Sir Francis Drake of course who landed near the Bay on June 17 1579.

   2. _____

3. Indians of course had lived in the area long before the Spanish arrived.

   3. _____

4. Father Serra we know established a number of missions in California.

   4. _____

5. In San Francisco for example he built Mission Dolores.

   5. _____

6. Mission Dolores you see was one of the last to be built.

   6. _____

7. In 1835 San Francisco indeed became the name of the city.

   7. _____

8. It wasn't until July 9 1896 of course that the U.S. flag flew over the city.

   8. _____

9. No doubt the discovery of California gold caused the city's population to grow.

   9. _____

10. San Francisco indeed became a bustling city.

   10. _____

91-B Practice Procedure Follow the procedure given for 91-A.

1. On April 18 1906 a strong earthquake hit the city.

   1. _____

2. The earthquake and fire moreover nearly destroyed San Francisco.

   2. _____

3. The fire it is said may have been more destructive than the earthquake.

   3. _____

4. San Francisco nevertheless recovered to become a major U.S. city.

   4. _____

5. The city indeed is home to people of many ethnic backgrounds.

   5. _____

6. The people of San Francisco you know are proud of their city's past.

   6. _____

7. The city moreover was the site of the signing of the United Nations Charter.

   7. _____

8. The U.N. Charter indeed was signed there on June 26 1945.

   8. _____

9. Views of the Bay from the city's many hills of course are often spectacular.

   9. _____

10. Indeed Twin Peaks is a favorite tourist attraction.

   10. _____

Your Total Score _____ /42

If your score was 33 or less for 91-A and 91-B, review Section 30-D, page 165, before continuing.

Stop and Go Practice

92-A Practice Procedure Fill in the necessary commas, periods, question marks, and exclamation points in the following sentences. This is a special practice for the use of commas before coordinating conjunctions in compound sentences and for introductory words. Score one point for each punctuation mark correctly placed.

Your Score

1. Hooray They have admitted me to music school

   1. _____

2. Yes my acceptance letter arrived today and it was none too soon

   2. _____

3. Mr G B Blue the director of the school signed the letter

   3. _____

4. Really I was surprised

   4. _____

5. Were you accepted

   5. _____

6. I learned that Pete Becky and Jodi were going to music school with me

   6. _____

7. My friend Ramona already is enrolled

   7. _____

8. When does the semester begin

   8. _____

9. Gee We have to be in New York City by next week

   9. _____

10. Can we get there on time

   10. _____

92-B Practice Procedure Follow the procedure given for 92-A.

1. Our train was to arrive in New York City at noon and by 1:00 p m we needed to be at the school

   1. _____

2. Honestly that was a tight schedule

   2. _____

3. We made it though

   3. _____

4. Ms Schmidt the harmony teacher greeted us

   4. _____

5. She invited me to enroll in her class

   5. _____

6. Pete my friend decided to take music theory

   6. _____

7. Is enrollment in lyric writing still open

   7. _____

8. Becky Jodi and I want to take lyric writing you see

   8. _____

9. That class no doubt is already closed

   9. _____

10. We will be placed on a waiting list I hope

   10. _____

Your Total Score _____ /50

If your score was 39 or less for 92-A and 92-B, review Section 30, pages 161-166, before continuing.

93-A Practice Procedure Fill in the necessary commas in the following sentences. Score one point for each comma correctly placed.

Your Score

1. When I visited the local junior college the director asked me about my career objectives.

1. _____

2. I replied that I planned to work in an office to sell or to design graphics.

2. _____

3. Miss Anderson my advisor encouraged me to take courses in office techniques sales and art.

3. _____

4. After I reviewed the curriculum offerings I decided to discuss the matter with my friends.

4. _____

5. My friends you know will help me think things through.

5. _____

6. They I hope will ask me the proper questions.

6. _____

7. When I arrived at the neighborhood center some of my friends were already there.

7. _____

8. Bill Henry Juan and Tony came later to join Loni Lori Hester and Jack for our discussion.

8. _____

9. After I presented the problem they all began to speak at once.

9. _____

10. Bill Tony Lori and Hester my best friends made the most sense.

10. _____

93-B Practice Procedure Follow the procedure given for 93-A.

1. Lori a nurse's aide encouraged me to consider a medical career.

1. _____

2. She to tell the truth thinks I would be an excellent physician.

2. _____

3. Bill Tony and Hester suggested that I should do something with my art abilities.

3. _____

4. The others especially Henry thought I would be a great salesperson.

4. _____

5. My former English teacher Mrs. Willett always told me to become a writer.

5. _____

6. When I mentioned this to the group they looked shocked dismayed and surprised by the thought.

6. _____

7. They you see never imagined that I would ever become a writer.

7. _____

8. When Bill re-emphasized my art skills I began to think that art might be my best field of choice.

8. _____

9. Both my art teachers Mrs. Stuart and Mr. Webb were enthusiastic about my drawings oils charcoals and graphics.

9. _____

10. My friends agreed that in some way painting drawing and designing must enter into any career choice I make.

10. _____

Your Total Score _____ /50

If your score was 39 or less for 93-A and 93-B, review Section 30-D, pages 163-166, before continuing.

94-A Practice Procedure Insert the necessary commas in the following sentences. This is an additional review for all comma usage. Score one point for each comma correctly placed.

Your Score

1. When we won the debate title everyone in our small town of Walters Oklahoma was excited.

   1. _____

2. Will Lisa Dwayne and Rita our debate team members did a great job.

   2. _____

3. Our team you know won hands down.

   3. _____

4. No team from our high school had won since June 2 1985.

   4. _____

5. Ms. Bell and Mr. Walton our team coaches were proud but they gave all the credit to the team members.

   5. _____

6. Will and Lisa the team captains planned the team's strategy well.

   6. _____

7. After the first part of the debate was completed Will Lisa Ms. Bell and Mr. Walton evaluated the team's progress.

   7. _____

8. Dr. Garcia our school principal and her administrative staff attended the semifinals in Lawton Oklahoma.

   8. _____

9. Mrs. Smith the English chairperson was present and she told the team members of her pride in them.

   9. _____

10. Indeed other faculty members were there also.

    10. _____

94-B Practice Procedure Follow the procedure given for 94-A.

1. When our team won the semifinals at Lawton someone shouted "Go Walters!"

   1. _____

2. Several of us students drove up to Norman Oklahoma for the finals.

   2. _____

3. Henry my friend from England rode with us.

   3. _____

4. Jack Elke Eva Larry Jon and Wes rode on the bus.

   4. _____

5. Because we wanted to show our support for the team everyone from our school sat together.

   5. _____

6. The opposing team in the finals Fort Sill High School arrived first.

   6. _____

7. After our opponents took their places our team arrived.

   7. _____

8. You know of course our opponents won the contest last year.

   8. _____

9. After their first argument it was clear that Will Lisa and Rita would win.

   9. _____

10. Mrs. Lewis chairperson for the debate judges announced that Walters High School had won the championship.

    10. _____

Your Total Score _____ /50

If your score was 39 or less for 94-A and 94-B, review Section 30-D, pages 163-166, before continuing.

95-A Practice Procedure Insert the necessary commas in the following sentences. This is a review for all comma usage. Score one point for each comma correctly placed.

Your Score

1. Jenny Cheri and Diane are scheduled to visit Alaska in July.   1. _____

2. Jenny and Cheri friends at my work chose ship bus and plane tours of the state.   2. _____

3. They said "Marie won't you go with us?"   3. _____

4. I replied "You know I've always wanted to go there."   4. _____

5. Diane their friend was pleased that I could go.   5. _____

6. We flew to Vancouver British Columbia and there we boarded a ship for the Inside Passage.   6. _____

7. Ketchican Alaska an old gold rush town was our first stop.   7. _____

8. When we got off the ship the rain came down in buckets.   8. _____

9. Sitka our next stop once was the capital of Russian Alaska but today it is an American fishing community.   9. _____

10. Jenny Cheri Diane and I enjoyed our visit to Sitka.   10. _____

95-B Practice Procedure Follow the procedure given for 95-A.

1. Juneau Alaska's capital can be reached only by ship or plane.   1. _____

2. After we left Juneau we flew to Anchorage Fairbanks and Point Barrow.   2. _____

3. After flying over the Columbia Glacier Marie exclaimed "That's truly a spectacular sight!"   3. _____

4. Mt. McKinley the highest mountain in North America is in Denali National Park.   4. _____

5. Moose sheep and grizzly bear are often seen in the park.   5. _____

6. Point Barrow Alaska's largest Eskimo village is located north of the Arctic Circle.   6. _____

7. In Point Barrow we purchased mukluks dolls and ceremonial masks as souvenirs.   7. _____

8. Since our luggage space was limited I said "Please send these to me at 2701 New Avenue Las Vegas Nevada."   8. _____

9. The people of Point Barrow you know are proud of their Eskimo culture.   9. _____

10. We to tell the truth now know why that culture is so rich.   10. _____

Your Total Score _____ /47

If your score was 37 or less for 95-A and 95-B, review Section 30-D, pages 163-166, before continuing.

95-C Practice Procedure On a separate sheet of paper, demonstrate your understanding of the use of commas in an interesting, well-written paragraph. Tell about a trip you have taken or hope to take, a film you have seen, or a book you have read.

/36

Score

Date

Name

96-A Practice Procedure Fill in the necessary periods, questions marks, and exclamation points in the following sentences. Score one point for each correct answer.

Your Score

1. Where is the closest travel agency

2. Now I remember It's near the bank

3. Wow That's a good location for a travel agency

4. I have many questions to ask the travel agent

5. My parents will pay a major part of the cost

6. That's a real help

7. How much will it cost to go to Camp Lucky

8. It's probably too expensive for me

9. Gee It costs too much

10. Can we find a less expensive camp

1. _____

2. _____

3. _____

4. _____

5. _____

6. _____

7. _____

8. _____

9. _____

10. _____

96-B Practice Procedure Follow the procedure given for 96-A.

1. The agent has a long list of lower-priced camps

2. Oh Camp Luhan really sounds great

3. Yes It is one we will want to consider

4. Is trout fishing available there

5. The size of this camp appeals to me

6. Watch out It might be over our budget

7. But it's in such a beautiful location

8. Camp Scott looks good too

9. Help me I can't decide between the two

10. Shall I flip a coin to decide

1. _____

2. _____

3. _____

4. _____

5. _____

6. _____

7. _____

8. _____

9. _____

10. _____

96-C Practice Procedure Write and punctuate correctly three sentences for each type of end punctuation—the period, question mark, exclamation point. Use a separate sheet of paper. Score one point for each correct sentence.

Your Total Score _____ /36

If your score was 28 or less for 96-A, 96-B, and 96-C, review Sections 30-A, 30-B, and 30-C, pages 161-163, before continuing.

30-E THE SEMICOLON ;

The semicolon is used to separate independent clauses of a compound sentence when they are not joined by a coordinating conjunction. It is used as a slow down signal, stronger than a comma, but not a complete stop. A semicolon looks like a comma with a period over it (;). You can remove a semicolon and put a period in its place, and you will have two complete sentences instead of one.

Examples

The textbook cost $30.00; the workbook cost $10.00.

The table is set; dinner will be served promptly.

The semicolon is used between independent clauses of a compound sentence when they are joined by a conjunctive adverb (moreover, however, consequently, nevertheless, therefore, besides, then).

Examples

The film was great for the most part; however, toward the end it dragged.

We arrived fifteen minutes late for the bus; consequently, we had to wait an hour for the next one.

The child fell off his pony; nevertheless, he got right back on and continued his lesson.

30-F THE COLON :

A colon looks like one period above another period (:). It is used before an example, a series of words, or a list. The colon often follows terms like as follows, thus, in the following manner, or for example.

Examples

He visited four Florida cities: Tampa, Miami, Palm Beach, and Vero Beach.

The directions to her house are as follows: go two blocks down to Ash, turn right on Ash and go one block to Holly, turn left on Holly and go three blocks to Linden, turn left on Linden to 2430.

A colon can be used after the salutation in a letter.

Examples

Dear Ms. Morrison:

Dear Dr. and Mrs. Cook:

Use the colon between the hour and minutes in writing the time.

Examples

The film begins at 1:20 p.m.

Our office is open from 8:00 a.m. to 5:00 p.m.

30-G THE DASH —

The dash (—) marks a sudden change in the sentence. It is used when a sentence is interrupted abruptly and an entirely different sentence or thought is added.

Examples

My cousin Dorothy—you remember she had bright red hair—is in college.

Saying goodbye at the airport—it was jammed with people—was difficult.

The teacher—tall and erect—has taught here for ten years.

The dash may be used in place of the comma where emphasis is desired.

Examples

There was only one vegetable he disliked—broccoli.

There's only one word to describe it—cold!

He had only one big fault—snoring.

30-H THE PARENTHESES ( )

Parentheses ( ) are used to set off additions or expressions that are not necessary to the sentence. Unlike the dash, parentheses tend to de-emphasize what they set off. Parentheses are also used to enclose figures within a sentence.

Examples

Only two students (Bob and Judy) were kept after school for talking in class without permission.

Thanksgiving (the fourth Thursday in November) is a national holiday in the United States.

We will celebrate her birthday (June 25) with a party.

Doing some type of exercise daily (swimming, aerobics, running) has improved her health.

30-I THE APOSTROPHE '

The apostrophe (') shows ownership or possession. (See pages 35-36 for additional examples.)

Examples

The neighbor's dog barked all night.
The childrens' toys fell on the ground.

The apostrophe is also used to show omission of a letter. These words are *contractions.*

Example 1

It's too early to call them.

Analysis:

It's—It is—The apostrophe takes the place of the *i* in the word *is*.

Example 2

They weren't to arrive until tonight.

Analysis:

weren't—were not—The apostrophe takes the place of the *o* in the word *not*.

Example 3

They're nice people to know.

Analysis:

They're—They are—The apostrophe takes the place of the *a* in the word *are*.

THE APOSTROPHE SHOWS OWNERSHIP.

Susy's dog won the blue ribbon.

30-J THE QUOTATION MARKS " "

Quotation marks (" ") are used to enclose the exact words of a person (direct quotation).

Examples

Bette said, "Let's go to the movies tonight."

"Don't ever talk to strangers," Joan's mother cautioned.

"Read Chapter 24 and be ready for a test tomorrow," the teacher said.

USE QUOTATION MARKS TO ENCLOSE EXACT WORDS.

"Eat to live, live not to eat."
—Benj. Franklin

A mistake is often made when the quotation is broken by the identification of the person speaking. Close the first part of the quotation and start again when the direct quote is continued. Place commas before and after the part of the sentence not enclosed with the quotation marks.

If the identifying expression ends the sentence and the quotation continues, put a period after the expression. Begin the rest of the quotation with a quotation mark and a capital letter.

Examples

"Wash the dishes," said their mother, "and your sister will dry them."

"It's too cold for me," I shouted. "I don't have a heavy jacket."

Use quotation marks to set off the titles of chapters within a book, magazine articles, and reports. Titles of books, magazines, plays, poems, and other whole publications should be underlined when written in longhand and italicized when printed.

Examples

"Safe Investments" is a biweekly column in her newsletter.

The Carpinteria Herald is our local newspaper.

Use quotation marks to enclose unusual words or expressions.

Example

Charles has a reputation of being a "stuffed shirt."

Follow these simple rules when placing quotation marks with other marks of punctuation.

1. Place periods and commas *inside* quotation marks. (I answered, "I am not needed." "You must go," he insisted.)
2. Place semicolons and colons *outside* quotation marks. (He always called it "my camp on the river"; actually, it was an estate with a view of the river.)
3. Place question marks or exclamation points *inside* the quotation marks if they are part of the quoted matter. (He asked, "When will we arrive?") Place question marks or exclamation points *outside* the quotation marks if they punctuate the entire sentence. (Why did she say, "We are too late"?)

Do not use quotation marks in an indirect quote. The statement must be the direct and exact words of a person for quotation marks to be used.

Example 1

I was told that the cleaning would be ready today.

Analysis:

No quotation marks are needed because this is an indirect quote.

Example 2

The announcer said that the technical difficulty would be corrected promptly.

Analysis:

No quotation marks are needed because this is an indirect quote.

30-K EXPRESSION OF NUMBERS

Two questions are always asked about numbers: (1) When do you write numbers in words? (2) When do you use figures instead of a number in words? Keep in mind the following rules about numbers.

Definite numbers above ten should be in figures.

Examples

The classroom had <u>40</u> student desks.

The plane was <u>20</u> minutes late.

He was <u>17</u> years old when he entered college.

There were <u>26</u> apartments in the building.

Indefinite numbers should be written in words.

Example 1

Over <u>twenty</u> people applied for the job.

Analysis:

twenty—written out because *Over* is indefinite

Example 2

There were nearly <u>thirty</u> people in line when we arrived at the theater.

Analysis:

thirty—written out because *nearly* is indefinite

Example 3

Almost <u>forty</u> students signed up for computer training.

Analysis:

forty—written out because *Almost* is indefinite

A number at the beginning of a sentence should be written in words. This is just like capitalizing the first letter of a sentence.

Examples

<u>Ten</u> students received A's on the test.

<u>Twenty</u> fiction books were on the reading list.

<u>Four</u> cruise ships arrived at the same time.

When writing a percentage, use figures with the word percent. The symbol % is used only in statistical copy. When you write out the word *percent*, use it as one word. This practice is preferred to that of writing *percent* as two words.

Examples

She won the election with <u>53 percent</u> of the vote.

It's a shame that only <u>27 percent</u> of our town's registered voters voted in the last election.

A common problem is not knowing when to use *st, th,* or *d* in a date. Remember, *if the figure (or date) follows the month, you do not use st, th, or d.*

Examples

July <u>4</u>, 1776

December <u>15</u>, 1791

If, however, the date comes before the month, use st, th, or d.

Examples

<u>4th</u> of July, 1776

<u>15th</u> of December, 1791

TRYOUT EXERCISE

Directions: Fill in the necessary punctuation in the following sentences. Check your answers on page 246 or with your teacher before continuing with your assignment.

1. It s a beautiful sunset she said It looks like the sky is on fire

2. Isn t it true that he prefers shellfish oysters scallops mussels to the following crabs lobsters and eels

3. My friend Bill he graduated with me is coming home from the service tomorrow

---

Complete Application Practices 97-98, pages 181-182, at this time.

Review of the Apostrophe in Contractions and of Numbers

97-A Practice Procedure In the space provided write the contraction for each underlined expression and place the apostrophe in the contraction to replace an omitted letter or letters or to show proper ownership. Score one point for each correct answer.

Answers

1. <u>Joans</u> paper won first prize. (singular possessive)
2. <u>It is</u> a beautiful day.
3. The <u>students</u> bus was late. (plural possessive)
4. The <u>womens</u> store closed. (plural possessive)
5. His books <u>were not</u> in the car.
6. <u>They are</u> not going to see him.
7. The photographer took the <u>girls</u> picture. (singular possessive)
8. He <u>was not</u> selected for the team.
9. <u>It is</u> too early to know the score of the game.
10. <u>They are</u> at the theater.

1. _____
2. _____
3. _____
4. _____
5. _____
6. _____
7. _____
8. _____
9. _____
10. _____

Your Total Score _____ /10

If your score was 7 or less, review Section 30-I, page 178.

97-B Practice Procedure Complete each of the following sentences by writing in the space provided the correct form of the word in the parentheses. Score one point for each correct answer.

1. The book fair was set to open on the (4, 4th) of August.
2. Because the announcements were late, it opened on the (5, 5th) instead.
3. (14, Fourteen) schools participated in the fair.
4. Almost (20, twenty) publishing houses were represented.
5. On the (4, 4th) of August, book stalls were set up.
6. Before the doors opened, over (20, twenty) people waited to get in.
7. Over (60, sixty) of the visitors were parents.
8. A book I liked was about Eli Whitney who, I learned, was born on January (8, 8th), 1825.
9. Did you say that Whitney was born on the (8, 8th) of January?
10. The prices for all books included the (6%, 6 percent) sales tax.
11. Our teacher ordered a (13, thirteen) volume set of reference books for our class.
12. (13, Thirteen) volumes take up a lot of room on a shelf.
13. Another teacher ordered an (11, eleven) volume set.
14. A book that was printed on December (7, 7th), 1941, was on display.
15. Total attendance at the fair numbered nearly (400, four hundred).

1. _____
2. _____
3. _____
4. _____
5. _____
6. _____
7. _____
8. _____
9. _____
10. _____
11. _____
12. _____
13. _____
14. _____
15. _____

Your Total Score _____ /15

If your score was 11 or less, review Section 30-K, page 180, before continuing.

98-A Practice Procedure Insert all necessary punctuation marks in the following sentences. This is a complete review of punctuation. Score one point for each mark correctly placed.

Your Score

1. The Bell family is to have a family reunion on June 5 1998

1. _____

2. It will take place in Chicago Illinois from 9 00 a m to 8 00 p m

2. _____

3. Mr J B Bell the family s oldest living member and Rena Lowe J B s sister plan to attend

3. _____

4. The family s happy that they ll be present

4. _____

5. Yes replied my aunt and I m sure you ll enjoy them

5. _____

6. Do you think Deanna my cousin from Portland Oregon and John my cousin from Vancouver B C will come I asked

6. _____

7. I ll bet that Sue Ron Rachel and Toby Bell from Cardiff Wales won t be there

7. _____

8. Those folks I believe live too far away

8. _____

9. If you don t mind I ll write a special letter encouraging them to come my father said

9. _____

10. Henry they ll really appreciate that I know my mother replied

10. _____

98-B Practice Procedure Follow the procedure given for 98-A.

1. The letter was sent to the Bell family in Cardiff Wales but it turned up in London England instead

1. _____

2. Cecil the Bell s long-lost uncle received it there

2. _____

3. Believing the letter was his Cecil read the message and called to his wife Nancy There s to be a Bell family reunion in America

3. _____

4. I d love to go Nancy responded

4. _____

5. Cecil replied that they d go but soon noted the letter was for his cousin in Cardiff Wales

5. _____

6. Tonight said Nancy I ll call your cousin

6. _____

7. Toby there s to be a Bell family reunion in America on June 5 1998 said Nancy

7. _____

8. Toby agreed that a reunion was a good idea

8. _____

9. Toby wrote a letter to America and said We ll all be there

9. _____

10. Say do you know where the Bells of Cardiff and London will be on June 5 1998

10. _____

Your Total Score _____ /120

If your score was 95 or less for 98-A and 98-B, review Section 30, pages 161-180, before continuing.

98-C Practice Procedure Choose a topic and write a paragraph or sentences on a separate sheet of paper to demonstrate your understanding of these types of punctuation: end punctuation, commas in a series and with appositives, commas with dependent clauses and quotations, quotation marks, and contractions.

Capital Letters

Capitalize the first word of every sentence. The first letter of a direct quotation or a sentence within a quotation is capitalized.

Examples

<u>The</u> ship docked this morning.

"<u>Answer</u> the telephone," she said.

<u>Then</u> Ned said, "<u>Hello</u>."

Always use capital "I" for the pronoun "I" any place in any sentence.

Examples

Will <u>I</u> be late for school?

Can't <u>I</u> leave now?

Capitalize the days of the week, months of the year, and holidays.

Examples

<u>Labor Day</u> is a holiday in <u>September</u>.

On <u>New Year's Day</u> I always watch the football games.

Her days off are <u>Sunday</u> and <u>Monday</u>.

<u>Easter</u> is a religious holiday.

Capitalize proper nouns, abbreviations of proper nouns, and proper adjectives. (See pages 25-26 for a review of proper nouns and page 127 for a review of proper adjectives.)

Examples

<u>Benjamin Franklin</u> was an <u>American</u> patriot.

<u>Atlanta</u> is the capital of <u>Georgia</u>.

<u>Aunt Sue</u> and <u>Uncle Melvin</u> live in <u>Pasadena</u>, <u>California</u>.

The professor speaks <u>German</u>, <u>French</u>, <u>Spanish</u>, and <u>English</u>.

<u>Dr. Otto</u> is a very good veterinarian.

Capitalize important events and documents.

Examples

Baseball fans look forward to the <u>World Series</u>.

The <u>U.S. Constitution</u> is a written document.

The <u>Versailles Treaty</u> ended <u>World War I</u>.

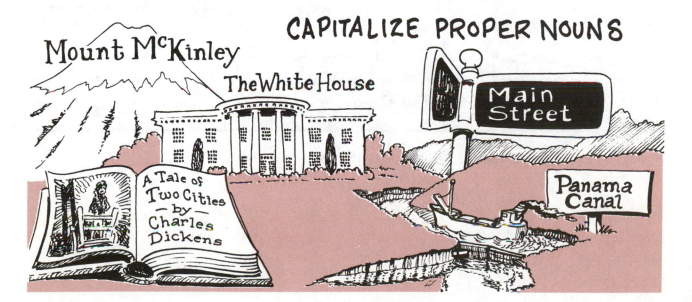

Mount McKinley   The White House   CAPITALIZE PROPER NOUNS   Main Street   A Tale of Two Cities — by — Charles Dickens   Panama Canal

Capitalize the principal words in the titles of complete literary and artistic works. Such titles include books, magazines, movies, plays, songs, paintings, sculptures, and poems. These titles are usually underlined or italicized.

Examples

Readers Digest is a favorite American magazine.

The New York Times is a famous newspaper.

All's Well That Ends Well is a comedy written by William Shakespeare.

Last week we enjoyed a production of Singing in the Rain.

I look forward to reading National Geographic.

Wuthering Heights is a classic film.

Children and adults continue to enjoy reading Swiss Family Robinson.

Look it up in the Encyclopedia Britannica.

Capital Letter Usage Summary

1. To begin every sentence.

2. For the pronoun *I* any place in a sentence.

3. For the days of the week, the months of the year, and holidays.

4. For proper nouns and proper adjectives.

5. For important events and documents.

6. For the principal words in the titles of literary and artistic works.

TRYOUT EXERCISE

Directions: In the following sentences, add the necessary capital letters by circling each small letter that should be capitalized. Check your answers on page 246 or with your teacher before continuing with your assignment.

1. the burden and the glory is a book written by president john f. kennedy.

2. thanksgiving, the fourth thursday in november, is my favorite national holiday.

3. on our vacation we visited erie, pennsylvania, and boston, massachusetts.

4. mary and i attended the rose bowl game last new year's day.

5. the american team arrived in paris on tuesday to play the french team next sunday.

Complete Application Practices 99-104, pages 185-190, at this time.

99-A Practice Procedure In the following sentences, add the necessary capital letters by circling each small letter that should be capitalized. Score one point for each correct response.

Your Score

1. our literary team (bill, lois, judy, and bob) is to write a paper about american writers of the past.

1. _____

2. research revealed that captain john smith published an account of the founding of jamestown.

2. _____

3. captain smith's account of his rescue by pocahontas is filled with descriptions of pioneer struggles.

3. _____

4. roger williams, founder of rhode island colony, was the author of *a key into the language of america.*

4. _____

5. in his travel book, *itinerarium*, alexander hamilton told of his journey from annapolis, maryland, to portsmouth, new hampshire.

5. _____

6. thomas paine's pamphlet, *common sense*, helped to stir the american patriots.

6. _____

7. his words, "these are the times that try men's souls," appeared in the first of a series of essays he called *the crisis*.

7. _____

8. benjamin franklin's book entitled *autobiography* is considered an american classic.

8. _____

9. washington irving and william cullen bryant were major literary figures in new york after 1815.

9. _____

10. in his book, *the sketch book*, irving wrote about rip van winkle.

10. _____

99-B Practice Procedure Follow the procedure given for 99-A.

1. ralph waldo emerson, another american man of letters, was born in boston, mass., on may 25, 1803, and died in concord, mass., on april 27, 1882.

1. _____

2. henry david thoreau, who lived for a time at walden pond, wrote a book entitled *walden*.

2. _____

3. one of new england's most famous writers was a harvard university medical professor, oliver wendell holmes.

3. _____

4. born on long island, n.y., walt whitman was the poet who wrote *leaves of grass.*

4. _____

5. another famous poet was henry wadsworth longfellow who was born in portland, maine, on february 27, 1807.

5. _____

6. we remember longfellow for many works but especially for the poem *the courtship of miles standish.*

6. _____

7. james russell lowell wrote against the mexican war in his *biglow papers.*

7. _____

8. the team's research provided us with more information than i expected they would find.

8. _____

9. it was decided that bill and lois would discuss the works of smith, williams, hamilton, paine, and franklin and write their report by new year's day.

9. _____

10. judy and bob agreed to concentrate on irving, bryant, emerson, thoreau, holmes, whitman, longfellow, and lowell, and their report was to be completed by christmas.

10. _____

Your Total Score _____ /136

If your score was 108 or less for 99-A and 99-B, review Section 31, pages 183-184, before continuing.

100 Practice Procedure Fill in all the necessary punctuation and capitalization in the following story. Indicate capital letters by circling each small letter that should be capitalized. Score one point for each correctly capitalized word and one point for each punctuation mark correctly placed.

Your Score

as we sat in our rambling gray and white home among the trees at 223 tioga falls road at little bear lake we watched the dreary rain fall all morning long finally the storm lessened and the dark gray clouds passed over the sun shone brightly on the wet grass yes the day soon was as pleasant as any other august day of course we knew that was usually true with a warm summer rain this time however the rain had swelled the river and washed away our small wooden bridge sally my youngest sister sat beside the destroyed bridge she was unhappy because of its loss it was then that a shiny red convertible drove up beside her the four of us our names are thomas helen loni and joshua watched as the car approached it was around 2 30 p m august 17 1991

the driver an ill-humored stranger hollered out the window in a sullen way how deep is this river kid

my young sister wrinkled her brow but she replied not too deep

can i make it if i drive through it right here the man asked speak up stupid i don t have all day the stranger demanded

i think so replied my sister in fact i m sure you can

the driver shifted into gear and started into the swift stream midway across the car began to settle into the mud the angry soaked and bedraggled driver sloshed through the raging water toward my sister soft mud clung to his jacket and trousers the fellow was purple with rage by the time he reached my sister

you dumb kid why did you tell me i could drive through that river water he yelled it s over five feet deep right there

with an innocent expression my young sister looked toward the sunken car then in a small voice she said slowly i don t understand it the water is only up to here on the ducks swimming out there

1. _____
2. _____
3. _____
4. _____
5. _____
6. _____
7. _____
8. _____
9. _____
10. _____
11. _____
12. _____
13. _____
14. _____
15. _____
16. _____
17. _____
18. _____
19. _____
20. _____
21. _____
22. _____
23. _____
24. _____
25. _____
26. _____
27. _____
28. _____
29. _____
30. _____
31. _____

Your Total Score _____ /133

If your score was 105 or less, review Sections 30-31, pages 161-184, before continuing.

/133

Score

Date

Name

Punctuation and Capitalization Review

101-A Practice Procedure Fill in all necessary punctuation and capitalization in the following sentences. Indicate capital letters by circling each small letter that should be capitalized. Score one point for each punctuation mark correctly placed and one point for each correctly capitalized word.

Your Score

1. the airline announcer said flight 406 to washington d c dallas and phoenix is ready for boarding

    1. _____

2. the riley family of new york city moved forward to the flight gate

    2. _____

3. bob carol and lauren riley and ronald and lucy their parents were eager to be on their way

    3. _____

4. ronald the father was taking the family to visit relatives in arizona

    4. _____

5. carol carried a copy of *victoria* magazine to read on the flight

    5. _____

6. she i believe likes *victoria* better than *the country living*

    6. _____

7. lauren and bob both like *business week* magazine and *time*

    7. _____

8. bob read an article in *time* entitled all about stress

    8. _____

9. he told lauren read it and it will help you

    9. _____

10. you re going to read that stuff questioned carol of her brother and sister

    10. _____

101-B Practice Procedure Follow the procedure for 101-A.

1. the rileys plane was delayed from 11 00 a m to 1 00 p m

    1. _____

2. the departure time change of course was a disappointment and it meant they would arrive at phoenix airport several hours late

    2. _____

3. when the delay was announced dr riley suggested to his family let s take a walk around kennedy international airport

    3. _____

4. carol the youngest riley daughter said you go and i ll stay here

    4. _____

5. bob explained that he was hungry and then he said let s eat instead

    5. _____

6. dr. and mrs riley lauren and bob walked to the airport restaurant the landings

    6. _____

7. just as his parents expected bob ordered a cheeseburger onion rings and a root beer

    7. _____

8. bob do you think that will hold you until we have lunch on the plane joked dr riley

    8. _____

9. gee said bob i guess it will but i sure wouldn t want to starve in the meantime

    9. _____

10. just then carol rushed to the table and said hurry the plane is leaving early

    10. _____

Your Total Score _____ /177

If your score was 141 or less for 101-A and 101-B, review Sections 30-31, pages 161-184, before continuing.

Punctuated and Capitalized Sentences

102-A Practice Procedure Fill in all necessary punctuation and capitalization in the following sentences. Indicate capital letters by circling each small letter that should be capitalized. Score one point for each correct response.

Your Score

1. peter do you know where the deepest lake in the u s is located asked ms sobul the teacher

    1. _____

2. yes peter replied i believe it is in oregon

    2. _____

3. peter continued by saying the name of the lake is crater lake and it s in crater lake national park

    3. _____

4. ms sobul then asked who knows when the lake was discovered and by whom

    4. _____

5. janet waved her arm and shouted i do

    5. _____

6. ms sobul said all right janet tell us

    6. _____

7. after she rose to her feet janet said that the lake was discovered in 1853 by john wesley hillman a prospector

    7. _____

8. you re correct said the teacher but in what book or magazine did you read about it

    8. _____

9. janet responded i used to live in oregon and in my other school i read about it in *national geographic*

    9. _____

10. did you visit the lake ms sobul asked and if you did is the water as blue and beautiful as they say

    10. _____

102-B Practice Procedure Follow the procedure given for 102-A.

1. janet responded yes the water is the deepest blue you can ever imagine

    1. _____

2. i ve seen it in photographs but i ve never visited the lake in person ms sobul commented

    2. _____

3. do they call it crater lake because it s in a volcanic crater wilma another student asked

    3. _____

4. who can respond to that question ms sobul asked

    4. _____

5. terry raised his hand and responded it was created by volcanic action but it isn t a crater

    5. _____

6. that s right terry but do you know the source of the lake s water said the teacher

    6. _____

7. yes responded terry the lake gets its water from melting snow and rainwater

    7. _____

8. when we still lived in oregon interjected janet i went with my family to mazama campground for a vacation

    8. _____

9. when we were there janet added i learned that it became a national park in 1902 the nation s sixth national park

    9. _____

10. although the park doesn t attract great hordes of tourists those who come really enjoy their visit

    10. _____

Your Total Score _____ /200

If your score was 160 or less for 102-A and 102-B, review Sections 30-31, pages 161-184, before continuing.

103 Practice Procedure Match each item in Column A with the item it describes in Column B. Write the identifying letter from Column A in the blank provided at the right. Items in Column A are used more than once. Score one point for each correct answer.

Column A	Column B	Answers
a. apostrophe	**1.** used to enclose exact words of a person	**1.** _____
b. capital letter	**2.** used at the end of an imperative sentence	**2.** _____
c. colon	**3.** used for holidays	**3.** _____
d. comma	**4.** used after an interrogative sentence	**4.** _____
e. dash	**5.** used after the salutation in a business letter	**5.** _____
f. exclamation point	**6.** used after words expressing sudden feeling	**6.** _____
g. period	**7.** used before a coordinating conjunction in a compound sentence	**7.** _____
h. question mark	**8.** used for principal words in a song title	**8.** _____
i. quotation marks	**9.** used to indicate sudden change in a sentence (the sentence is suddenly broken off)	**9.** _____
j. semicolon	**10.** used to set off an appositive	**10.** _____
	11. used for separation in dates and addresses	**11.** _____
	12. used to show the omission of a letter	**12.** _____
	13. used to set off titles of articles from a magazine	**13.** _____
	14. used for proper nouns	**14.** _____
	15. used after introductory words that are separated from the rest of the sentence	**15.** _____
	16. used to separate independent clauses of a compound sentence not joined by a coordinating conjunction	**16.** _____
	17. used before a series or list introduced by "as follows"	**17.** _____
	18. used for important events and documents	**18.** _____
	19. used to start every sentence	**19.** _____
	20. used at the end of a declarative sentence	**20.** _____
	21. used after an abbreviation or initial	**21.** _____
	22. denotes ownership or possession	**22.** _____
	23. used between hours and minutes	**23.** _____
	24. used to set off unrelated words in a sentence	**24.** _____
	25. used to separate words in a series	**25.** _____

Your Total Score _____ /25

If your score was 19 or less, review Sections 30-31, pages 161-184, before continuing.

Punctuation Review

104-A Practice Procedure Insert all necessary punctuation marks in the following sentences. Score one point for each mark correctly placed.

Your Score

1. The letter from the contest sponsor arrived I was almost too nervous to open it

    1. _____

2. Your entry has won our contest I read

    2. _____

3. The prize I d won was a trip for four to the Hawaiian Islands Kauai Oahu Maui Hawaii and Molokai all five islands

    3. _____

4. My entry was an essay entitled The Rule of Law Why

    4. _____

5. To prepare for the essay I d consulted all kinds of literature books reports magazine articles

    5. _____

6. My teacher said Congratulations We weren t surprised that you won therefore we ve already planned a celebration

    6. _____

7. She planned the party for the 2d of December from 5 00 p m to 6 30 p m

    7. _____

8. My grandfather you remember that he d once served as a sailor in Hawaii was invited

    8. _____

9. All of my friends from school church and the club were invited too

    9. _____

10. The teacher s invitation read You re invited to help us celebrate Terri s winning the essay contest

    10. _____

104-B Practice Procedure Follow the procedure given for 104-A.

1. Mrs Anderson Kirsten s mother asked When do you leave for Hawaii

    1. _____

2. My mother responded It s up to the sponsors They re saying sometime next week Monday Tuesday or Wednesday

    2. _____

3. A friend asked Weren t you surprised to win

    3. _____

4. Hawaiian foods pineapple papaya poi were served to the guests

    4. _____

5. My friend Judy remarked Poi takes getting used to doesn t it

    5. _____

6. Please read your essay to the group Terri my teacher requested

    6. _____

7. When I finished everyone shouted Well done

    7. _____

8. Our principal Mr Lake announced Terri is the first student from our school to win a national essay contest

    8. _____

9. Everyone was pleased I d won but I was the most pleased of all

    9. _____

10. I announced Thanks for your good wishes and I m off to Hawaii

    10. _____

Your Total Score _____ /118

If your score was 93 or less for 104-A and 104-B, review Section 30, pages 161-180, before continuing.

Word Blunders

OBJECTIVES
1. To recognize misused words in everyday speech and writing.
2. To learn the proper usage of frequently misused words.

Have you ever been misunderstood or embarrassed by mispronouncing a word or by using the wrong word to convey your thought? The simple mistakes we make in speaking and writing may be called *word blunders*. How many of these word blunders do you avoid?

32-A WHO'S AND WHOSE

Who's is the contraction for *who is*. Remember that a contraction has an apostrophe (') for the omitted letter or letters.

Example 1

Who's your favorite performer?

Analysis:

Who's—contraction for *who is*—*Who is* your favorite performer?

Example 2

Miss Simms, who's a bank president, is our neighbor.

Analysis:

who's—contraction for *who is*—*who is* a bank president

Whose shows ownership or possession. It is used as a possessive adjective and modifies a noun. *Whose* is the possessive case of *who*.

Example 1

Whose car is blocking the driveway?

Analysis:

Whose—possessive adjective—modifies the noun *car*

Example 2

Whose dog was barking all night?

Analysis:

Whose—possessive adjective—modifies the noun *dog*

32-B IT'S AND ITS

It's is the contraction for *it is*. The apostrophe (') takes the place of the letter *i* which is omitted. The contraction *it's* acts as the subject and the verb of a clause or sentence.

Example 1

It's a new type of health food.

Analysis:

It's—contraction for *it is*—*It is* a new type of health food.

Example 2

It's the best present I have ever received.

Analysis:

It's—contraction for *it is*—*It is* the best present I have ever received.

Its shows ownership or possession. It is used as a possessive adjective and is followed by a noun. *Its* is the possessive case of *it*.

Example 1

Its paw got caught in the door.

Analysis:

Its—possessive adjective—modifies the noun *paw*

Example 2

The museum with its gardens attracted a crowd.

Analysis:

its—possessive adjective—modifies the noun *gardens*

32-C THEIR, THERE, AND THEY'RE

There is an adverb. It is never used to show ownership. Be careful in your choice of the verb form with *there*. *There* is never used as a subject and therefore does not determine the singular or plural form of the verb. The subject is usually the noun or pronoun that follows the verb form. If that noun or pronoun is singular, the verb form should be singular. If it is plural, the verb form should be plural.

Example 1

There is often a noisy student in class.

Analysis:

There—adverb—modifies the verb *is*. The singular verb form *is* agrees with the singular subject *student*

Example 2

There were five jobs available at the new store.

Analysis:

There—adverb—modifies the verb *were*. The plural verb form *were* agrees with the plural subject *jobs*

Example 3

When we arrived there, we didn't mind the rain.

Analysis:

there—adverb—modifies the verb *arrived*

Their denotes ownership or possession. It is used as a possessive adjective and modifies a noun. *Their* is the possessive case of *they*.

Example 1

Their picnic was postponed due to the weather.

Analysis:

Their—possessive adjective—modifies the noun *picnic*

Example 2

Jules and Boris left their coats in the back room.

Analysis:

their—possessive adjective—modifies the noun *coats*

They're is the contraction for *they are*. Remember that a contraction has an apostrophe (') for the omitted letter or letters.

Example

They're glad to get jobs.

Analysis:

They're—contraction for *they are. They are* glad to get jobs.

TRYOUT EXERCISE   **Directions:** Complete each of the following sentences by writing in the blank provided at the right the correct form of the word in the parentheses. Check your answers on page 246 or with your teacher before continuing with your assignment.

1. (Who's, Whose) going to the beach?   1. _____

2. (They're, Their, There) planning to study accounting.   2. _____

3. (It's, Its) a new company that sells calculators.   3. _____

4. (Who, Whose) car was stolen last night?   4. _____

5. We went (there, their, they're) with Ms. Perkins.   5. _____

6. The car with (it's, its) recent paint job looked new.   6. _____

7. (Their, There, They're) families traveled to Canada.   7. _____

Complete Application Practices 105-106, pages 193-194, at this time.

105 Practice Procedure Complete each of the following sentences by writing in the blank provided at the right the correct word in the parentheses. Score one point for each correct response.

Answers

1. (Who's, Whose) idea was it to visit our national parks?　　　1. _____

2. Miss Pew, (who's, whose) the librarian, suggested it.　　　2. _____

3. (It's, Its) a large national park system in the U.S.　　　3. _____

4. (Who's, Whose) the director of our parks and historic sites?　　　4. _____

5. The responsibility and (it's, its) authority are with the Interior Department.　　　5. _____

6. We saw a bear and (it's, its) cubs walk in Yellowstone National Park.　　　6. _____

7. Mrs. Healy, (who's, whose) father worked there, told us about the Grand Canyon.　　　7. _____

8. (It's, Its) an experience to drive through Zion National Park.　　　8. _____

9. The travel agent, (who's, whose) firm handled our trip, gave us maps.　　　9. _____

10. Doris, (who's, whose) a pilot, enjoyed the auto ride.　　　10. _____

11. Zion National Park with (it's, its) gorge was unusual.　　　11. _____

12. If you are there before (it's, its) sunset, you will enjoy the sight.　　　12. _____

13. (Who's, Whose) expected to pay for lunch today?　　　13. _____

14. The travel agency and (it's, its) staff arranged for our lodging.　　　14. _____

15. Jack Vaughn lived near Everglades National Park with (it's, its) many water-ways.　　　15. _____

16. (Who's, Whose) going to visit the San Antonio Mission?　　　16. _____

17. Please tell us (who's, whose) assignment it is.　　　17. _____

18. (Who's, Whose) an authority on Valley Forge?　　　18. _____

19. Amy Cruz, (who's, whose) degree is in American history, was the lecturer.　　　19. _____

20. Kitty Osborne, (who's, whose) cousin worked there summers, showed a film.　　　20. _____

21. (It's, Its) historical value is important to all citizens.　　　21. _____

22. (Who's, Whose) never as happy as when he is in the wilderness?　　　22. _____

23. The park and (it's, its) rangers made it interesting.　　　23. _____

24. (It's, Its) fortunate you can visit our historical sites.　　　24. _____

25. (Who's, Whose) mistake is it if you never see or read about them?　　　25. _____

Date

Score

/25

Your Total Score _____ /25

If your score was 19 or less, review page 191 before continuing.

106 Practice Procedure Complete each of the following sentences by writing in the blank provided at the right the correct form of *there, their,* or *they're*. Remember that *there* is an adverb, *their* shows ownership, and *they're* is a contraction for *they are*. Score one point for each correct response.

Answers

1. (There, Their, They're) comes a time to prepare for a job.

   1. _____

2. The career counselor gave Walt and Sue (there, their, they're) application forms.

   2. _____

3. Walt asked, "Are (there, their, they're) people who start at the top?"

   3. _____

4. What are (there, their, they're) chances for career courses?

   4. _____

5. (There, Their, They're) willing to enroll in classes.

   5. _____

6. (There, Their, They're) first jobs were with a movie studio.

   6. _____

7. They had an uncle who worked (there, their, they're).

   7. _____

8. The studios had some openings in (there, their, they're) mail rooms.

   8. _____

9. Some of (there, their, they're) friends wanted to be actors.

   9. _____

10. (There, Their, They're) smart and learned on the job.

   10. _____

11. However, (there, their, they're) boss advised them to get steady work.

   11. _____

12. They were fortunate to get temporary work (there, their, they're) as stage hands.

   12. _____

13. (There, Their, They're) friend, Kelsey, enrolled in drama classes.

   13. _____

14. Are (there, their, they're) any jobs open in the studios?

   14. _____

15. Eric and Sandy were allowed to read (there, their, they're) lines for the producer.

   15. _____

16. (There, Their, They're) going to be in a new production.

   16. _____

17. Was it (there, their, they're) they received their first jobs?

   17. _____

18. They met more gifted actors (there, their, they're) than ever before.

   18. _____

19. (There, Their, They're) sorry to hear that.

   19. _____

20. It was (there, their, they're) that they decided on business careers.

   20. _____

Your Total Score _____ /20

If your score was 15 or less, review page 192 before continuing.

32-D GOOD AND WELL

Good is an adjective meaning skillful, admirable, or having the right qualities. It describes a noun and answers the question "what kind of."

Example 1

Angie and Alec are <u>good</u> friends.

Analysis:

> <u>good</u>—adjective—describes the noun *friends*—answers the question "what kind of"

Example 2

The pie was <u>good</u>.

Analysis:

> <u>good</u>—predicate adjective—describes the noun *pie*

Well is an adverb telling how something is done. It usually modifies a verb and answers the question "how."

Example 1

Gloria speaks Spanish <u>well</u>.

Analysis:

> <u>well</u>—adverb—modifies the verb *speaks*—answers the question "how"

Example 2

The nurses work together <u>well</u>.

Analysis:

> <u>well</u>—adverb—modifies the verb *work*—answers the question "how"

32-E IN AND INTO

In is a preposition and means "within a place." The person or thing is already there.

Example 1

The children swim <u>in</u> the pool.

Analysis:

> <u>in</u>—preposition—children are already *in* the pool

Example 2

Ellie and Teresa were <u>in</u> the kitchen.

Analysis:

> <u>in</u>—preposition—Ellie and Teresa are already *in* the kitchen

Into is also a preposition, but it means "the moving or going from outside to inside."

Example 1

The lifeguard jumps <u>into</u> the pool.

Analysis:

> <u>into</u>—preposition—shows movement from outside to inside the pool

Example 2

The cat ran <u>into</u> the house.

Analysis:

> <u>into</u>—preposition—shows movement from outside to inside the house

32-F ALMOST AND MOST

Almost is an adverb meaning "nearly."

Most is an adjective or adverb meaning "the greatest in number or quality."

Example 1

Carol <u>almost</u> finished her homework.

Analysis:

<u>almost</u>—adverb—means nearly

Example 2

The driver <u>almost</u> had an accident.

Analysis:

<u>almost</u>—adverb—means nearly

Example 1

Priscilla is the <u>most</u> intelligent student in the school.

Analysis:

<u>most</u>—adverb—means the best or greatest

Example 2

My <u>most</u> embarrassing moment happened yesterday.

Analysis:

<u>most</u>—adverb—means greatest in quality

32-G BESIDE AND BESIDES

Beside means "to be next to or at the side of something."

Besides means "in addition or extra."

Example 1

She parked her car <u>beside</u> the new motorcycle.

Analysis:

<u>beside</u>—next to or at the side of

Example 2

My cousin sat <u>beside</u> the coach during the game.

Analysis:

<u>beside</u>—next to or at the side of

Example 1

<u>Besides</u> the lunch table, she brought the salad and dessert.

Analysis:

<u>Besides</u>—in addition to

Example 2

My brother received a snapping turtle <u>besides</u> two hamsters.

Analysis:

<u>besides</u>—in addition to

32-H SURE AND SURELY

Sure is an adjective meaning "to be certain or positive."

Surely is an adverb meaning "certainly." If you can replace *surely* with *certainly*, you know *surely* is correct.

Example 1

She is always <u>sure</u> she knows the answers.

Analysis:

<u>sure</u>—adjective—means certain or positive

Example 2

Fritz was <u>sure</u> he passed the test.

Analysis:

<u>sure</u>—adjective—means certain or positive

Example 1

He will <u>surely</u> report the accident to the police.

Analysis:

<u>surely</u>—adverb—means certainly

Example 2

Tina <u>surely</u> will ask Ben to the company's picnic.

Analysis:

<u>surely</u>—adverb—means certainly

32-I REAL AND VERY

Real is an adjective meaning "genuine." It describes a noun.

Example 1

It was a <u>real</u> painting by Van Gogh.

Analysis:

real—adjective—describes the noun *painting*—means genuine

Example 2

Her gloves are made of <u>real</u> leather.

Analysis:

real—adjective—describes the noun *leather*—means genuine

Very is an adverb meaning "extremely." It usually modifies an adjective.

Example 1

This is the <u>very</u> best restaurant in town.

Analysis:

very—adverb—modifies the adjective *best*—means extremely

Example 2

Rubens was a <u>very</u> famous artist.

Analysis:

very—adverb—modifies the adjective *famous*—means extremely

32-J TO, TOO, AND TWO

To is a preposition that is followed by a noun or a pronoun in the objective case. (See pages 141 and 149 for a review of prepositional phrases.) Another use of *to* is with the infinitive phrase (*to* plus a verb form). (See page 150 for an explanation of infinitive phrases.)

Example 1

Mrs. Leonard took us <u>to</u> the harbor.

Analysis:

to—preposition

Example 2

Penny brought her record collection <u>to</u> school.

Analysis:

to—preposition

Example 3

Today I have <u>to</u> introduce the speaker.

Analysis:

to—beginning of infinitive phrase—*to* plus the verb form *introduce* and its object

Too is an adverb. It means "also" or "besides." In addition it can mean "very" or "excessively."

Example 1

Lucy came to the lecture <u>too</u>.

Analysis:

too—adverb—modifies the verb *came*—means also

Example 2

Mr. Woods was <u>too</u> nice most of the time.

Analysis:

too—adverb—modifies the adjective *nice*—means excessively

Two is a number and is usually an adjective.

Example 1

The <u>two</u> doctors performed the operation.

Analysis:

two—adjective—number

Example 2

There were <u>two</u> minutes left in the game.

Analysis:

two—adjective—number

32-K THEN AND THAN

Then is an adverb meaning "at that time." It answers the question "when" of the verb.

Example 1

The singer <u>then</u> sang my favorite song.

Analysis:

then—adverb—answers the question "when" of the verb *sang*

Example 2

When I finished mowing the lawn, Mrs. Polk <u>then</u> paid me.

Analysis:

then—adverb—meaning "at that time"—answers the question "when" of the verb *paid*

Than is a conjunction and makes or shows a comparison of two or more things.

Example 1

Mark runs faster <u>than</u> Kevin.

Analysis:

than—conjunction—shows a comparison of two people, *Mark* and *Kevin*

Example 2

Laureen is taller <u>than</u> her twin sister.

Analysis:

than—conjunction—shows a comparison between *Laureen* and *twin sister*

Different from is always used in comparing different things. Never use *different than*.

Example 1

The author's last book was <u>different from</u> his previous books.

Analysis:

different from—used in comparing different things—never *different than*

Example 2

Racing an automobile is <u>different from</u> paddling a canoe.

Analysis:

different from—used in comparing different things—never *different than*

32-L BETWEEN AND AMONG

Between is used when referring to two people or things.

Example 1

Erin ran <u>between</u> Martha and Emily.

Analysis:

between—referring to two people, *Martha* and *Emily*

Example 2

The mouse hid <u>between</u> the garage and the trash bin.

Analysis:

between—referring to two things, *garage* and *trash bin*

Among is used when referring to more than two people or things.

Example 1

<u>Among</u> the students, parents, and teachers, there are similar concerns.

Analysis:

Among—referring to more than two people or groups

Example 2

<u>Among</u> my favorite collections are coins, stamps, and baseball cards.

Analysis:

Among—referring to more than two things

Whenever you use either *between* or *among*, the pronoun that follows is always in the objective case (*me, him, her, us, them*). (See pages 44-46 for a review of the case forms of pronouns.)

Example 1

My father settled the argument between <u>her</u> and <u>me</u>.

Analysis:

<u>her</u>, <u>me</u>—objects of the preposition *between*—objective case

Example 2

The police rushed among <u>them</u> and arrested three of the rioters.

Analysis:

<u>them</u>—object of the preposition *among*—objective case

32-M LIKE AND AS

Like is a preposition followed by a noun or pronoun in the objective case.

Example 1

My twin brother looks <u>like</u> me.

Analysis:

<u>like</u>—preposition—has object *me*

Example 2

Grace talks <u>like</u> him.

Analysis:

<u>like</u>—preposition—has object *him*

Example 3

His handwriting is <u>like</u> old script.

Analysis:

<u>like</u>—preposition—has object *script*

As is a conjunction and introduces a clause.

Example 1

<u>As</u> he danced, he watched his feet.

Analysis:

<u>As</u>—conjunction—introduces the clause *As he danced*

Example 2

<u>As</u> the rain began, we ran for cover.

Analysis:

<u>As</u>—conjunction—introduces the clause *As the rain began*

Example 3

The defendant listened <u>as</u> the jury read the verdict.

Analysis:

<u>as</u>—conjunction—introduces the clause *as the jury read the verdict*

32-N AS—AS, SO—AS

As—as is used in comparing equal things.

Example 1

Holidays <u>as</u> well <u>as</u> weekends are happy occasions.

Analysis:

<u>as</u>, <u>as</u>—compares equal things.

Example 2

Cats <u>as</u> well <u>as</u> dogs make nice pets.

Analysis:

<u>as</u>, <u>as</u>—compares equal things

So—as is used in making a negative comparison.

Example 1

Her roses are not <u>so</u> sweet smelling <u>as</u> last year's.

Analysis:

<u>so</u>, <u>as</u>—negative comparison

Example 2

Her new job is not <u>so</u> good <u>as</u> her previous one.

Analysis:

<u>so</u>, <u>as</u>—negative comparison

TRYOUT EXERCISE

Directions: Complete each of the following sentences by writing in the blank provided at the right the correct form of the word in the parentheses. Check your answers on page 246 or with your teacher before continuing with your assignment.

1. Movies are different (from, than) live television.　1. _____

2. (Between, Among) the berries, apples, and bananas there were grapes.　2. _____

3. It was (to, too, two) scary a movie for my friends.　3. _____

4. There was an age difference between Mr. Diaz and (she, her).　4. _____

5. Dodie is (sure, surely) an excellent driver.　5. _____

6. The store sold clothes and hardware (beside, besides) shoes.　6. _____

Complete Application Practices 107-108, pages 201-202, at this time.

107 Practice Procedure Complete each of the following sentences by writing in the blank provided at the right the correct word in the parentheses. Score one point for each correct response.

Answers

1. That new book was (sure, surely) an informative one.   1. _____

2. Did you know any other patriots (beside, besides) George Washington?   2. _____

3. It wasn't (to, too, two) long before she told us.   3. _____

4. Who was the more famous patriot (among, between) Jefferson and Adams?   4. _____

5. Thomas Jefferson was a (real, very) educated person.   5. _____

6. During the Revolutionary War, the minutemen waited (beside, besides) the road.   6. _____

7. (Who's, Whose) Betsy Ross and why is she remembered?   7. _____

8. The teacher put his history book (in, into) the desk.   8. _____

9. Politicians today are not (as, so) good as they were in the 1770s.   9. _____

10. Washington's battle strategy was better (then, than) any British general's.   10. _____

11. (Who's, Whose) the patriot who said, "Give me liberty or give me death"?   11. _____

12. (Who's, Whose) remark was "When the well's dry, we know the worth of water"?   12. _____

13. Professor Case spoke (to, too, two) our class about famous Americans.   13. _____

14. He (sure, surely) was an expert on our Civil War.   14. _____

15. His wife was a (good, well) student of our history.   15. _____

16. Pattie Case was a (real, very) exciting speaker.   16. _____

17. She lectures (like, as) him.   17. _____

18. The last speaker was (as, so) interesting as the previous one.   18. _____

19. Dr. Case lectures (good, well).   19. _____

20. Mr. Wells was different (from, than) other teachers.   20. _____

21. We recognized the book by (it's, its) cover.   21. _____

22. Benjamin Franklin was a (real, very) American statesman.   22. _____

23. Grant and Lee planned their campaigns (good, well).   23. _____

24. Was (there, their, they're) a reason for the Civil War?   24. _____

25. It was (than, then) that I realized what it means to be a good citizen.   25. _____

Your Total Score _____ /25

If your score was 19 or less, review Section 32, pages 191-200, before continuing.

Name

Date

Score

/25

/30

Score

Date

Name

108 Practice Procedure Construct sentences using the following pairs or groups of words. You may use each pair or group in the same sentence or write a separate sentence for each word. Score one point for the correct use of each word.

1. beside
   besides

2. good
   well

3. than
   then

4. to
   too
   two

5. who's
   whose

6. like
   as

7. real
   very

8. as—as
   so—as

9. it's
   its

10. almost
    most

11. between
    among

12. their
    they're
    there

13. in
    into

14. sure
    surely

Your Total Score _____ /30

If your score was 23 or less, review Section 32, pages 191-200, before continuing.

Speech Duds

Use:	Don't Use:
almost everybody	most everybody
an hour	a hour
anyway	anyways
anywhere	anywheres
aren't you	ain't you
back of	in back of
better	more better
brought	brung
burst	busted
can hardly	can't hardly
different from	different than
drowned	drownded
feel bad	feel badly
grew up	growed up
have a	have got a
have gone	have went
he doesn't	he don't
he says	he sez
inside the	inside of the
kind of	kind of a
long way	long ways
might have	might of
not nearly	nowhere near
off the	off of the
ought not	hadn't ought
ought to have gone	ought to of gone

Use:	Don't Use:
plan to go	plan of going
prohibit from	prohibit to
seldom	seldom ever
should have	should of
sort of	sort of a
this (tie, dress)	this here (tie, dress)
this kind	these kind
those (shoes)	them (shoes)
thrown	throwed
try to	try and
very good	awfully good
was scarcely	wasn't scarcely
were you	was you
where	where at
wished on	wisht on
with regard to	with regards to

TRYOUT EXERCISE

Directions: Complete each of the following sentences by writing in the blank provided at the right the correct word or words in the parentheses. Check your answers on page 246 or with your teacher before continuing with your assignment.

1. The owner thought he (might have, might of) a map of Ireland.

1. _____

2. Miss Dole (can hardly, can't hardly) afford them.

2. _____

3. We (seldom, seldom ever) get to see the map of Central America.

3. _____

4. (Try and, Try to) buy a used map of Australia.

4. _____

5. Great Britain's map was (inside the, inside of the) store.

5. _____

6. The clerk (doesn't, don't) know where anything is.

6. _____

Complete Application Practices 109-110, pages 205-206, at this time.

109 Practice Procedure Complete each of the following sentences by writing in the blank provided at the right the correct word or words in the parentheses. Check the list of Speech Duds on the previous pages to make your choice. Score one point for each correct answer.

Answers

1. Pete's new job is different (than, from) his last one.   1. _____

2. (Anyway, Anyways) he is pleased with his employment.   2. _____

3. The owner was a (very good, awfully good) friend.   3. _____

4. Now he (don't, doesn't) have to work weekends.   4. _____

5. What (kind of a, kind of) job is it?   5. _____

6. He (can't hardly, can hardly) wait to go to work.   6. _____

7. Mr. Orr has large computers (inside of the, inside the) inner office.   7. _____

8. His friends (seldom, seldom ever) saw Pete so happy.   8. _____

9. The boss (growed up, grew up) in St. Louis.   9. _____

10. Ann and Karen will (try to, try and) get jobs there.   10. _____

11. It was an unusual (sort of a, sort of) job.   11. _____

12. (This, This here) company pays high salaries.   12. _____

13. I (have a, have got a) friend who works for the city.   13. _____

14. You (hadn't ought to, ought not) be jealous.   14. _____

15. The job is (nowhere near, not nearly) as good as he claims.   15. _____

16. I still travel a (long way, long ways) to go to work.   16. _____

17. In fact, I would go (anywheres, anywhere) for a job.   17. _____

18. It (seldom ever, seldom) is as good as he says.   18. _____

19. (Anyway, Anyways) they think of their careers.   19. _____

20. Ruth (was scarcely, wasn't scarcely) in the running for supervisor.   20. _____

21. What (sort of a, sort of) job would you want?   21. _____

22. Maud broke her leg when she fell (off of a, off a) chair.   22. _____

23. She (don't, doesn't) feel too good.   23. _____

24. (This here, This) accident was unfortunate.   24. _____

25. Maud waited (an hour, a hour) for the doctor.   25. _____

Your Total Score _____ /25

If your score was 19 or less, review Section 33, pages 203-204, before continuing.

110 Practice Procedure Complete each of the following sentences by writing in the blank provided at the right the correct word or words in the parentheses. Score one point for each correct answer.

Answers

1. (Try and, Try to) list our three most populated cities.

1. _____

2. You (hadn't ought, ought not) to have listed Buffalo.

2. _____

3. He (doesn't, don't) know any of the five largest cities.

3. _____

4. (Was, Were) you able to list New York and Los Angeles?

4. _____

5. Our friends (plan to go, plan on going) to Disneyland.

5. _____

6. The Valdez family (can't hardly, can hardly) wait to return to San Antonio.

6. _____

7. (Aren't you, Ain't you) glad you went to Arizona?

7. _____

8. (Almost everybody, Most everybody) wants to visit Washington, D.C.

8. _____

9. (This kind of a, This kind of) trip would be fun.

9. _____

10. San Francisco is (different from, different than) Los Angeles.

10. _____

11. We (brought, brung) back souvenirs from Philadelphia.

11. _____

12. My great grandfather (might have, might of) been related to Sam Houston.

12. _____

13. (Where, Where at) is the Alamo?

13. _____

14. (Anyways, Anyway) we saw the movie about Sam Houston.

14. _____

15. She (seldom, seldom ever) heard of the California gold rush.

15. _____

16. It was a (long ways, long way) from San Diego to Memphis.

16. _____

17. There (was scarcely, wasn't scarcely) a book in our library about Pittsburgh.

17. _____

18. Some cities are (better, more better) than other cities.

18. _____

19. Baltimore was a (awfully good, very good) city to see historic areas.

19. _____

20. (Anywhere, Anywheres) you walk in our nation's capital is interesting.

20. _____

21. Vic and Lydia should (have went, have gone) to Boston.

21. _____

22. What (sort of, sort of a) car did you have in Boston?

22. _____

23. Lydia (says, sez) that she drove a rental car.

23. _____

24. Komuro and Kato (have got, have) a chance to work in Salem.

24. _____

25. Our trip last summer was (nowhere near, not nearly) as much fun as I had expected.

25. _____

Your Total Score _____ /25

If your score was 19 or less, review Section 33, pages 203-204, before continuing.

Classification of Sentences

OBJECTIVES
1. To recognize and use simple, compound, and complex sentences.
2. To recognize and use topic sentences.
3. To recognize and use linking words and phrases.
4. To write paragraphs applying the rules of grammar.

34-A THE SIMPLE SENTENCE

You have already learned that a *simple sentence* expresses a complete thought and has a subject and a verb (page 1).

Example 1

Connie played golf on Saturday.

Analysis:

Connie—subject
played—verb

Example 2

Bob visited his mother on Sunday.

Analysis:

Bob—subject
visited—verb

Example 3

Roberto lives in New York.

Analysis:

Roberto—subject
lives—verb

A simple sentence may have a *compound subject* (more than one) or a *compound verb* or both in the same sentence.

Example 1

Jack and Phyllis saw plays in London.

Analysis:

Jack, Phyllis—compound subject
saw—plural verb—agrees in number with the plural (compound) subject

Example 2

The sleeper tossed and turned.

Analysis:

sleeper—subject
tossed, turned—compound verb

Example 3

Toby and Bart ran and played in the park.

Analysis:

Toby, Bart—compound subject
ran, played—compound verb

34-B THE COMPOUND SENTENCE

A *compound sentence* contains two or more simple sentences connected by a coordinating conjunction (*and, but, or, nor, yet*). In a compound sentence, each simple sentence is called an independent clause. Each independent clause expresses a complete thought.

Example 1

The roses in our garden are beautiful, but our irises didn't do well.

Analysis:

Each of the underlined independent clauses expresses a complete thought and can stand alone as a simple sentence. Since the clauses are equal in rank, they are joined by the coordinating conjunction *but*.

Example 2

Carmen's birthday is in May, and my birthday is in January.

Analysis:

The independent clauses are joined by the coordinating conjunction *and*.

Example 3

The cactus will bloom tonight, or it may wait until tomorrow night.

Analysis:

The independent clauses are joined by the coordinating conjunction *or*.

34-C THE COMPLEX SENTENCE

A *complex sentence* contains an independent clause and one or more dependent clauses. An independent clause contains a subject and a verb (either or both of which may be compound) and expresses a complete thought. A dependent clause cannot stand alone and needs the independent (main) clause to make its meaning clear.

Example 1

Vince Mezzio, who scored the winning touchdown, lives in my hometown.

Analysis:

The underlined dependent clause does not make a complete statement and cannot stand alone. It needs the independent clause for its understanding.

Example 2

When the fog came in, everyone left the beach.

Analysis:

The underlined dependent clause needs the independent clause for its understanding.

Example 3

Before the starting gun sounded, Julie dashed ahead.

Analysis:

The underlined dependent clause needs the independent clause for its understanding.

Example 4

I don't think it will storm although the clouds look ominous.

Analysis:

The underlined dependent clause needs the independent clause for its understanding.

Example 5

The river, which overflowed its banks yesterday, is back to normal today.

Analysis:

The underlined dependent clause needs the independent clause for its understanding.

TRYOUT EXERCISE

Directions: Identify the following sentences as simple, compound, or complex. Write your answers in the blanks provided at the right. Check your answers on page 246 or with your teacher before continuing with your assignment.

1. The doors to the aircraft's cabin closed, and the plane moved away from the gate.

1. _____

2. Because the rain was especially heavy, the road washed out.

2. _____

3. The fog lifted in the afternoon.

3. _____

Complete Application Practices 111-112, pages 209-210, at this time.

111 Practice Procedure Identify the following sentences as simple (*S*), compound (*C*), or complex (*Cx*). Write your answers in the blanks provided at the right. Score one point for each correct answer.

Answers

1. A low tide provides good views of tide pools.

1. _____

2. The tidal area, which is divided into three zones, is home to many plants and animals.

2. _____

3. Plants and animals adapt to their environments in different ways.

3. _____

4. Some sea creatures live in their own armor, but some live in the armor of others.

4. _____

5. A few sea creatures live under rocks, and others live in the sea's sandy bottom.

5. _____

6. The starfish, which attaches itself to rocks, is strong enough to withstand the movement of the waves.

6. _____

7. The mussel is a favorite food of the starfish.

7. _____

8. Crabs, although a common sight at tide pools, hide in the rocks to avoid detection.

8. _____

9. Because hermit carbs live in empty snail shells, one must look carefully to find them.

9. _____

10. The sea cucumber, which resembles a cucumber, actually has tube feet like a starfish.

10. _____

11. The sea urchin lives on the outer rocks, and it is able to remain there despite heavy surf.

11. _____

12. Because sea urchins can't move around, the tide brings food to them.

12. _____

13. Sea urchins usually live in clusters on the rocks.

13. _____

14. The octopus can change colors, and it can squeeze itself into cracks of almost any size.

14. _____

15. The sea slug, which is brilliantly colored, has a soft and unarmored body.

15. _____

16. When the tide is out, barnacles remain closed to keep from drying out.

16. _____

17. Black turban snails, which are high up on rocks, look like pebbles.

17. _____

18. Chitons are well camouflaged.

18. _____

19. Chitons are oval shaped and colorful, and they usually can be found under rocks and in crevices.

19. _____

20. Anemones, which are frequently green or red, are known as the flowers of the tide pool.

20. _____

21. Tentacles, though harmless to humans, are used to paralyze an anemone's prey.

21. _____

22. In some tide pools, barnacles are forced out by mussels.

22. _____

23. Creatures in a tide pool fight for food and space.

23. _____

24. Because of jagged rocks, shoes should be worn when visiting tide pools.

24. _____

25. Visitors should enjoy the tide pools, but they should not disturb or remove anything there.

25. _____

Your Total Score _____ /25

If your score was 19 or less, review Section 34, pages 207-208, before continuing.

Name

Date

Score

/25

112-A Practice Procedure Construct complete sentences by adding *independent clauses* to the dependent clauses listed below. The dependent clause may be used any place in the sentence. Try to make your sentences interesting. Write them on a separate sheet of paper. Score one point for each correct sentence.

1. whenever he leaves

2. after I talked

3. if she answers my letter

4. while I was waiting for the bus

5. before I left home

6. as I read the newspaper

7. when the doorbell rang

8. although I was accepted

9. unless you call me

10. because he didn't write the letter

11. if mother answers the phone

12. when the video ended

13. although he liked cake

14. since the telephone was busy

112-B Practice Procedure Construct complete sentences by adding *dependent clauses* to the independent clauses listed below. The dependent clause may be used any place in the sentence. Try to make your sentences interesting. Write them on a separate sheet of paper. Score one point for each correct sentence.

1. she ran for club president

2. the bus was early

3. school starts next week

4. the play was sold out

5. Shauna was elected treasurer

6. the huge wave crashed over the boat

7. the cat's name was Ebony

8. Rita is a physician

9. the road was flooded

10. he asked a key question

11. the bike was stolen

12. she always is a good sport

13. John left the room

14. Elaine spoke to the principal

112-C Practice Procedure Make compound sentences from the independent clauses listed below. Match a clause from Column A with a clause from Column B using an appropriate coordinating conjunction. In the space provided, write the letter of the clause and the conjunction. Score one point for each correct match and one point for each correct conjunction.

Column A	Column B	Answers
1. The lawn will be cut today	A. we found seats anyway	1. _____
2. The streets were flooded	B. I couldn't eat it	2. _____
3. Fritz arrived early	C. they canceled school	3. _____
4. The dessert looked good	D. I may do it tomorrow	4. _____
5. The bus was crowded	E. he missed the bus	5. _____

Your Total Score _____ /38

If your score was 29 or less for 112-A, 112-B, and 112-C, review Section 34, pages 207-208, before continuing.

The Paragraph

Almost every part of our lives is directed by rules. We learn to play games, drive our cars, and govern ourselves by them. Rules have also been developed to help us talk with each other and to express ourselves in written form so that we understand each other. Most people pattern their speech and writing after these rules. Those who don't are often misunderstood.

The real purpose of learning grammar rules is to learn to express ourselves clearly so that other people can understand what we are trying to say or write. We have already studied the rules. Now we are going to apply them.

Do you remember what a sentence is? A *sentence* is a group of words expressing a complete thought. It contains at least a subject and a verb.

Do you know what a paragraph is? A *paragraph* is a group of sentences working together to explain or describe a single topic. It is usually short but must be long enough to make the topic clear. Details, reasons, or examples in paragraphs are arranged in a logical manner. The amount and kinds are left up to the writer. Each detail, however, is related to the paragraph's single topic. Identify the topic and the details that support it in the following paragraph:

There is a saying that reads, "After the wreck comes the reckoning." If you were involved in an automobile accident, however

minor, at any time in your life, you know that the reckoning wasn't easy. Even if there were no doctor bills or lawsuits to worry about, you probably found that there were questions to be answered, official forms to be filled out, property damage to be paid for, and perhaps days and weeks of irritating delay and inconvenience. Multiply all the details of your accident by several million, and you will realize that the task of reckoning last year's history of automobile smashups was both difficult and distressing.

In the preceding paragraph about the aftermath of an automobile accident, the first sentence attracts your attention and makes you want to continue reading. The listing of the various details (bills, damage, inconvenience, and so on) helps to further stimulate the reader's attention and maintain interest.

In order to write a good paragraph, the following qualities should be applied:

1. Look with an observing eye so that you can actually describe the details you see.
2. Select the right words to tell what you see.
3. Develop the ability to share your experiences through the correct use of words.
4. Keep to the point.

35-A THE TOPIC SENTENCE

A *topic sentence* expresses the central thought of the paragraph. The first sentence in a paragraph is usually the topic sentence. Sometimes it is repeated in a summary sentence to conclude the paragraph. Occasionally, for a particular effect, experienced writers prefer to place it at the end of the paragraph only. But wherever it is placed, the topic sentence should catch the

reader's interest so that he or she will want to continue reading.

After the topic sentence, the paragraph should be developed by using other sentences to expand on the topic sentence. Ideas should be presented in a sensible, concise, and natural order. Each sentence should include additional details that keep to the point.

35-B LINKING WORDS AND PHRASES

Linking words and phrases make it possible for sentences within a paragraph to hold together in a proper or smooth manner. That is, the reader is led through the paragraph without experiencing sudden gaps in thought. Linking words and phrases are used to tie the sentences together.

Example 1

First bait your hook. Then drop your line in the water.

Analysis:

First—linking word
Then—linking word
Each word shows a proper time relationship between the two sentences.

Example 2

Over the mantel hung an Early American print. On the mantel sat a brass clock.

Analysis:

Over the mantel—linking phrase
On the mantel—linking phrase
Each phrase locates the details as seen by the writer.

Example 3

In the spring Hannah played tennis. In the summer she practiced swimming.

Analysis:

In the spring—linking phrase
In the summer—linking phrase
Each phrase makes a contrast between the two sentences.

Example 4

This semester Joshua studied hard every night. As a result, he earned good marks.

Analysis:

As a result—linking phrase—It states the effect of the sentence preceding it.

Example 5

Lee is a good comedian. For example, her material is new and up-to-date. Likewise, her delivery is clear and appropriate.

Analysis:

For example—linking phrase which gives an example
Likewise—linking word which adds to the example previously given

TRYOUT EXERCISE   **Directions:** Construct topic sentences from the suggestions below. Check your sentences with your teacher before continuing with your assignment.

1. first day at a new school _____

_____

_____

2. the food was delicious _____

_____

_____

Complete Application Practices 113-120, pages 213-220, at this time.

Writing Topic Sentences

113 Practice Procedure The most important sentence in a paragraph is the topic sentence. It states in general terms what the paragraph is all about. Choose 10 of the 15 suggestions for paragraph topics listed below and write 10 topic sentences. Score one point for each correct topic sentence.

1. television sitcoms _____

   _____

2. an earthquake _____

   _____

3. a favorite sports personality _____

   _____

4. cleaning the house _____

   _____

5. a headache _____

   _____

6. a hotdog with mustard _____

   _____

7. a visit _____

   _____

8. redecorating _____

   _____

9. a new brother or sister _____

   _____

10. a first date _____

    _____

11. selecting a college _____

    _____

12. aerobics _____

    _____

13. life in a small town _____

    _____

14. fishing _____

    _____

15. making someone happy _____

    _____

Your Total Score _____ /10

If your score was 7 or less, review Section 35-A, page 211, before continuing.

114-A Practice Procedure Identify the following sentences as simple (*S*), compound (*C*), or complex (*Cx*). Write your answers in the blanks provided at the right. Score one point for each correct answer.

Answers

1. The U.S. Supreme Court is in Washington, D.C.

   1. _____

2. Washington, D.C., which is the nation's capital, is a beautiful city.

   2. _____

3. The White House is near the Washington Monument, and the tidal basin includes the Jefferson Memorial.

   3. _____

4. The Capital subway train may be ridden by visitors, but the train has priority seating for Senators.

   4. _____

5. The Smithsonian Institute, which is a wonderful museum, is housed in several buildings.

   5. _____

6. Although a tram takes visitors around to most Capital sights, there is still much walking to do.

   6. _____

7. Arlington Cemetery is across the Potomac River in Virginia.

   7. _____

114-B Practice Procedure Three topic sentences are given below. Following each topic sentence are a number of statements. Three of these statements support the topic sentence. Identify these by underlining them. Score one point for each correct response.

Your Score

1. It was probably the most enjoyable circus I've ever seen.

   1. _____

   a. The ringmaster was tall, had a good voice, and kept the show moving along smartly.
   b. The acrobats fell down.
   c. The wild animals were well trained and performed without a hitch.
   d. The clowns were terrible.
   e. In the middle of the show the tent blew down.
   f. The high flyers were spectacular.

2. The blue carpeting was a good economical choice for the living room.

   2. _____

   a. The blue color faded almost immediately.
   b. The blue color went well with the sofa.
   c. It had a rough texture that I liked.
   d. It didn't show spots.
   e. It was too expensive.
   f. The color clashed with everything in the room.

3. The town was a good place for us to live.

   3. _____

   a. Traffic on the town streets was congested.
   b. It wasn't too big and it wasn't too small.
   c. The elementary school was badly overcrowded.
   d. The nearest hospital was forty miles away.
   e. The house we bought was just right.
   f. The people in the town are friendly.

Your Total Score _____ /16

If your score was 12 or less, review Section 34, pages 207-208, and Section 35-A, page 211, before continuing.

115-A Practice Procedure Underline the linking words and linking phrases in the following paragraphs. These words make it possible for the sentences in a paragraph to relate smoothly to one another and to achieve unity in the paragraph. Score one point for each correct answer.

1. From the outset, I knew my driving trip was going to be a disaster. First, my alarm clock failed to wake me up. Then, rushing to the shower I slipped and hit my head on the bathroom sink. A short time later, my suitcase wouldn't lock, and I had to repack in one borrowed from my parents. Finally, my car wouldn't start. As a result, I stayed home! Do you blame me?

2. The view from our hotel balcony was truly spectacular! To begin with, the color of the sea was a striking azure blue. Next, the pounding white breakers made a dramatic contrast to the lovely sea. To the left, a sandy white beach dotted by waving palm trees awaited us. To the right, a sparkling, oval-shaped swimming pool was an inviting attraction. Last of all, a cloudless blue, blue sky framed the whole scene to perfection.

3. Preparing the soil for a garden is important. For instance, if the soil isn't properly prepared, the garden may fail. In the first place, the soil should be moist but not soggy. So, waiting to begin your work until a few days after the garden has been watered is a good idea. Then, select a suitable spade or shovel. Dig and loosen the soil to a depth of about a foot. Next, mix in some mulch and fertilizer and level the soil with a rake. When the soil is level, you're ready to plant. Last of all, weed it, water it, and enjoy it.

115-B Practice Procedure Try your hand at using linking words and phrases and see how much your writing will improve. On a separate sheet of paper, write two short paragraphs selected from the topic sentences below. Title the paragraphs. Score ten points for each properly written paragraph.

1. It's really fun to read!

2. That old desk is an heirloom.

3. The school year opened with a bang!

4. Exercising is good for you.

5. The film was the worst I've ever seen.

Your Total Score _____ /38

If your score was 29 or less for 115-A and 115-B, review Section 35-B, page 212, before continuing.

Paragraph Order and Development

116-A Practice Procedure As you have learned, the topic sentence tells the reader what the paragraph is about. It is a preview of coming attractions. The rest of the sentences provide the details promised by the topic sentence. The total paragraph should flow in an orderly way from sentence to sentence. In the paragraph below, there is no sentence order. Rearrange the sentences on a separate sheet of paper until they are properly placed and the paragraph holds together. Score one point for each sentence properly placed.

Finally, a U.S. Navy ship brought up the rear, the decks lined with white uniformed sailors waving and calling out to the crowds along the way.   First, the old sternwheeler, *Delta Countess*, passed by with flags flying and bunting draped from the railings.   The program was divided into three parts.   As the navy ship moved along, red, white, and blue rockets were fired off its bow.   This year's Fourth of July Harbor Festival was the best ever.   Next came a group of some forty sailboats of various sizes.   Each boat had brightly colored sails that billowed in the steady breeze.   Without question, the rockets were a spectacular climax to a thoroughly enjoyable holiday treat.

116-B Practice Procedure In this exercise you are given the beginnings of two paragraphs. Complete one of the paragraphs in your own words. Remember to add the details in a logical order and to link the sentences so that there is smoothness from one sentence to another. Score ten points for a complete and logical paragraph.

1. It was a cold, dark, rainy day in early December. _____

_____

_____

_____

_____

_____

_____

2. The black and white photograph showed a man, a woman, and a small child standing on the porch of a house. _____

_____

_____

_____

_____

_____

_____

Your Total Score _____ /18

If your score was 13 or less for 116-A and 116-B, review Section 35, pages 211-212, before continuing.

Paragraph Construction

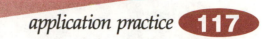

117-A Practice Procedure Select one of the following topic sentences and expand it into a short paragraph of five to ten sentences. Remember to use sentences that give reasons, details, facts, similarities and differences, or examples to support the topic sentence. List your ideas on a separate sheet of paper before including them in your paragraph. Score ten points for a complete and orderly paragraph.

1. Choosing the right automobile isn't always easy.
2. I enjoy chicken, but I don't like fish.
3. The car ran out of gas at the bottom of the hill.
4. TV can be both boring and exciting.

_____

_____

_____

_____

_____

_____

_____

_____

_____

_____

117-B Practice Procedure Follow the procedure given for 117-A.

1. The brochure about the trip sounded wonderful.
2. When I returned to my room, the money was missing.
3. The TV news program lasted for a full hour.
4. The letter from them was in this morning's mail.

_____

_____

_____

_____

_____

_____

_____

_____

_____

_____

Your Total Score _____ /20

If your score was 15 or less for 117-A and 117-B, review Section 35, pages 211-212, before continuing.

Name

Date

Score

/20

/15

Score

Date

Name

118-A Practice Procedure Match each item in Column A with the item it describes in Column B. Be especially careful, as some of them are similar. Write the identifying letter from Column A in the blank provided at the right. Score one point for each correct answer.

Column A	Column B	Answers
a. expresses the central thought of a paragraph	**1.** paragraph	**1.** _____
b. linking words	**2.** topic sentence	**2.** _____
c. contains an independent clause and one or more dependent clauses	**3.** compound sentence	**3.** _____
	4. That <u>boy and girl</u> are members of the team.	
d. contains a compound subject		**4.** _____
e. contains a dependent clause	**5.** as a result, for instance	**5.** _____
f. a group of words (with subject and verb) that expresses a complete thought	**6.** The secretary <u>who took the dictation</u> is absent.	**6.** _____
g. a group of sentences dealing with a single topic	**7.** The owner of the sailboat <u>scraped and painted</u> it.	**7.** _____
h. contains two or more independent clauses connected by a coordinating conjunction	**8.** next, first, finally	**8.** _____
	9. simple sentence	**9.** _____
i. linking phrases	**10.** complex sentence	**10.** _____
j. contains a compound verb		

118-B Practice Procedure Follow the procedure given for 118-A.

Column A	Column B	
a. topic sentence	**1.** Because it rained, we left.	**1.** _____
b. compound sentence	**2.** Keeps to the point	**2.** _____
c. complex sentence	**3.** the first or last sentence in a paragraph	**3.** _____
d. linking words or phrases		
e. paragraph	**4.** Mother's birthday is in June, and Father's birthday is in January.	**4.** _____
	5. hold sentences in a paragraph together	**5.** _____

Your Total Score _____ /15

If your score was 11 or less for 118-A and 118-B, review Unit 11 before continuing.

119-A Practice Procedure Identify the following sentences as simple (*S*), compound (*C*), or complex (*Cx*). Write your answers in the blanks provided at the right. Score one point for each correct answer. In addition, fill in all the necessary punctuation and draw a circle around each inserted punctuation mark. Score one point for each correct response.

Answers

1. Tanya is a good golfer

2. Leon who is our best golfer will play in the tournament

3. Jack is a better player than Tanya

4. Tim and Debbie play golf once in awhile

5. Tim and Debbie have a 10 a m starting time and Tanya and Jack will start playing at noon

6. Elise took golf lessons but she did not improve her golf game

7. Because the heavy rain ruined the greens the tournament was canceled

8. All of us waited for the rain to stop

9. The game of golf which originated in Scotland is a popular sport in America

10. Although golf can be expensive I still play as often as possible

1. _____
2. _____
3. _____
4. _____
5. _____
6. _____
7. _____
8. _____
9. _____
10. _____

Your Total Score _____ /30

119-B Practice Procedure Underline the linking words and phrases in the following paragraph. In addition, fill in all the necessary punctuation and capitalization. Draw a circle around each punctuation mark added and a circle around each letter that should be capitalized. Score one point for each correct response.

i planned a surprise birthday party for my friend and it went off without a hitch first i made a list of all her relatives and friends next i eliminated the names of people who would be away on the date of the party finally i cut out people who might not enjoy coming for one reason or another as a consequence i ended up with a list of some fifty people before doing anything else i made certain that both the recreation room in our apartment complex and the caterer would be available the night of the birthday this confirmed i selected the invitations addressed them included notes to everyone that the party was to be kept a surprise and took them to the post office as a final safeguard i invited my friend to accompany me to a play on the night of her birthday and she accepted as you can see she was set up but good

Your Total Score _____ /47

If your score was 59 or less for 119-A and 119-B, review Sections 34-35, pages 207-208 and 211-212, before continuing.

120 Practice Procedure Utilizing the topic details given below, prepare paragraphs, including topic sentences, that support the requirements for a paragraph as described in Section 35, page 211. Write your paragraphs in the space provided. Score five points for each correct paragraph.

1. Topic: Oysters

Details:
a. Oysters can produce pearls.
b. Oysters are usually 2-10 inches in length.
c. Oysters have irregular shells.
d. Oysters are bivalves.
e. Oysters are common in warm waters.

_____

_____

_____

_____

_____

_____

_____

_____

2. Topic: New York's Central Park

Details:
a. Central Park attracts many people.
b. In 1857 Central Park was created out of a swampland and a city dump.
c. Central Park is known to many as a beautiful green refuge from the surrounding city life.
d. Central Park covers over 843 acres.
e. Central Park contains everything from a world famous museum to a sheep meadow.

_____

_____

_____

_____

_____

_____

_____

_____

Your Total Score _____ /10

If your score was 7 or less, review Section 35, pages 211-212.

121 Practice Procedure Complete each of the following sentences by writing in the blank provided at the right the correct word or words in the parentheses. This is a review quiz of all of the preceding units. Score one point for each correct answer.

Answers

1. (Who's, Whose) teacher visited Washington, D.C.?　　1. _____

2. With (who, whom) did she travel?　　2. _____

3. The Declaration of Independence is different (from, than) our Constitution.　　3. _____

4. Who (don't, doesn't) know the difference?　　4. _____

5. Which one of the two documents (was, were) signed first?　　5. _____

6. (What, Which) one is more important—the Constitution or the Declaration?　　6. _____

7. (Who's, Whose) signature was first on the Declaration?　　7. _____

8. What (is, are) the Bill of Rights?　　8. _____

9. Who else (beside, besides) Jefferson signed both those documents?　　9. _____

10. How many signers of our Constitution (was, were) there?　　10. _____

11. (Their, There) were 38 signatures.　　11. _____

12. Was it your aunt (who, whom) has a copy of the Bill of Rights?　　12. _____

13. From (who, whom) did she get it?　　13. _____

14. Mr. Garrick paid more for his copy than (she, her).　　14. _____

15. (Between, Among) the 38 signatures were many patriotic Americans.　　15. _____

16. George Washington didn't look (as, like) Hamilton.　　16. _____

17. Washington (sure, surely) deserved to be our first President.　　17. _____

18. His military strategy was better (than, then) that of the British.　　18. _____

19. (Where, Where at) is our Constitution displayed?　　19. _____

20. My cousin took my brother and (I, me) to see both historic documents.　　20. _____

21. (It's, Its) really worth visiting our nation's capital.　　21. _____

22. We flew there and (than, then) we rented a car.　　22. _____

23. The White House is a (real, very) fine building.　　23. _____

24. (Ain't, Isn't) that an exciting city to visit?　　24. _____

25. What (kind of, kind of a) trip are you planning next?　　25. _____

Your Total Score _____ /25

122 Practice Procedure Complete each of the following sentences by writing in the blank provided at the right the correct word or words in the parentheses. This is a review quiz of material in all the preceding units. Score one point for each correct answer.

Answers

1. Just between you and (I, me) that was an interesting Career Day.   1. _____

2. If anyone gets a job (their, there), Ann will.   2. _____

3. The personnel managers gave (us, we) applicants some hints.   3. _____

4. We (sat, set) quietly and listened to them.   4. _____

5. Amy (lies, lays) her papers on the manager's desk.   5. _____

6. The speaker's notes (lay, laid) on my desk for a week.   6. _____

7. (Lie, Lay) your application forms next to your seat.   7. _____

8. My notes about jobs are still (lying, laying) there.   8. _____

9. The clerk (sat, set) my form in the file.   9. _____

10. (Let, Leave) your resume with the employment office.   10. _____

11. Miss Ruiz (learned, taught) us about job opportunities.   11. _____

12. Mr. Grant (shall, will) call if a job becomes available.   12. _____

13. Miss Thomas (don't, doesn't) like to promise any jobs.   13. _____

14. I would have (gone, went) with you if I had heard.   14. _____

15. Neither of the applicants (is, are) certain of a job.   15. _____

16. I (saw, seen) the results of the interviews.   16. _____

17. Each of the workers there (offer, offers) ideas to the company.   17. _____

18. (Who, Whom) do you see for a promotion?   18. _____

19. From (who, whom) did you get references?   19. _____

20. Several of them and (us, we) were called for another interview.   20. _____

21. Gerry, (who, whom), I believe, has an aunt in the firm, was offered a job.   21. _____

22. (Bring, Take) me the book about office procedures.   22. _____

23. All of us (has, have) our ideas about work habits.   23. _____

24. Lydia was offered (to, too, two) jobs.   24. _____

25. She (ought not, hadn't ought) to refuse any job.   25. _____

Your Total Score _____ /25

123 Practice Procedure Complete each of the following sentences by writing in the blank provided at the right the correct word or words in the parentheses. This is a short review quiz on material in the preceding units. Score one point for each correct answer.

Answers

1. A good writer is one (that, which) is entertaining.

1. _____

2. (Us, We) pupils have read fascinating books this year.

2. _____

3. The class (was, were) interested in *A Tale of Two Cities* by Dickens.

3. _____

4. Either Paul or Heidi (has, have) copies of Dickens' books.

4. _____

5. (Who, Whom) do you think reads his stories now?

5. _____

6. Kimberly likes to read any book (which, that) is funny.

6. _____

7. Edgar Allan Poe's mysteries scare Colin and (she, her).

7. _____

8. Our librarian recommends good books to them and (I, me).

8. _____

9. Nancy, (who, which) was once an actress, likes plays.

9. _____

10. We borrowed Tom Clancy's new novel from Jodi and (he, him).

10. _____

11. Many of my friends read (his, their) reports aloud.

11. _____

12. Puzo's latest book was (better, more good) than his previous novel.

12. _____

13. Ms. Cody (brought, brung) back some books from Wales.

13. _____

14. What (kind of, kind of a) writer was Ms. Cody?

14. _____

15. Some students (seldom, seldom ever) visit their library.

15. _____

16. Max (can hardly, can't hardly) wait to read a good book.

16. _____

17. (Who, Whom) has seen the rare books in the Huntington Library?

17. _____

18. (This, This here) library has many famous manuscripts.

18. _____

19. (Inside the, Inside of the) library is the first Bible printed.

19. _____

20. Our teachers (plan to go, plan on going) there soon.

20. _____

21. Mrs. Chan (don't, doesn't) want to miss the lectures.

21. _____

22. Our town library is (not nearly, nowhere near) as large as yours.

22. _____

23. Did you plan to go with Gordie and (they, them)?

23. _____

24. The teacher will give a pass to (whoever, whomever) wants to go.

24. _____

25. She is a teacher (who, whom) we respected.

25. _____

Your Total Score _____ /25

124 Practice Procedure Complete each of the following sentences by writing in the blank provided at the right the correct word or words in the parentheses. This is a review quiz on material in the preceding units. Score one point for each correct answer.

Answers

1. (Try and, Try to) find a book that lists the great rivers of the world. 1. _____

2. Freddie and Carla (grew up, growed up) along the Mississippi River. 2. _____

3. (Was, Were) you aware that the Mississippi is a long river? 3. _____

4. (It's, Its) the longest river in the United States. 4. _____

5. (Who's, Whose) grandfather was a river pilot? 5. _____

6. It (sure, surely) is a pleasure to sail down the river. 6. _____

7. Everyone (know, knows) what "down the river" means. 7. _____

8. It is a good feeling to (lie, lay) in bed and watch the stars. 8. _____

9. Julie sat (beside, besides) the captain of the boat at dinner. 9. _____

10. (What, Which) is the longer river—the Missouri or the Snake? 10. _____

11. (Anyway, Anyways) we all had a good laugh. 11. _____

12. You (shall, will) enjoy floating along the shoreline. 12. _____

13. How many lakes (is, are) there in the Great Lakes? 13. _____

14. (Their, There) are five of them. 14. _____

15. Between Heidi and (I, me) we came up with the answer. 15. _____

16. One of the (most pretty, prettiest) rivers is the St. Lawrence. 16. _____

17. We (saw, seen) a travelogue about the Nile River. 17. _____

18. (Their, There) uncle knew the captain of the *Delta Queen*. 18. _____

19. The captain of the boat, (who, which) is an American, is friendly. 19. _____

20. What is the (worse, worst) boat ride imaginable? 20. _____

21. Our teacher told us to (bring, take) our charts of the world's artificial lakes to class tomorrow. 21. _____

22. On the boat trip Sal and Jennie dived (in, into) the river. 22. _____

23. (Their, There) bathing suits never did dry. 23. _____

24. At the harbor Jennie (than, then) bought a new robe. 24. _____

25. Andrea tried to behave (as, like) me. 25. _____

Your Total Score _____ /25

To spell correctly is an important part of the communication process. When you allow misspelled words to creep into your writing, such words stand out as if they were sore thumbs. You should do everything possible to avoid misspellings, for they can be a source of embarrassment to you, the writer, and can be misleading or confusing to the reader.

Historically, the English language was heavily influenced by other languages. Principally, these languages were those brought to the British Isles by invaders over many hundreds of years. English, therefore, is filled with words, pronunciations, and spellings borrowed from Old English (Anglo-Saxon), Old French, Latin, and Greek.

Over a long period of time, numerous attempts were made to standardize or otherwise make sense of the spelling of English words, especially in keeping with how the words were pronounced, but these met with little success. Even printers tried their hand at it. Finally, Dr. Samuel Johnson's dictionary, published in 1765, became a true spelling guide for the British.

The English colonists brought their language with them to America where Johnson's work proved to be useful in the colonies, as well. Soon, however, the spellings of some British words were simplified by Noah Webster, an American interested in furthering correct spelling. Webster's spelling changes resulted in such words as *color* and *connection* (American) replacing *colour* and *connexion* (British).

A greater problem for spellers than different British and American spellings is that the spelling of English words is not logical. Sounds are spelled in many different ways, and even though some words sound alike, they frequently are not spelled the same (*ate* and *eight, their* and *there*). There is no uniform relationship between spelling and pronunciation. Another obstacle is that many English words contain letters that are silent and are not pronounced aloud (*debt* and *receipt*).

Despite these many problems, useful spelling rules do exist. If studied and mastered, the following rules will help you become a good speller and writer.

1. *Make a distinction between* ie *and* ei.

   Memorize this jingle:
   > Use *i* before *e*
   > Except after *c*
   > Or when sounded like *a*
   > As in *neighbor* or *weigh*.

   Examples

i before *e*	*ei* after *c*	*ei* when sounded like *a*
achieve	ceiling	eight
brief	deceiving	freight
piece	receiving	weight

2. *Drop the final* e *when a suffix (end of the word) beginning with a vowel is added, but not before a suffix beginning with a consonant.*

   a. Drop the final *e* before a suffix beginning with a vowel:

Examples	advise + able = advisable
	locate + ion = location
	score + ing = scoring
	sense + ible = sensible

Exceptions	dye + ing = dyeing (distinguished from *dying*)
	service + able = serviceable (keeps *c* sound soft before *a* or *o*)
	outrage + ous = outrageous (keeps *g* sound soft before *a* or *o*

   b. Keep final *e* before a suffix beginning with a consonant:

Examples	arrange + ment = arrangement
	entire + ly = entirely
	hate + ful = hateful
	nine + ty = ninety

Exceptions	Some words adding *ful* or *ly* drop the final *e*:
	awe + ful = awful
	due + ly = duly
	Some words adding *ment* drop the final *e*:
	argue + ment = argument
	judge + ment = judgment

3. *Final* y *when preceded by a consonant is usually changed to* i *when a suffix is added except before a suffix beginning with* i.

Examples   busy + er = busier
easy + ly = easily
nasty + ness = nastiness
try + es = tries

Exceptions   baby + ish = babyish
carry + ing = carrying

4. *Double the final single consonant before adding a suffix that begins with a vowel when a single vowel precedes the consonant and the consonant ends an accented syllable or a single syllable word.*

Examples   admit + ed = admitted
big + er = bigger
commit + ed = committed
forget + able = forgettable
get + ing = getting
refer + ing = referring

5. *Make nouns plural by adding* s *or* es.

a. Add *s* when the noun ends in a sound that can be smoothly united with an *s*.

Examples   bell = bells
chat = chats
night = nights
stair = stairs

Exceptions   buffalo = buffaloes
echo = echoes

b. Add *es* when the noun ends in a sound that cannot be smoothly united with an *s*.

Examples   couch = couches
dish = dishes
rash = rashes
tax = taxes

c. Change *y* to *i* and add *es* when the noun ends in a *y* that is preceded by a consonant.

Examples   berry = berries
lady = ladies
sky = skies
trophy = trophies

d. Add *s* when the noun ends in a *y* that is preceded by *a, e, o,* or *u*.

Examples   bay = bays
day = days
toy = toys
tray = trays

6. *Pronounce words properly, establish spelling as a habit, and use a quick and easy drill.*

a. Pronunciation:

Some words are spelled just as they sound; others are not. Still, pronunciation of words can be of assistance to you in learning how to spell.

If you mispronounce a word, you're almost certain to misspell it too. For example, it's athlete, not athalete; drowned, not drownded; perspire, not prespire; lightning, not lightening. If you pronounce a word correctly, you will have a better chance of spelling it correctly.

b. Habit:

Spelling is really a habit. Learn to spell a word correctly and you will probably never misspell it. Eventually you will correctly spell words without thinking about them. You will have established a good spelling habit.

c. Easy drill:

Use the following drill to help you establish a good spelling habit:

(1) Look at the word.
(2) Say the word to yourself.
(3) If the word is more than one syllable, break it into syllables.
(4) Look at each letter.
(5) In your mind, ''write'' the word.
(6) On paper, write the word.
(7) Check the spelling of the word with your list.
(8) On paper, write the word a second and a third time.
(9) If you correctly wrote the word on paper three times, you've probably learned it for good.
(10) If you were unable to correctly write the word on paper three times, you will need to restudy the word.

ie and *ei* Words

Spelling 1-A Practice Procedure Study the spelling of the following *ie* and *ei* words. In each group of words, one is misspelled. Circle the misspelled word. Score one point for each correct response. For assistance refer to Spelling Rule 1 on page 225.

Your Score

1. achieve, anxiety, beleive, ceiling   1. _____

2. efficient, fiery, greif, handkerchief   2. _____

3. hurriedly, neice, piece, receive   3. _____

4. hygiene, liesure, notoriety, prairie   4. _____

5. frieght, obedience, reign, forfeit   5. _____

6. deceit, decieve, science, tries   6. _____

7. neighbor, shriek, seize, seige   7. _____

8. ceiling, mischievous, rien, sleigh   8. _____

9. conciet, field, priest, weight   9. _____

10. cheif, deceive, lenient, relieve   10. _____

Your Total Score _____ /10

Spelling 1-B Practice Procedure These 24 words contain an *ie* or *ei*. Write each word twice, spelling it correctly. Refer to the *ie* and *ei* spelling rules on page 225.

1. brief _____ _____	13. yield _____ _____
2. either _____ _____	14. alien _____ _____
3. weigh _____ _____	15. quiet _____ _____
4. seize _____ _____	16. weird _____ _____
5. height _____ _____	17. niece _____ _____
6. shriek _____ _____	18. neither _____ _____
7. piece _____ _____	19. fiend _____ _____
8. thief _____ _____	20. freight _____ _____
9. their _____ _____	21. siege _____ _____
10. rein _____ _____	22. chief _____ _____
11. eight _____ _____	23. feint _____ _____
12. grief _____ _____	24. friend _____ _____

The Final e; Commonly Misspelled Words

Spelling 2-A Practice Procedure In the spaces provided at the right, correctly spell each word with the suffix added. Score one point for each correct response. For assistance refer to Spelling Rule 2 on page 225.

Answers

1. divide + ed   1. _____

2. rescue + ed   2. _____

3. sure + ly   3. _____

4. change + able   4. _____

5. fine + ed   5. _____

6. like + ness   6. _____

7. elevate + ing   7. _____

8. use + ing   8. _____

9. pleasure + able   9. _____

10. hoe + ing   10. _____

Your Total Score _____ /10

Spelling 2-B Practice Procedure Here are 40 words that are frequently misspelled. Study them carefully and be prepared to write them from memory.

absence	develop	neighbor	rhythm
all right	efficient	original	ridiculous
altogether	embarrass	pertain	safety
appetite	favorite	piece	seize
basically	fourth	pledge	separate
believe	imagine	practice	shining
choose	loose	pursue	sponsor
chose	lose	receive	therefore
coarse	maintenance	relief	thorough
desperate	morale	religion	weird

228

The Final *y*; Commonly Misspelled Words

Spelling 3-A Practice Procedure In the spaces provided at the right, correctly spell each word with the suffix added. Score one point for each correct response. For assistance refer to Spelling Rule 3 on page 226.

Answers

1. easy + er   1. _____
2. individuality + es   2. _____
3. dignity + es   3. _____
4. worry + ing   4. _____
5. beauty + ful   5. _____
6. inferiority + es   6. _____
7. industry + es   7. _____
8. chatty + ness   8. _____
9. swarthy + ness   9. _____
10. hurry + ing   10. _____

Your Total Score _____ /10

Spelling 3-B Practice Procedure Here are 40 words that are frequently misspelled. Study them carefully and be prepared to write them from memory.

ambulance	breathe	disease	leisure
appreciate	brilliant	eliminate	prompt
arithmetic	carpenter	equipped	quart
arrange	chorus	fiftieth	relieve
athletes	clothes	genuine	satisfy
athletics	commit	hundred	sophomore
audience	committed	interrupt	stationary
aviator	concise	journey	stationery
bachelor	consonant	laughter	tenant
biography	disappear	legible	truly

Doubling the Final Single Consonant

Spelling 4-A Practice Procedure In the spaces provided at the right, correctly spell each word with the suffix added. Score one point for each correct response. For assistance refer to Spelling Rule 4 on page 226.

/20

Score

Date

Answers

1. sun + ing   1. _____

2. run + er   2. _____

3. remit + ed   3. _____

4. stir + ed   4. _____

5. buff + er   5. _____

6. bud + ing   6. _____

7. read + er   7. _____

8. stamp + ed   8. _____

9. get + ing   9. _____

10. lead + er   10. _____

Spelling 4-B Practice Procedure Follow the procedure given for Spelling 4-A.

Name

1. stop + ed   1. _____

2. omit + ing   2. _____

3. begin + er   3. _____

4. gap + ed   4. _____

5. butter + ed   5. _____

6. dent + ed   6. _____

7. gab + er   7. _____

8. recur + ing   8. _____

9. sit + ing   9. _____

10. stick + ing   10. _____

Your Total Score _____ /20

Spelling 5-A Practice Procedure In the spaces provided at the right, correctly spell each noun in its plural form. Score one point for each correct response. For assistance refer to Spelling Rule 5 on page 226.

Answers

1. picture   1. _____

2. bay   2. _____

3. hero   3. _____

4. dash   4. _____

5. nursery   5. _____

6. dart   6. _____

7. pouch   7. _____

8. chief   8. _____

9. dairy   9. _____

10. crane   10. _____

Spelling 5-B Practice Procedure Follow the procedure given for Spelling 5-A.

1. sale   1. _____

2. buoy   2. _____

3. baby   3. _____

4. bale   4. _____

5. canal   5. _____

6. lunch   6. _____

7. delivery   7. _____

8. snake   8. _____

9. majority   9. _____

10. fox   10. _____

Your Total Score _____ /20

Alphabetizing; British and American Spellings

spelling practice **6**

Spelling 6-A Practice Procedure Alphabetize the following words in the spaces provided at the right. Score one point for each correct response.

Answers

1. remiss
2. respect
3. release
4. reason
5. rights
6. recent
7. responsibilities
8. recognize
9. review
10. refuse

1. _____
2. _____
3. _____
4. _____
5. _____
6. _____
7. _____
8. _____
9. _____
10. _____

Your Total Score _____ /10

Spelling 6-B Practice Procedure Some of the following words are spelled in the British manner; some are spelled in American English. In the spaces provided, identify each and then label and spell each correctly (see the examples). Use your dictionary for help. Note that American dictionaries list American English spellings first because these are the preferred spellings. Score one point for each correct response.

Examples:

a. theatre	*British*	*theater*	*American*
b. apologize	*American*	*apologise*	*British*
1. clamor			
2. sombre			
3. mould			
4. inflection			
5. acknowledgment			
6. humor			
7. centre			
8. odor			
9. traveler			
10. plow			

Your Total Score _____ /30

Spelling Practice; Commonly Misspelled Words

Spelling 7-A Practice Procedure In each of the following pairs of words, one word is spelled correctly and one is not. Circle the misspelled word in each pair. Use your dictionary for help. Score one point for each correct response.

Your Score

1. fourth, fuorth   1. _____

2. absence, absense   2. _____

3. appriciate, appreciate   3. _____

4. disapline, discipline   4. _____

5. busness, business   5. _____

6. arrears, arears   6. _____

7. bookkeeping, bookeeping   7. _____

8. budget, bugget   8. _____

9. maintenence, maintenance   9. _____

10. embarass, embarrass   10. _____

Your Total Score _____ /10

Spelling 7-B Practice Procedure Here are 40 words that are frequently misspelled. Study them carefully and be prepared to write them from memory.

abundant	carefully	fabulous	package
accumulate	character	formerly	partner
advertisement	committee	government	physician
alphabet	consider	intelligence	pleasant
annual	continue	interfere	privilege
answer	describe	jealous	quite
applause	difficult	laboratory	responsible
argument	doesn't	launch	sentence
aviation	engineer	missile	specimen
between	existence	obedient	thousand

/100

Score

Date

Name

Spelling 8 Practice Procedure Here are 100 words that are frequently misspelled. Study them carefully and be prepared to write them from memory.

accommodate	descend	marvelous	recollect
acknowledge	desirable	messenger	recommend
aggravate	determined	mischievous	reliable
allegiance	dialogue	mortgage	relieve
amateur	distinguish	mosquito	respectfully
analysis	disappoint	mysterious	respectively
apparent	document	nuisance	riddle
appointment	eligible	occasion	salmon
approximately	embargo	opportunity	sergeant
assignment	emphasize	organized	significant
attendance	enthusiastically	parliament	soldier
auditorium	essential	particular	straightened
benefited	eventually	peculiar	substitute
chimney	exaggerate	permissible	surgeon
circumstance	extraordinary	politician	syllable
comparison	grammar	possession	sympathetic
competition	gymnasium	preparation	tongue
congratulate	hesitate	proceed	tremendous
congressional	immediate	prominent	unconscious
consequently	initiative	properly	unnecessary
correspondence	interpret	prosperous	valuable
courteous	irresistible	publicity	vegetable
deceive	license	receipt	view
decision	lieutenant	recipe	villain
delicious	loneliness	recognize	witty

Vocabulary Practice

Definitions

Vocabulary 1-A Practice Procedure Select the one word in the series that is closest in meaning to the numbered word. Write the letter that identifies the correct word in the blank provided at the right. Score one point for each correct answer.

Answers

1. fragile   **(a)** breakable   **(b)** sweet   **(c)** sturdy   **(d)** remains   **(e)** little   1. _____

2. distinctive   **(a)** usual   **(b)** unique   **(c)** matched   **(d)** improper   **(e)** chic   2. _____

3. reason   **(a)** proof   **(b)** faith   **(c)** refute   **(d)** answer   **(e)** motive   3. _____

4. recognize   **(a)** meet   **(b)** regard   **(c)** rework   **(d)** identify   **(e)** settle   4. _____

5. terminate   **(a)** frisk   **(b)** begin   **(c)** end   **(d)** graduate   **(e)** grow   5. _____

6. frank   **(a)** cute   **(b)** grouchy   **(c)** willing   **(d)** bored   **(e)** candid   6. _____

7. avoid   **(a)** abandon   **(b)** refuse   **(c)** ignore   **(d)** shun   **(e)** lessen   7. _____

8. frivolous   **(a)** violent   **(b)** serious   **(c)** trivial   **(d)** tardy   **(e)** monumental   8. _____

9. rectify   **(a)** reduce   **(b)** add   **(c)** correct   **(d)** satisfy   **(e)** strengthen   9. _____

10. contradict   **(a)** confirm   **(b)** regret   **(c)** pay   **(d)** contrast   **(e)** deny   10. _____

Vocabulary 1-B Practice Procedure Follow the procedure given for Vocabulary 1-A.

1. realistic   **(a)** put on   **(b)** lifelike   **(c)** varied   **(d)** fragile   **(e)** rigid   1. _____

2. remiss   **(a)** negligent   **(b)** despondent   **(c)** paid   **(d)** punctual   **(e)** avoid   2. _____

3. forecast   **(a)** mold   **(b)** fortune   **(c)** predict   **(d)** review   **(e)** fish   3. _____

4. stress   **(a)** boldness   **(b)** silence   **(c)** emphasis   **(d)** concern   **(e)** withdraw   4. _____

5. reluctant   **(a)** enthusiastic   **(b)** willing   **(c)** fresh   **(d)** fashionable   **(e)** unwilling   5. _____

6. obsolete   **(a)** outdated   **(b)** stubborn   **(c)** new   **(d)** topical   **(e)** reluctant   6. _____

7. skeptical   **(a)** frugal   **(b)** insulting   **(c)** tender   **(d)** feverish   **(e)** suspicious   7. _____

8. potential   **(a)** strong   **(b)** weak   **(c)** light   **(d)** possible   **(e)** frivolous   8. _____

9. rational   **(a)** logical   **(b)** illogical   **(c)** occasional   **(d)** unreasonable   **(e)** lazy   9. _____

10. appraise   **(a)** inform   **(b)** estimate   **(c)** verify   **(d)** laud   **(e)** near   10. _____

Your Total Score _____ /20

Antonyms

Vocabulary 2-A Practice Procedure Select the one word that is the *antonym* (word that means the opposite) for each numbered word. Write the letter of the word you select in the blank provided at the right. Score one point for each correct response.

Answers

1. dense   **(a)** rigid   **(b)** loose   **(c)** compact   **(d)** dark   **(e)** straight   1. _____

2. impede   **(a)** instruct   **(b)** defy   **(c)** condense   **(d)** assist   **(e)** block   2. _____

3. famine   **(a)** abundance   **(b)** starvation   **(c)** relative   **(d)** turmoil   **(e)** levity   3. _____

4. cautious   **(a)** sterile   **(b)** wistful   **(c)** reckless   **(d)** careful   **(e)** shy   4. _____

5. terse   **(a)** wordy   **(b)** concise   **(c)** bold   **(d)** silent   **(e)** taut   5. _____

6. apparent   **(a)** glaring   **(b)** obvious   **(c)** obscure   **(d)** visible   **(e)** assured   6. _____

7. elegant   **(a)** lofty   **(b)** stately   **(c)** coarse   **(d)** beautified   **(e)** lengthy   7. _____

8. frigid   **(a)** chilly   **(b)** warm   **(c)** cool   **(d)** vain   **(e)** formal   8. _____

9. contempt   **(a)** scorn   **(b)** criticism   **(c)** difference   **(d)** disgrace   **(e)** praise   9. _____

10. consumer   **(a)** contemporary   **(b)** seller   **(c)** teacher   **(d)** buyer   **(e)** contact   10. _____

Vocabulary 2-B Practice Procedure Follow the procedure given for Vocabulary 2-A.

1. surly   **(a)** suspicious   **(b)** obedient   **(c)** pleasant   **(d)** rude   **(e)** understanding   1. _____

2. obscure   **(a)** unique   **(b)** dirty   **(c)** hidden   **(d)** obvious   **(e)** old   2. _____

3. petty   **(a)** precious   **(b)** small   **(c)** inferior   **(d)** large   **(e)** exciting   3. _____

4. sarcastic   **(a)** sassy   **(b)** polite   **(c)** biting   **(d)** eager   **(e)** imposing   4. _____

5. jubilant   **(a)** happy   **(b)** trusting   **(c)** joyous   **(d)** inspiring   **(e)** unhappy   5. _____

6. despair   **(a)** fear   **(b)** hope   **(c)** anger   **(d)** depression   **(e)** hate   6. _____

7. explicit   **(a)** precise   **(b)** specific   **(c)** cold   **(d)** unclear   **(e)** outspoken   7. _____

8. contagious   **(a)** immune   **(b)** wary   **(c)** diseased   **(d)** opposite   **(e)** grateful   8. _____

9. commence   **(a)** begin   **(b)** succeed   **(c)** near   **(c)** speak   **(e)** end   9. _____

10. tumult   **(a)** event   **(b)** registration   **(c)** bubble   **(d)** turmoil   **(e)** order   10. _____

Your Total Score _____ /20

Homonyms and Homophones

Vocabulary 3 Practice Procedure *Homonyms* are words that sound the same and often have the same spelling, but differ in meaning. *Homophones* are words that sound the same, but have different spellings and differ in meaning. Both can be problems in spelling and understanding. Complete each of the following sentences by writing in the blank provided at the right the correct form of the word in the parentheses. Score one point for each correct answer.

Answers

1. We crossed the (boarder, border) into Mexico.   1. _____

2. The farmer (sheared, sheered) his sheep.   2. _____

3. They took a (plain, plane) to New York.   3. _____

4. It was a (tail, tale) told by an excellent writer.   4. _____

5. The expensive (stationary, stationery) was on sale.   5. _____

6. That (bolder, boulder) is heavy.   6. _____

7. We put a new (grate, great) in the fireplace.   7. _____

8. The city (waists, wastes) its funds.   8. _____

9. The price for the suit was (fair, fare).   9. _____

10. His foot slipped off the (brake, break).   10. _____

11. (Their, There) home was on a lake.   11. _____

12. He used all the (flour, flower) for a cake.   12. _____

13. The (oar, ore) was mined in Colorado.   13. _____

14. The pelicans (pray, prey) on fish.   14. _____

15. His (role, roll) in the play was that of the villain.   15. _____

16. The team took (forth, fourth) place in the race.   16. _____

17. All she wanted was (peace, piece) and quiet.   17. _____

18. The bells (pealed, peeled) at midnight.   18. _____

19. She was our school's (principal, principle).   19. _____

20. The rancher opened the (gait, gate) for her horse.   20. _____

Your Total Score _____ /20

Synonyms

Vocabulary 4-A Practice Procedure Select the correct *synonym* (word that has about the same meaning) from the lettered words to match the italicized word in the sentence. Write the letter of the word you select in the blank provided at the right. Score one point for each correct response.

Answers

1. A *forlorn* person is (a) argumentative (b) foolish (c) unhappy (d) athletic.   1. _____

2. A *gigantic* mountain is (a) hilly (b) pretty (c) rocky (d) huge.   2. _____

3. An *incredible* trip is (a) inconsistent (b) ordinary (c) unbelievable (d) realistic.   3. _____

4. A *gruesome* sight is (a) beautiful (b) pretentious (c) horrible (d) genuine.   4. _____

5. An *obnoxious* customer is (a) pleasant (b) objectionable (c) tactful (d) unconcerned.   5. _____

6. A *pampered* baby is (a) teased (b) changed (c) praised (d) spoiled.   6. _____

7. An *amiable* person is (a) insolent (b) foreign (d) amazing (d) friendly.   7. _____

8. A *remote* campground is (a) restricted (b) neglected (c) distant (d) expensive.   8. _____

9. An *inflammatory* remark is (a) soothing (b) unrehearsed (c) inflexible (d) arousing.   9. _____

10. An *artificial* flower is (a) wilted (b) fake (c) pretty (d) genuine.   10. _____

Vocabulary 4-B Practice Procedure Follow the procedure given for Vocabulary 4-A. Notice how all the italicized words begin with the letters *im*. Look at the words carefully before you make your choice.

1. An *immaculate* house is (a) spotless (b) painted (c) enormous (d) expensive.   1. _____

2. An *imminent* danger is (a) delayed (b) approaching (c) great (d) fleeting.   2. _____

3. An *impetuous* child is (a) hasty (b) cautious (c) naughty (d) poor.   3. _____

4. An *immaterial* piece of evidence is (a) significant (b) lengthy (c) unimportant (d) restricted.   4. _____

5. An *impartial* statement is (a) prejudiced (b) incomplete (c) truthful (d) fair.   5. _____

6. An *impeccable* person is (a) faultless (b) unusual (c) unethical (d) virtuous.   6. _____

7. An *impassive* attitude is (a) emotional (b) unemotional (c) inflexible (d) forceful.   7. _____

8. An *impertinent* child is (a) polite (b) sensitive (c) talented (d) rude.   8. _____

9. An *imposing* building is (a) old (b) ordinary (c) contemporary (d) impressive.   9. _____

10. An *impudent* clerk is (a) respectful (b) untidy (c) wise (d) rude.   10. _____

Your Total Score _____ /20

Definitions

vocabulary practice **5**

Vocabulary 5-A Practice Procedure In the blank at the right, place the letter of the word that is closest in meaning to the numbered word. Score one point for each correct response.

Answers

1. rely   **(a)** ignore   **(b)** agree   **(c)** distrust   **(d)** alter   **(e)** depend   1. _____

2. tirade   **(a)** vitality   **(b)** spanking   **(c)** beverage   **(d)** scolding   **(e)** speed   2. _____

3. typical   **(a)** characteristic   **(b)** many   **(c)** exceptional   **(d)** motley   **(e)** special   3. _____

4. bragged   **(a)** boasted   **(b)** laughed   **(c)** belittled   **(d)** arched   **(e)** smoothed   4. _____

5. oafish   **(a)** settled   **(b)** clumsy   **(c)** polished   **(d)** beginning   **(e)** fat   5. _____

6. obstinate   **(a)** cruel   **(b)** steady   **(c)** faltering   **(d)** stubborn   **(e)** impulsive   6. _____

7. veer   **(a)** finish   **(b)** halt   **(c)** abate   **(d)** swerve   **(e)** snake   7. _____

8. frugal   **(a)** thrifty   **(b)** free   **(c)** extravagant   **(d)** rhythmic   **(e)** brotherly   8. _____

9. despicable   **(a)** capable   **(b)** contemptible   **(c)** helpful   **(d)** reckless   **(e)** marked   9. _____

10. grisly   **(a)** bony   **(b)** tough   **(c)** horrifying   **(d)** neat   **(e)** fat   10. _____

Vocabulary 5-B Practice Procedure Follow the procedure given for Vocabulary 5-A.

1. squander   **(a)** presume   **(b)** dirty   **(c)** waste   **(d)** duck   **(e)** double   1. _____

2. prohibit   **(a)** forbid   **(b)** agree   **(c)** decline   **(d)** reject   **(e)** consent   2. _____

3. ideal   **(a)** perfect   **(b)** important   **(c)** useful   **(d)** unsound   **(e)** correct   3. _____

4. regal   **(a)** common   **(b)** liquid   **(c)** basic   **(d)** royal   **(e)** feminine   4. _____

5. fascinate   **(a)** endure   **(b)** annoy   **(c)** tolerate   **(d)** calm   **(e)** charm   5. _____

6. apprehend   **(a)** understand   **(b)** arrest   **(c)** release   **(d)** hit   **(e)** leave   6. _____

7. prim   **(a)** formal   **(b)** informal   **(c)** cautious   **(d)** loose   **(e)** forceful   7. _____

8. alleviate   **(a)** worsen   **(b)** control   **(c)** relieve   **(d)** hurt   **(e)** break   8. _____

9. fabulous   **(a)** limited   **(b)** bright   **(c)** petty   **(d)** incredible   **(e)** additional   9. _____

10. conformity   **(a)** pride   **(b)** control   **(c)** agreement   **(d)** body   **(e)** rebellion   10. _____

11. germane   **(a)** relevant   **(b)** bacterial   **(c)** European   **(d)** flashy   **(e)** pert   11. _____

12. notorious   **(a)** renowned   **(b)** infamous   **(c)** recluse   **(d)** beloved   **(e)** quiet   12. _____

13. superficial   **(a)** small   **(b)** haughty   **(c)** sound   **(d)** enormous   **(e)** shallow   13. _____

14. objective   **(a)** statue   **(b)** goal   **(c)** disagreement   **(d)** speech   **(e)** constable   14. _____

15. franchise   **(a)** reason   **(b)** tax   **(c)** clash   **(d)** license   **(e)** credit   15. _____

Your Total Score _____ /25

239

Vocabulary 6-A Practice Procedure In the following sentences, select one word that has the same meaning as the italicized word (*synonym*). Also, select one word that has the opposite meaning (*antonym*). Each lettered group of words contains a word that means the same and one that means the opposite of the italicized word. Write the letter of the synonym and that of the antonym in the blanks provided. Check your dictionary. Score one point for each correct response.

	Synonym	Antonym
Example: An *expensive* radio is (a) pretty (b) costly (c) useless (d) cheap.	*b*	*d*
1. A *fragile* dish is (a) flowery (b) cheap (c) strong (d) breakable.	1. _____	_____
2. A *casual* meeting is (a) unexpected (b) planned (c) frantic (d) bitter.	2. _____	_____
3. A *diligent* worker is (a) hardworking (b) tardy (c) careless (d) tiny.	3. _____	_____
4. An *imminent* departure is (a) approaching (b) distant (c) sad (d) unusual.	4. _____	_____
5. *Scandalous* behavior is (a) scientific (b) proper (c) shameful (d) sarcastic.	5. _____	_____
6. A *logical* ending is (a) secluded (b) reasonable (c) unlikely (d) open.	6. _____	_____
7. A *cordial* greeting is (a) friendly (b) exciting (c) indifferent (d) unexpected.	7. _____	_____
8. A *memorable* week is (a) forgettable (b) expensive (c) noteworthy (d) merciful.	8. _____	_____
9. A *robust* person is (a) sturdy (b) sickly (c) right (d) untruthful.	9. _____	_____
10. A *torrid* day is (a) chilly (b) hot and dry (c) topsy-turvy (d) orderly.	10. _____	_____

Vocabulary 6-B Practice Procedure Follow the procedure given for Vocabulary 6-A.

	Synonym	Antonym
1. An *absurd* story is (a) humorous (b) sensible (c) tragic (d) ridiculous.	1. _____	_____
2. A *malicious* act is (a) kind (b) spiteful (c) mature (d) childish.	2. _____	_____
3. A *humid* day is (a) baking (b) moist (c) freezing (d) dry.	3. _____	_____
4. An *odious* statement is (a) repugnant (b) charming (c) short (d) lengthy.	4. _____	_____
5. A *rabid* dog is (a) docile (b) toy (c) large (d) mad.	5. _____	_____
6. An *obscure* village is (a) prominent (b) unclean (c) unnoticed (d) clean.	6. _____	_____
7. A *hostile* customer is (a) friendly (b) eager (c) angry (d) relaxed.	7. _____	_____
8. A *precarious* location is (a) lovely (b) insecure (c) ugly (d) stable.	8. _____	_____
9. A *dismal* day is (a) gloomy (b) quiet (c) busy (d) cheery.	9. _____	_____
10. A *valid* excuse is (a) flimsy (b) convincing (c) simple (d) complicated.	10. _____	_____

Your Total Score _____ /40

Application Practice Score Summary

Unit 4   Verbs

Page	Application Practice	Drill	Points Possible	Student Score
75	43	Find the Verb	50	
76	44	Helping Verbs	55	
77	45	Predicate Nouns, Pronouns, and Adjectives	50	
78	46	Extra Practice on Verbs	60	
83	47	Verb and Subject Agreement	20	
84	48	Verb and Subject Agreement	25	
89	49	Verb and Subject Agreement	20	
90	50	Verb Agreement with Indefinite Pronouns, *There*, and *Or*	20	
91	51	Verb Agreement with Collective Nouns	20	
92	52	Verb Agreement with Indefinite Pronouns, Collective Nouns, *There*, and *Or*	20	
93	53	Noun, Verb, and Pronoun Review	20	
94	54	Noun, Verb, and Pronoun Review	20	

Unit 5   The Time of Verbs

Page	Application Practice	Drill	Points Possible	Student Score
99	55	Present and Past Tenses	20	
100	56	Future and Present, Past, and Future Tenses	20	
103	57	Perfect Tense	19	
104	58	Tense Review	21	
109	59	Irregular Verbs	25	
110	60	Active and Passive Voices	20	
115	61	Lie-Lay Practice	25	
116	62	Sit-Set Practice	25	
121	63	Shall-Will and Should-Would Practice	30	
122	64	May-Can Practice	30	
123	65	Verb Review I—Past, Present, Future	20	
124	66	Verb Review II—Perfect Tenses	19	
125	67	Verb Review III—Irregular Verbs, Active and Passive	20	
126	68	Verb Review IV—Summary Verb Review	25	

Unit 6   Adjectives and Adverbs

Page	Application Practice	Drill	Points Possible	Student Score
129	69	Descriptive, Proper, and Possessive Adjective Identification	17	
130	70	Adjective Drill	22	
133	71	Degrees of Comparison	50	
134	72	Degrees of Comparison	25	
137	73	Adverb Practice	50	
138	74	Adjective and Adverb Recognition	86	
139	75	Adjective Drills	20	
140	76	Adjective and Adverb Recognition	102	

Unit 7   Prepositions and Conjunctions

Page	Application Practice	Drill	Points Possible	Student Score
143	77	Recognizing Prepositions and Prepositional Phrases	50	
144	78	Objective Case after Prepositions	25	
147	79	Conjunction Recognition	24	
148	80	Using Conjunctions	40	

Unit 8   Phrases and Clauses

Page	Application Practice	Drill	Points Possible	Student Score
155	81	Prepositional and Participial Phrases	30	
156	82	Infinitive Phrases	40	
157	83	Independent and Dependent Clauses	60	
158	84	Noun Clauses	30	
159	85	Matching	20	
160	86	Phrases and Clauses	40	

Unit 9   Punctuation and Capitalization

Page	Application Practice	Drill	Points Possible	Student Score
167	87	End Punctuation	20	
168	88	Abbreviation Practice	50	
169	89	Comma Usage—Series and Appositives	60	
170	90	Comma Usage—Dependent Clauses and Quotations	24	
171	91	Comma Usage—Addresses, Dates, and Unrelated Expressions	42	
172	92	Stop and Go Practice	50	
173	93	Comma Usage	50	
174	94	Comma Usage	50	
175	95	Complete Comma Review	47	
176	96	End Punctuation Review	36	
181	97	Review of the Apostrophe in Contractions and of Numbers	25	
182	98	Punctuation Review	120	
185	99	Capitalization	136	
186	100	Punctuation and Capitalization	133	
187	101	Punctuation and Capitalization Review	177	
188	102	Punctuated and Capitalized Sentences	200	
189	103	Punctuation Matching Practice	25	
190	104	Punctuation Review	118	

Unit 10   Word Choice

Page	Application Practice	Drill	Points Possible	Student Score
193	105	It's, Its—Who's, Whose	25	
194	106	Their, There, They're Practice	20	
201	107	Frequently Misused Words Practice	25	
202	108	Frequently Misused Words Practice	30	
205	109	Speech Duds	25	
206	110	Speech Duds	25	

Unit 11   Writing Sentences and Paragraphs

Page	Application Practice	Drill	Points Possible	Student Score
209	111	Sentence Classification	25	
210	112	Sentence Construction	38	
213	113	Writing Topic Sentences	10	
214	114	Sentence Classification, Topic Sentences	16	
215	115	Linking Words and Phrases	38	
216	116	Paragraph Order and Development	18	
217	117	Paragraph Construction	20	
218	118	Matching	15	
219	119	Sentence Review	77	
220	120	Writing Paragraphs	10	

Answers for Tryout Exercises

UNIT 1

Tryout Exercise, Page 1
1. guide explained
2. We watched
3. friend lives
4. Mrs. Mauro mailed
5. Grant bought
6. Christy sent

Tryout Exercise, Page 2

	D	Int	Excla	Imp
1.		✔		
2.	✔			
3.				✔
4.			✔	

Tryout Exercise, Page 10
1. They, gave, speeches
2. He, lost, votes
3. people, gave, them, cheers
4. She, read, speech, students

Tryout Exercise, Page 14
1. The, experienced, flew, the, skillfully
2. Heavy, frequently, cancel, some
3. The, eager, flight, worked, quickly, quietly
4. The, flies, north, a, regular

Tryout Exercise, Page 18
1. Hurrah!, and, with, from
2. Wow!, in, and, and, to
3. Gosh!, and, with
4. or, near
5. and, and, to

UNIT 2

Tryout Exercise, Page 28
1. Shirley Modesti [P], leader [C], class [Col], trip [C], Australia [P], August [P]
2. committee [Col], parents [C], students [C], Los Angeles International Airport [P]
3. band [Col], school [C], group [Col], airport [C], Cairns [P], Australia [P]
4. morning [C], faculty [Col], Outer Barrier Reef [P], view [C], fish [C], coral [C]
5. Miss Oswald [P], Palace Hotel [P], staff [Col], tours [C], students [C]

Tryout Exercise, Page 32
1. roads
2. armies
3. benches
4. potatoes
5. shelves
6. teeth

Tryout Exercise, Page 36
1. the cat's tail, the cats' tails
2. the author's book, the authors' books
3. the mother's chair, the mothers' chairs

1. uncles'
2. man's
3. owner's

UNIT 3

Tryout Exercise, Page 46
1. I
2. she
3. me
4. he
5. My

1. He, him, me
2. We, him, us, them

Tryout Exercise, Page 50
1. his
2. their
3. his
4. their
5. his
6. their

Tryout Exercise, Page 57
1. Who
2. Who
3. Which
4. Who
5. Which
6. Whom

Tryout Exercise, Page 60
1. who
2. whom
3. who
4. whoever
5. whomever

UNIT 4

Tryout Exercise, Page 73
1. is used — S
2. Can operate — Q
3. will begin — S
4. can write — S
5. can help — S
6. Can store — Q
7. Will reduce — Q
8. Can improve — Q
9. must teach — C
10. will learn — C

Tryout Exercise, Page 74
1. old — A
2. he — P
3. expert — N

Tryout Exercise, Page 82
1. are
2. were
3. were
4. has
5. was

Tryout Exercise, Page 88
1. was or were
2. was
3. is
4. is
5. are
6. were
7. is
8. are
9. were
10. was

UNIT 5

Tryout Exercise, Page 96
1. buys
2. practice
3. has
4. doesn't

Tryout Exercise, Page 98
1. lived
2. traveled
3. were
4. drove

Tryout Exercise, Page 98
1. Shall
2. will
3. Shall
4. Will

Tryout Exercise, Page 102

1. have started	4. will have known
2. will have selected	5. has replied
3. had practiced	

Tryout Exercise, Page 108

1. fell   2. heard   3. will keep

Tryout Exercise, Page 114

1. set   2. lies   3. laid   4. sat

Tryout Exercise, Page 120

1. should	3. Let	5. lend	7. Raise
2. May	4. teach	6. take	

UNIT 6

Tryout Exercise, Page 132

1. most skillful	3. smarter	5. happiest
2. best	4. worst	6. tamer

Tryout Exercise, Page 136

1. <u>Probably</u>, <u>there</u>   3. <u>Finally</u>, <u>very</u>
2. <u>Where</u>, <u>recently</u>   4. <u>often</u>, <u>seldom</u>

UNIT 7

Tryout Exercise, Page 142

1. (with) the Legal Aid Foundation
2. (for) the district attorney
3. (of) the court

1. us   2. me   3. her

Tryout Exercise, Page 146

1. correlative, words	4. coordinating, words
2. subordinating, clauses	5. correlative, phrases
3. coordinating, words	

UNIT 8

Tryout Exercise, Page 150

1. <u>in the living room</u>, adj
2. <u>to the office</u>, adv
3. <u>by the river</u>, adj

Tryout Exercise, Page 151

1. <u>to the game</u>, adv
2. <u>to win the scholarship</u>, adj
3. <u>To write a composition</u>, n

Tryout Exercise, Page 151

1. <u>Fighting a cold</u>, Pam
2. <u>given a new coat of paint</u>, house
3. <u>wearing the red dress</u>, girl

Tryout Exercise, Page 154

1. <u>Because the bus was late</u>, we missed the first act. (adv)
2. The birds <u>that flew overhead</u> were sea gulls. (adj)

Tryout Exercise, Page 154 (continued)

1. <u>What the newscaster said</u>, subject
2. <u>that they will go with us</u>, object
3. <u>that his watch was broken</u>, predicate noun
4. <u>whatever school accepts me</u>, object of preposition

UNIT 9

Tryout Exercise, Page 163

1. Don't shove me (**!**)
2. Are you the new teacher (**?**)
3. Let's take a walk on the beach (**.**)

1. memo	1. quart
2. St.	2. number
3. Ave.	3. volume

Tryout Exercise, Page 166

1. Myron, my uncle, is from Ohio.
2. I bought apples, oranges, and grapes.
3. Yes, I can see you tonight.
4. Bart was born on March 8, 1980, in Texas.
5. Her father said, "You must be home by midnight."

Tryout Exercise, Page 180

1. "It's a beautiful sunset," she said. "It looks like the sky is on fire."
2. Isn't it true that he prefers shellfish (oysters, scallops, mussels) to the following: crabs, lobsters, and eels?
3. My friend Bill — he graduated with me — is coming home from the service tomorrow.

Tryout Exercise, Page 184

1. (the), (burden), (glory), (president), (john) (f.) (kennedy)
2. (thanksgiving), (thursday), (november)
3. (oh), (erie), (pennsylvania), (boston), (massachusetts)
4. (mary), (i.) (rose), (bowl), (new) (year's), (day)
5. (the), (american), (paris), (tuesday), (french), (sunday)

UNIT 10

Tryout Exercise, Page 192

1. Who's	3. It's	5. there	7. Their
2. They're	4. Whose	6. its	

Tryout Exercise, Page 200

1. from	3. too	5. surely
2. Among	4. her	6. besides

Tryout Exercise, Page 204

1. might have	3. seldom	5. inside the
2. can hardly	4. Try to	6. doesn't

UNIT 11

Tryout Exercise, Page 208

1. compound   2. complex   3. simple

Tryout Exercise, Page 212

1. Answers will vary.   2. Answers will vary.

Index